Mannership

Claire and Saul

Mannership

Seeking a Source of Self-Destruction

Mark

Mark Goodwin

Matador
Unit E2 Airfield Business Park,
Harrison Road, Market Harborough,
Leicestershire. LE16 7UL
Tel: 0116 2792299
Email: books@troubador.co.uk
Web: www.troubador.co.uk/matador
Twitter: @matadorbooks

ISBN 978 1803131 467

British Library Cataloguing in Publication Data.
A catalogue record for this book is available from the British Library.

Printed and bound by CPI Group (UK) Ltd, Croydon, CR0 4YY

Matador is an imprint of Troubador Publishing Ltd

Preface

Around the age of just fifteen months, following a long illness, I lost my hearing. The next six years were silent for me. Other senses became somehow enhanced to compensate, particularly sight. Just as the blind are not aware how their hearing is more acute, there was nothing to indicate that my way of watching was any different from others. There was, however, an immediate effect. The absence of sound developed within me a hunger to '*see* other connections'; looking to replace the loss with another form of attachment. Seeking links thus became one of my strongest drives.

As soon as crawling became an option to move around, I would rock the pram until it fell over to crawl out and explore. This insatiable curiosity to wander has been another giant in my life. Just as a toddler becomes surprised by unexpected discoveries, my fascination for new lands and connections grew.

The familiarity with quietness in my childhood permitted much time for reflection. During my silent years nature fascinated me. The animals in those early years were mostly very small, particularly mice and insects. Much larger animals have subsequently taught me priceless lessons. Elephants are great teachers.

Although these two giants of curiosity and keen observation have propelled my life since infancy, there is a third force which took hold of me as a late teenager. Having wandered through much of Africa and Asia between the age of seventeen and twenty-one, my attention was captivated by the way 'intact' people communicated. With my 'deaf-sight' there was no doubt which tribes were communicating on a different dimension from others. Some nomadic tribes adopted me as if they had found their long lost son, opening my eyes to another level of deliciousness and safety. Their warmth led me to explore more; the crawling simply embraced greater distances.

My university education seemed destined for an academic career, but my heart yearned for those times spent with peoples who 'took me' in a way my own culture had not. Academia was easily and naturally swapped, without a second thought, for beginning my career with indigenous peoples in the Gilbert and Ellice Islands. In the beauty and warmth of life among Pacific Islanders began an unconscious knowledge to help with the eventual task of this book. Perhaps the variety of lessons from different societies around the world enabled me to collect clues which were just waiting for a germination of all fitting together. Writing this book guided me to orientate the jigsaw pieces so their connections were revealed.

The subsequent global spread of my careers has been the flowering of my curiosity. But, more than that, the diversity has produced a spider's web of connections without which the challenges of this book could not have been grasped. Looking back, some parts of my career did not seem to 'fit' with a path. But, in an uncanny way, they provided clues and answers that were required in my search. Everything was needed in the end.

We should start with how this exploration began. The book has a life of his own, the course quite unexpected. It wasn't my plan to search for a source of self-destruction. Nothing was further from my mind. Instead, the book took me there, initially unawares.

Meredith Belbin is renowned for his research at Henley Business School on 'team roles'. Over a million people have used his 'instrument' to determine their most effective role in a team. This research with 'management teams – why they succeed or fail' was also well known to my daughter Alika. While she had studied Belbin's work in her psychology degrees, it was one of my preferred instruments in consulting work for organisations. We both admired the power and simplicity of the Belbin model. An idea took root that we should explore this subject more. Having discovered that the Belbin office was scarcely three miles from my parents' house at Madingley, near Cambridge, we decided to stop by.

As we drove down the narrow gravel lane, Alika asked me: "Is Meredith Belbin still alive?" Her question took me by surprise. Not having any idea, it seemed easier to reply, "Perhaps we could find out." Opening the front door of his office, we were struck with a joyous surprise to find him very much alive, in good spirits and with a cup of coffee in hand. That energy stayed with us and continued all day. By noontime we had visited Meredith's garden, collected his wife Sheila and adjourned to my village pub, the Three Horse Shoes at Madingley, for lunch. The conversation never slowed as we wandered through my family garden to admire the trees. It was very easy to forget why we had come to meet Meredith in the first place, such was the richness of conversation we had that day.

Over the next few months we met regularly to continue our sprawling discussions. Meredith has a lovely conservatory on the sunny side of his garden with a sumptuous sofa and armchairs. We would sit there for hours, pausing for occasional teas, admiring the view of his so English garden whilst among piles of books in the warm sunshine or protected from a gentle rain.

Meredith is an avid reader with the advantage of Cambridge University Library on his doorstep. My travelling experience, or fieldwork, complemented his research. Quickly we decided to write a joint book on the 'future of civilisations'. Chapters grew by themselves like creeping vines.

After some months, Meredith wrote the foreword, which began:

The 'Garden of Eden' was typified as idyllic in an age of innocence. Evidence from early, low density, communities does lend some support to this generally peaceful picture in primordial society. In this harmonious beginning, humans being part of the fauna belonged to the land.

A little later, he added: *From this juncture human society took a new road that forked, with one path leading to an emergence of civilisation, and the other leading to plunder creating the dominance of a warrior society. Thereafter, through much of human history, it has been a struggle between these two paths with great civilisations meeting such destruction. Vicious wars have been prevalent in every part of the world, increasingly about ideology. In the twentieth century, wars intensified to become global with the machinery of war proving ever-more technically advanced. The scale of suffering became unparalleled, operating to the detriment of both winners and losers.*

Since humans possess intelligence and a capacity to learn far in excess of all other species, what explanation can one offer for human society apparently operating against its self-interest? Is the span of human attention so limited that it is fixed primarily on the recent past and can learn nothing from history? How can it be that this 'naked ape', so seemingly harmless in its physical form, has evolved so unmistakeably into such a killer? Why is this patent human propensity for destruction blithely disregarded by academics and experts in evolutionary theory?

How did this reversal of civilized progress happen? What can we do about it? Why have these crucial questions been so conspicuously disregarded? Here I count myself very fortunate to have encountered Mark Goodwin. Taking on major responsibilities at a very early age, Mark's activities have taken him into, remarkably, 169 countries, always sharply observing as he goes. He has had six separate careers; in diplomatic service, management consultancy, tropical farming, global manufacturing, leadership coaching, as well as experience as a group psychoanalyst. Along the way he has lived and travelled extensively with primordial and tribal societies, whilst experiencing some of their rituals.

However, the 'joint book' – animated by our unpredictable discussions – turned out to have a different idea in mind. The question which Meredith asked: *What explanation can one offer for human society apparently operating against its self-interest?* was a subject which we conspired initially to avoid; as most cultures do. There was an unexpected fork in the road one morning for our joint book. Meredith wished to continue with the future of civilisation whilst the question of human self-destruction had grabbed my attention like an octopus which would not let go. The solution was simple; two books. My journey with the octopus had begun. This unavoidable question, with the psychological depth asked of me, took a few more years to explore and digest. The wrestling was mutual; I became captivated by the subject, which is just as the octopus had wanted.

My journey with an octopus as guide contained many unexpected explorations and fresh connections. The greatest joy in writing has been the discoveries and how much they have taught me. Several chapters were begun with an idea in mind, only to discover that this idea was not only wrong but the opposite of reality. Many of my earlier thoughts and assumptions had to be abandoned. But, replacing them by something better has been such a pleasure. It turns out that wandering and wondering have much in common. Perhaps a long time ago they were the same.

Just like many of my teenage journeys, this quest to seek possible causes for self-destruction began without an answer or destination in mind. My hope was that a source might indicate a possible cure. Many 'dead ends' were explored before chancing on some possible clear explanations for the greatest distress in our society.

We cannot ignore the fact that the rate of suicide and self-harm is increasing dramatically. In the last 45 years the suicide rate has increased by 60% globally. In the United Kingdom, the rate of self-harm among those as young as ten years increased by over 70% between 2012 and 2014. In many countries suicide is now a leading cause of death during optimal child rearing years between the ages of 16 and 30. This cannot have a genetic root or our species would not be here. Additionally, death cannot be our greatest fear or suicide would not be possible.

The challenge was to find a source which is more 'scary than death' and not genetic. Without the illumination of 'deaf-sight', developed in infancy, my way could have become as lost as if the octopus tentacles had obscured my eyes.

Suicide and self-harm are the most obvious aspects of self-destruction. But there is so much more. We could consider everything else we do which inhibits us as a possible act of self-harm. Addictions are relatives of self-harm. Once we scratch the surface, the affliction is much more prevalent than we thought.

There seem to be three questions to explore.

- How does an individual mind become 'poisoned' by a self-destructive tendency?
- How is the poison hidden, and harboured, in a part of the mind which is 'out of reach' or 'unknown to us' so we cannot simply 'deal' with it?
- How did our environment or culture develop in such a way that this 'poison' became thrust so deep into our children's minds?

These questions spawned my journey of exploration. The sources and variety of cultural distinctiveness in diverse parts of the world guided me towards clues which had already been found but not understood.

*****

The title, *Mannership*, has his own story.

In the early 1990s, after the major responsibilities of my early career, I decided to offer my experience to coach other leaders. The time was just after the fall of the Berlin Wall and the demand for my support came primarily from organisations in Central Europe seeking to learn about a world outside of the Soviet Union.

I explained that Management and Leadership are quite different. 'Management' derives from the Latin 'manus' for hand and 'agere' to act and means 'acting with the hands'. Like a farmer ploughing the land, organising the flow of water since winter, and seeking to transform nature. By contrast, 'Leadership' has roots in ancient North European languages as someone who gives confidence to follow them. The Old English *lædan* is more than a guide and implies 'faith to follow'. Leadership is more like a shepherd concerned for the safety of the flock whilst seeking greener pastures and co-existing with nature in the wild.

To remember the differences as well as the need for a fresh relationship between the farmer and the shepherd, I merged Management and Leadership into a new word *Mannership*. I liked that *manners* were implied as well as the sense of a journey in a *ship*.

When this book began his journey on the future of culture, the title *Mannership* seemed a possibility. Once the octopus took charge and the book's course changed, I trusted that a different title would emerge. However, as my journey progressed, I discovered that a source of self-destruction could not be understood without addressing the relationship of our culture to our nature. The cure for self-destruction requires a fresh relationship between the part of us who exercises self-control, or 'manages us' and our inspired nature. Like a new relationship between a farmer and a shepherd. I knew then that *Mannership* had quietly intended to be the title all along.

MARK GOODWIN

Part One

There is little doubt the explorations of this book would not have been possible without a different way of looking. John Hanning Speke was the first European to glimpse the source of the Nile in August, 1858, having heard rumours of two seas in the deepest interior; the seas of Ujiji and Ukerewe. After many struggles, he was guided to *a vast expanse* of *pale-blue waters*. In typical British fashion of the day, he gave her the name Lake Victoria. Although very hard to find for a struggling Englishman, the vast inner sea was unmissable once in view. A source of self-destruction is hard to find and well hidden by her own 'prickly jungle'. But she can remain hidden, even when in plain view, until we have a 'right way of looking'.

The first part is chronological and begins with the struggles of my silent years to help explain my 'way of watching' as well as the energies behind my drives.

Wandering as a teenager through Asia and Africa helped me to understand differences between cultures; those times taught me how peoples think quite differently. There was an invaluable lesson in discovering which aspects of human communication are universal. By seeing what is not the same everywhere gives extra clues to the ways our minds can develop 'differently' from other cultures. These travels have many anecdotes, and metaphors, which were needed as guides on the later quest. Three chapters trace the long journeys during my adolescence before a career began.

The years in the Pacific Ocean, among such a warm and wonderful group of Gilbertese Islanders, may have been the closest my path came to the Garden of Eden. They have so much light to shine on the darker parts of my research. Back then, I was in heaven. Many lessons only came to life in retrospect, re-examining contrasts between cultures later in my career.

Returning to Europe, and far from a hot climate, it was not too long until the magnetism of warm people captured me again during my tropical farming years. Acute observations of differences between societies in Africa, South-East Asia, the Pacific and the Caribbean taught me a great deal about the culture of the land of my infancy.

These journeys were gliding 'over the surface of the earth' until willing to plunge into observing my own mind; the subject of part two of this book.

Note: Most of the photographs are memories from my journeys. The cover picture was taken while crossing from Darfur to Chad in June, 1973 accompanied by the Zaghawa people.

Part Two

Whereas the first part of the book is chronological in following my development from infancy until my 'thirties', the second part searches for an understanding of the three questions:

How does an individual mind become 'poisoned' by a self-destructive tendency?

How is the poison hidden, and harboured, in a part of the mind which is 'out of reach' or 'unknown to us' so we cannot simply 'deal' with it?

How did our environment or culture develop in such a way that this 'poison' became thrust so deep into our children's minds?

Many of my initial inquiries led to a dead end. But, some of these yielded clues of where else to look or showed that 'the way of looking' had been misguided. To understand the depth behind the three questions required me to learn from unexpected guides. I hope that my reader can 'hang in there' as the pieces of the puzzle which were needed for me are set out before later being joined together. In addition to providing vital clues, these chapters brought discoveries which fascinated and sustained me. I hope my reader can also enjoy the variety of sprouting discoveries along the way.

The journey would not have been possible without some exceptional guides. These remarkable sages are introduced as 'stepping stones' and include learnings from twenty-five years of working with indigenous tribal shamans. Understanding afflictions in my own mind was essential to see some of the struggles within others.

My instincts suggested that other species have much to tell us about our minds. Some of our friends, the birds, have a brain weighing barely a gram; a raisin really. But the contents of the raisin are extraordinary. A whole array of separate intelligences is already imprinted before hatching; for flight; navigation; migration; botany and zoology; hunting for nourishment and so much more. To refer, in a derogatory way, to a 'bird-brain' is quite absurd. Science has recently discovered the New Caledonian crow has superior cognition to the great apes. But maybe we are considering this question backwards. A wise bird might well ask, through their piercing eye, why some of their neighbours, the human species, have so much difficulty with human instincts. Could our self-destruction be somehow connected with a fear of our instincts? The birds teach us more. Many of our instincts atrophy if we are kept in captivity.

My attention was captured by the navigational skills of birds and fishes. Both species have several independent navigational systems which 'resonate' to enable them to find the same nest or spawning ground after many thousands of miles. Despite my background in physics, I hadn't considered the other senses which birds and fishes possess. Perhaps we have more than five senses too. No individual navigation system is sufficient but a resonance or combination of them becomes attracted to a safe destination. I wondered if this could teach something about the way the human mind wrestles with internal conflicts while we navigate our lives.

The lessons of birds and fishes with their supreme navigator instincts gave me keys to explore subsequent subjects.

Adrian Raine's unique research *Anatomy of Violence* provides insights and pointers to the roots of violence. His study of the brains of murderers shows that neither genetics nor nurture is sufficient to produce a violent destiny. Other factors are also important, but how the different contributors combine is far more significant. Raine found that the nature versus nurture debate comes out as a tie. This seems like the inter-relation of the different navigation systems in birds and ocean creatures. Maybe in a bird's mind the debate between magnetic direction and a sense of smell also comes out as a tie. The nature / nurture debate has missed the point. Having two equal systems enables the mind to weigh up choices in combination with other critical guidance factors. The relationship between nature and nurture is more important than either of them.

Adrian Raine's research illustrates the criticality of other factors. He shows how a relationship between our birth experience and initial reception cannot be ignored. My experiences with shamans reminded me how this this dynamic is still visible. A conversation with a midwife helped to understand the effect of our mortal beginning on future characters.

Much of our life is influenced by events before we had a mind capable of 'processing the experience'. Suddenly, I began to wonder whether some of the ancient cultural stories and sacred texts might have hidden keys to a time before we had a vocabulary to describe events.

James Kugel's thorough analysis of authors of the Book of Genesis during the Babylonian captivity of the Hebrews in the 6th Century BCE highlights the influence of earlier Mesopotamian stories.

Samuel Noah Kramer's detailed explorations of cuneiform records on clay tablets since the 4th millennium BCE show the Babylonian culture had absorbed most of the earlier Sumerian myths. Many stories in Genesis are thus of Sumerian origin. Kramer says the Sumerian word 'Eden' means 'steppe' or the land further east where their people came from before arriving in Sumer in the 4th millennium BCE.

Kramer was most interested by his comparison of the Genesis story and the Sumerian poems relating to the fashioning of Eve, she who makes live, from the rib of Adam. Kramer tells us that the Sumerian word for rib, 'ti', also means 'to make live'. The pun in Sumerian loses validity once translated into Hebrew. Sacred texts are often designed to fall on the mind in more than one way of looking. A hidden meaning may be lost because a pun only 'works' in the original language. In subsequent chapters of this book, other ancient stories reclaim another meaning once the original puns are restored.

An idea sprouted that the Genesis story of Cain and Abel might have another meaning. Could the shepherd Abel, who offered up the spontaneity of first born animals, refer to our nature or instincts? Then the farmer Cain, who relied on culture or cultivation, could be seen as representing culture or nurture. Effectively, the culture represented by Cain buries Abel's instincts or nature in the ground.

The dynamic of our nature's domestication by culture seems to be critical. Where better to learn more than from our largest mammalian friend on land? My oldest friend in Sri Lanka used to have three elephants. Conversations with the mahouts helped me understand other vital clues. Elephants know about the subject of 'taming' or 'domestication' by humans. Unlike us, they do not forget the experience.

Next, by chance, my 'deaf-sight' witnessed the cultural domestication of a small girl one afternoon and the scene shocked me. Suddenly, she helped me to connect the pieces from all of the preceding chapters.

Although only two years old; the key she revealed enabled a different way of looking. Many ancient metaphors immediately made sense and this small girl's key enabled me to unlock other sacred portals.

My global wandering had taught me that a 'Cain and Abel' or 'Nurture and Nature' dynamic was almost universal, although with very significant differences. On a visit to Greenland, I remembered how some cultures have rituals to 'repair' this internal and potentially damaging relationship so that the two brothers can dwell together in unity like Emesh and Enten of the Sumerian 'Cain and Abel'.

Another significant clue comes from how different cultures relate to shame. Sacred stories have much to say on this subject. For Confucius, shame is a gateway to our energy. An individual mind, or a culture, which has not learned how to metabolise shame is at risk of spreading humiliation around themselves. Sadly we have seen a rash of this in some Western democracies recently.

My hunger since infancy to see links and connections was sated with every discovery of parallels among different religions. Finding a phrase of Moses which fitted perfectly with a teaching of Christ made my heart jump. A tear of joy flowed in reading how Confucius and Socrates agreed, or the Buddha and Lao-Tzu had the same ideas. Differences between religions have never interested me. Such 'pieces' of the jigsaw were left to one side until finding how they might fit together. Just as the stars in the night sky enable us to find Polaris or 'true north', perhaps when a significant number of different prophets and philosophers seem to agree we cannot ignore their combined suggestions of a better path. Suppose that Moses, the Buddha, Confucius, Lao-Tzu, Heraclitus, Socrates, Christ, Plotinus and Muhammad were to have met. Surely, what they agree upon must help us find a true north? What would this mean for us if the Kingdom mentioned by Confucius is the same land which Moses and Christ refer to? Allowing or entertaining this idea might open other doors. The surprise discovery was how much they all agreed upon.

More significantly, the way 'intact' people communicate, which had guided my early travels, also points towards a similar place of deliciousness and safety.

It is one of our greatest mistakes to assume that people all over the world think in the same way. They don't. For our safety we need to recognise the different paradigms coming from an evolution of culture.

CONTENTS

A Childhood without Noise

Much of my childhood cannot be remembered, so glimpses and suppositions have to fill the gaps. Having two elder sisters always chattering helped me to speak early, even before a year old. But when silence enveloped me as an infant, nobody noticed initially. My father observed a 'quaint habit' whenever sitting on his knee of my grasping his chin in my small hands and turning his head to face me. A new observation skill was beginning to develop as the sudden silence must have 'told me' something was missing. A little sister was born at this time providing another excitement and distraction. Unknown to my family, lip-reading and watching intently became my way of staying in the world. Without a witness to my deafness, maybe I didn't understand my predicament either.

It was at my first pre-school, aged three, that a teacher noticed something odd. Each morning, during a period when we all listened to the radio, she saw how my attention was always distracted by something else. She suggested that my hearing be tested. A few days later, the hospital said: "He doesn't hear anything, nothing at all." The family story is how my father then remembered that the 'quaint habit' had begun after my infant illness; the deafness must have begun then. Explaining how my bedridden three months included chicken pox, measles, German measles, mumps and whooping cough convinced the doctors that my auditory nerves had become damaged somehow.

My earliest memory, aged three, is of the stay in hospital for an operation to remove my adenoids and tonsils. I wet my pyjamas in the fear, and was furious that the nurses could only provide a replacement nightie. In those days there were few family visits in hospitals. The image which remains is of a ward of cots and all us infants standing forlornly clutching our wooden bars. Of course, the picture is a silent one with visible tears. The nurses stole my multi-coloured sweets and ate them all.

The hospital doctors had no answers when the operation made no difference. "He will never hear," they suggested. A life of permanent deafness they said. We all got used to the situation; that was how it was.

Other memories in my early childhood are how destructive I became, destroying most of my toys. When my father bought me something 'indestructible', a way was found to throw it from a great height. A fury about the loss of contact when enveloped by silence was perhaps being 'externalised somehow'. Eventually, I learned how to 'behave myself better'. In the struggle, my sleep was disturbed by night terrors.

I would play on my own for endless hours with a humming 'mmennum' which comforted me. Not hearing the sound of the hum, but feeling the body vibrations, made me feel less alone. Many years later, my family told me how they had known where to find me by following the humming sound. My interest in nature was much greater than a desire for toys. Initially fascinated by insects, as a four or five-year-old, I made a castle for them out of mud. If touched gently, a woodlouse curled into a ball and rolled down a sloping path to the castle door. Once stationary, they unfurled while extending their legs and wandered in.

Photographs from my childhood highlight a particularly intense way of looking. Six decades later, and only after writing this book, has enabled me to understand this look from deep behind the eyes.

There were several states of mind which accompanied me. On the one hand fascination in the mud of nature with my humming sound, and an ambivalent relationship to toys on the other hand. When not destroying the small 'dinky cars' there was a need to meticulously order them in a cupboard; perfectly arranged in lines with nobody allowed to touch them. Was this trying to 'put order into my loneliness'?

Later on, two white mice became my friends. They were called Pyramus and Thisbe, living in a cage next to my bed. In the middle of one night, Pyramus escaped into the parental bedroom and climbed onto my father's ear. The two mice were consequently exiled to the garage. They bred until seventy small mice were being fed daily. I enjoyed watching the way they held sunflower seeds on the side in their tiny hands to chew, just like I might hold a melon slice.

A little older, around the age of five or six, there was a distress which a hearing person might not notice. The silence is manageable and familiar. That is not the problem. A strong sense of shame and a fear of my own voice came because of the embarrassment of not speaking 'properly'. This could lead to strange looks when I uttered something. Sometimes strangers winced as if thinking me 'deformed'. Also, having been able to lip-read something and think about the words carefully, by the time I responded to what *I had seen*, the conversation had moved on beyond me. There were different embarrassing looks, as if someone was thinking, "Where did that come from; we were speaking about it five minutes ago." My silent years thus included a feeling of being generally 'out of order in society' or 'at fault' and ashamed. Luckily I wasn't born a couple of generations before, as in earlier times about a third of deaf children found themselves committed to psychiatric institutions.

Perhaps an autistic child or those with Asperger's might share some of my experience, particularly the shame. Once the vicious circle starts it is hard to get out and the path towards introversion becomes a preferred option.

Unexpectedly, my hearing started to reappear very slowly from the age of seven. One of my elder sisters would walk with me after school to weekly appointments with Miss O'Kell at Addenbrooke's hospital. She taught how to improve my lip-reading and elocution, supplemented by a little more sound filtering through. The weekly supply of bright yellow paper from the radiography department for me to draw on was a real incentive for these lessons. Miss O'Kell was a kind and determined teacher; I didn't have the heart to tell her not to wear all that bright red lipstick just for me; her lips were very easy to read without the extra paint.

To help *visualise* more of the experience, perhaps there is something my reader can try. In front of a mirror, say the word 'now'. At the beginning, the 'n' resembles a faint wrinkle in the nose like a rabbit alert to a smell. It is not easy to say 'n' without opening up the nostrils and slightly parting the lips first. At the end, the 'w' looks like the kind of dry kiss on the cheek which my great aunt Maud favoured. The 'o' in the middle is how we breathe. Many years later, it didn't surprise me to discover how the earliest form of writing with words, the Phoenician alphabet, did not have vowels. A deaf child sees the consonants as facial architecture whereas the vowels are how we breathe.

The teachers at St. Faith's clearly understood the struggle of not hearing. A first school report at the age of seven says, "It may not be entirely his fault that he has come bottom in this subject, as he is not always able to hear. He must watch carefully when spoken to and when listening to stories." Coming bottom in class was not a problem for any of us. Nobody minded or expected anything else. Or, has my memory become distorted and the distress carefully buried?

Meanwhile, we all missed the significance of the shame about my voice. The teachers noticed something which they could not quite put their finger on to grasp the significance. They seem to have been very close in two reports; "He reads with speed and understanding but finds reading aloud with clarity and expression difficult." And a year later; "He reads without expression, which may not be his fault." Neither the teachers, nor me, realised that this was the continuing effect of a deeper shame which was not just about the voice. Later in this book we will return to shame as one of the ingredients of 'self-destruction'.

Although having a large and bulky hearing aid, this didn't really help; actually I hated it. The headmaster wrote to my parents soon after my eighth birthday; "He does not often wear his hearing aid: should he?" Looking back now, it is clear that the development of a 'sound based hearing system' was a struggle and mixed blessing. Having felt able to see what was going on, the extra 'noise' was initially a distraction. This was not just a 'struggle in the mind'; my body struggled too. In the early 1960s it was quite common for cinema films to be 'dubbed' rather than subtitled. Once my 'second hearing' began, we sometimes went to the Regal cinema on St. Andrew's Street in Cambridge. If a film was dubbed, it usually made me feel queasy and as if about to be sick. Often it was necessary for me to leave. The visual movement of the lips being at complete variance with the sound was awful, and unbearable. It was as if two different voices came out of the mouth at the same time. Was this what American Indians meant by the phrase, "The white man speaks with a forked tongue?"

Reading my school reports yields another clue around 'shame of the voice'. Just before my ninth birthday, our curriculum was expanded to include French. At once, I found a freedom of voice. Maybe the way the whole class struggled with embarrassment in pronouncing a new language made my path easier, being already seasoned with a tough hide of shame about my voice. The French teacher's first termly report states, "He has made an excellent start – right on the ball every minute." She placed me 'top of the class' which was the opposite of almost all other subjects. Looking back, the shame of my voice was not present in a foreign language; that's interesting. However, the unconscious shame about my 'English' voice stayed with me until my early thirties. An Irish public speaking champion finally coached me how to overcome the struggle. We will come to that in the sequence of things.

The slow recovery in hearing continued until declared fully normal by Addenbrooke's hospital at the age of thirteen. I had also learned how to manage comfortably the 'two hearing systems' in parallel. My interest and progress in school accelerated, leading to a series of joyous memories with sustained increases in motivation while achieving much more than was expected of me every school year.

In early December, 1971, having sat the examinations for entrance to Magdalen College, Oxford to study nuclear physics, I was anxiously awaiting the results. My father had invited a Yorkshire farming client and his wife to stay the weekend with our family. Together with my mother, the four attended a formal dinner in Darwin College, Cambridge. During the pre-dinner drinks there was a surprise. Professor Dirk ter Haar, visiting from Oxford, had sought my father out. "Are you the father of Mark Goodwin? We have awarded your son Mark the Mackinnon Scholarship." Rather than telephoning me at once they decided that it would be better to hold on to this joyous news all evening until returning home to share the excitement with me in person. It was not just my parents but also their farming guests who all jumped into the sitting room with beaming smiles.

Out to Ceylon and Back from Sri Lanka

Unlike other British universities, Oxford and Cambridge had their own examinations in late autumn for admission the following October. Thus, if successful, there was an obligatory 'gap year' until admission. The design was to encourage students to use the intervening time to develop themselves and avoid thinking of university as an extension of school.

A few years previously, my father had become a fellow of Darwin College, the first mixed and uniquely post-graduate college at Cambridge. He was one of the founding lecturers at the Cambridge Veterinary School before developing a veterinary practice for farm animals. Actually, that reminds me, he took me to the farms sometimes as a small boy. Luckily squealing pigs didn't trouble my ears. Darwin College began in Newnham Grange, the family home of the son and grandson of Charles Darwin. The college started with just four students so they all came to Sunday lunch at our home. Among them we took a particular liking to a fine man from Ceylon, Vikramabahu Karunaratne, or 'Bahu' as he suggested we called him. Although ten years my senior, we had much in common. Bahu had come to write his doctorate in plasma physics, but his wisdom in philosophy interested me much more. We were instantly kindred spirits and often shared tea in his college rooms which were along the bicycle route from my school to home. Stories of Ceylon mesmerised me and he is my eldest friend.

A couple of years before my university entrance exam, a plan germinated for me to spend my 'gap year' visiting India and Ceylon. To make this possible, I saved up the money necessary by working for the Royal Mail in the Christmas holidays and by labouring on building sites during the Easter breaks. Most of my time around Easter seemed to involve mixing cement for bricklayers.

Immediately after Christmas 1971, and soon after my eighteenth birthday, I set off on my first major journey with the princely sum of ninety pounds. This was enough for six months, if very cautious, an Indian couple from Darwin had said. Landing in New Delhi, a railway ticket in 4th class with a further half price student reduction was purchased for less than £9. This would allow me to travel nine thousand miles on Indian trains.

My childhood experiences had equipped me in an unexpected way. India has such colours, smells, texture and taste, which senses had been enhanced since my infancy. There was no trace of shame or fear of my voice in such a different land with many languages. It was much easier to be myself once out of my culture. A natural open-heartedness to all those I met opened many doors. Also, my instincts taught me whenever a situation should make me wary and guided me to embrace more quickly the situations which were safe, 'deaf-sight' was my guide. Even though far from home, my heart felt nearer as if riding the horse of my nature and trusting the future.

I cannot remember meeting anybody in India who was unkind to me and most were so helpful with guidance. But, sometimes I was pointed in the wrong direction. My instincts told me that my questioner wanted to please me and to receive my gratitude for his guidance, even if he didn't know the way. Once wise to this, the solution was simple. I asked more often. This enabled me to meet more people and have greater enjoyment whilst sharing my gratitude more widely. The choice of direction came from a sense among several guides' suggestions. We all benefitted from the arrangement. This was perhaps one of my first lessons on how other cultures think in different ways.

I could not remember feeling freer or happier as this great adventure began to unfold from the North of India all the way down to Ceylon. Whenever someone spoke a seemingly unintelligible language, the 'first hearing system' could be relied upon for us to communicate with warm smiles.

The journey began with a visit to the Golden Temple at Amritsar where pilgrims were allowed to stay with free accommodation and food. They also invited me in and made me so welcome without even troubling my modest budget.

Travelling southwards led me to Agra with her beautiful fort and exquisite Taj Mahal. Next was Fatehpur Sikri where Emperor Akbar had founded his capital of the Mughal Empire in 1571. He had a giant chess set where people had performed as the chess pieces and sometimes suffered if 'taken'.

I had a Russian Zenit E camera with three rolls of Fuji film for 35 millimetre slides with me. Once a roll was completed, I posted it to the Fuji laboratory in London while adding my Cambridge home as the return address. Thus it was not necessary for me to send any postcards; my family could look at the slides to keep track of my progress. If they wanted to contact me, the only possibility was to write to Bahu where a letter could wait until my journey finally took me to his house some months later.

Before leaving home my father had asked me to make only one promise. As a veterinary surgeon, he was very anxious about rabies. He had asked me, if bitten by a bat, dog or monkey, then to immediately come home. The only way to protect against rabies was a two to three week course of injections in the stomach which might be very risky in India, he worried. A veterinary friend of his had died of rabies, when bitten by a puppy in The Gambia, and the details of his suffering were particularly gruesome. This life saving promise did not seem unreasonable. However, rather sooner than expected, my promise was to be tested.

The train, full of such social company and colourful saris, rattled west to Jaipur with her fascinating Hawa Mahal. This is the Palace of Winds by Maharaja Singh, with many small viewing rooms for each of his wives to enjoy the view without intruding on each other.

Close to the Hawa Mahal, Jaipur also boasts the Jantah Mantar observatory with many astronomical instruments and apparently the world's largest sundial. It was possible to climb into some of the instruments for a better view. After wandering around several of them in a small park, I rested on the grass. Several monkeys were sitting quietly a few yards from me, but causing no concern. Just behind me, a family with small children were having a picnic. A very pleasant afternoon until suddenly the children started throwing stones over my shoulders at the monkeys without any provocation. I ducked to avoid their stone throwing which was the wrong response. The monkeys were enraged and jumped shrieking towards the stone-throwing children. But they found me first on their way. Two jumped on my shoulder and one climbed on my back and bit me on the backside. Suddenly, my instincts took over and I rose up with a roar like a gorilla which surprised everybody in the park, but shocked the monkeys even more and they fled. My relief was short-lived. The monkeys had left, a small victory, but one of them had bitten me and the earlier promise flooded my mind. I was scared and had to do something quickly; to find a doctor at once. Not so easy on a Sunday afternoon. Rushing back into the centre of Jaipur, I asked several people for a doctor and followed their guidance. Their suggestions did not seem right but several suggested an alleyway with a small rickety external staircase. I climbed up onto a roof terrace where four men in vests and sarongs were playing cards.

Asking them again where I could find a doctor, one kind man asked what my trouble was. Having explained the story, he put down his cards to ask if he could examine the monkey bite. Trembling somewhat, I explained my fear of rabies. He nodded and thought about it carefully. "I think you are going to be alright. It is true that the monkey has scratched you but your skin is not significantly broken. Rabies is carried in the monkey saliva and you are very lucky here as he bit you in an area where you are wearing two layers of clothing, your trousers and underpants. My advice would be to do nothing but if you are still worried then you can come tomorrow to my surgery at the Jaipur hospital."

I thanked him and wished them all well with their afternoon. But, in the morning I was still worried. On the other hand, his advice made sense. Also, my adventure in India was so interesting that to give up so early would be a very difficult choice to make. Oscillating between two opposite courses, an easier decision was made to visit his surgery in the hospital. He looked rather different than the one playing cards on the terrace but was still very kind. Although he had made up his mind not to worry, he saw I was undecided. He suggested taking a break from hospital work to show me around. We went out to his motorcycle and drove to Amer Hill. The palace has magnificent silver doors. By the afternoon, my fear of rabies had waned and it was easier to stay in India. From time to time in the following months the thought still troubled me. A memory of the doctor's patience and kindness in showing me around will always stay with me, as will my guilt for the other patients who had to wait longer or see someone else that afternoon.

After two nights in Jaipur, my railway ticket whisked me to Udaipur with a Maharaja's palace in the centre of a lake. Arriving after lunch and admiring the view, I decided to take a photograph of the city from the far side of the lake. It was easy by bus, they said. Once the bus seemed far enough around, and beginning to veer in the wrong direction, I hopped off and walked twenty minutes or so down to the water. However, once there, my surroundings were quite different from what I had imagined. Just open grass and a few trees, with nobody else there to ask which bus to take back. It seemed simpler to just walk around the lakeshore rather than go back over open ground to the road and attempt to find a bus. I guessed a walk along the shore couldn't be more than three miles to get back to town. Probably not much more than an hour's walk. But waiting for sunset was not wise after all. Darkness would make my shoreline return to town alone tricky. As the sun started to wane, I took just one picture as the budget for photographs was equally tight.

Walking along briskly, after a quarter of an hour I came to a very high wall which ran straight into the lake. The wall was several feet higher than the water for fully fifty yards. This seemed very odd. Not knowing what it was or why it was there, I found a tree to climb and look over. The grass and trees seemed the same on the other side. So I found a way to climb over this wall and drop down about fifteen feet onto the grass before continuing my shoreline walk. Except, about fifteen minutes later I came across another very similar wall, also going down into the lake like before. Since the town was still in full view on my right, in the twilight,

I was clearly not lost. There was no choice but to find a way to climb over this wall too, but it was much harder than the first one even if about the same height. I hoped there were not any more such walls on this obstacle course. Luckily there weren't. Almost an hour later I arrived in the centre of town and settled in a small stall for rice and lentils, and of course a garam chai or hot tea. The others all asked me about my adventures and were fascinated by my tales. Suddenly remembering climbing the walls, I asked them about those walls which went into the lake. "Oh that's an enclosure where the maharajah kept his tigers," they said.

Six months in the Indian subcontinent warrants a whole book, particularly with the generosity and kindness received from so many of them. Although travelling alone, I was never alone. However, on fast forward, the trains meandered through many exquisite cities and villages to Rameshwaram where a ferry took me to Talaimannar on the north shore of Ceylon one full moon. Bahu had instructed me, on arrival in Colombo, to pass by the office of his uncle who would look after me in his village until Bahu came down from Kandy to collect me. I hadn't known that his uncle designed stamps. In his office were lovely paintings of Ceylonese scenes. They were shrunk in printing from wall hanging size for the first edition of Sri Lankan stamps when Ceylon changed her name, on 22nd May 1972, shortly after my arrival coincidentally.

A few days later Bahu turned up. I had just developed a very high fever with bloody diarrhoea and was in extreme pain. He took me at once to a witch doctor in the neighbouring village, an elderly lady who seemed very wise. After translating my symptoms, she collected some ingredients and mixed up a bright red liquid, which had to be drunk at once. Although feeling better immediately, she gave me enough to take for a few days.

The following morning we set off together by bus up to Kandy. Arriving in the central Colombo station from his uncle's village, Bahu suddenly remembered he had forgotten something. "Wait here," he said, "I just need to get something. There are some aunts in my house and I need some poison powder." He said it so calmly, it was odd. Clutching my bottle of red liquid from the witch doctor while waiting, I wondered what else about him I didn't know. But he had said that so normally. It was puzzling and perturbing, making me wonder how to address this awkward subject. On his return, just as calmly, my question was, "How many aunts are there in your house?" He replied, "Hundreds and they are quite big." As he demonstrated their approximate size with his thumb and forefinger, I told him of my relief that he had meant to say ants and he laughed enough to infect the whole bus.

His house was two hundred yards uphill from the Kandy central bus station, and very comfortable. The shower was in the garden with a bucket and rope next to a well. He had a cook who loved to tease me, and many interesting books.

Kandy, being in the centre of Sri Lanka, was perfectly placed for my radial daily tours. There were many temples and ancient monuments which were easily accessible by bus. After breakfast, when Bahu set off to teach at the university, I went down to the bus station and selected a bus from the list he made for me. Except, later that morning, the bus did not go to the destination written on the front. This didn't really matter as the bus went somewhere else which was also on my list. Perhaps the bus driver hadn't set the destination properly, I mused. But, the next morning, the same thing happened. This was clearly not a coincidence. Were the buses in Sri Lanka playing the same tricks on me as directions given in India? It was very intriguing. Over dinner that evening, even with our logical physics brains, we couldn't make heads or tails of it. Bahu suggested the following morning I find someone who spoke English and asked where the bus was going, never mind what it said on the front. I did. Again they didn't match. My interpreter saw the problem immediately.

The bus drivers had a long roll with a list of places to choose from which they wound forward or backward with a key until finding their chosen destination. Each destination was written in Sinhala, Tamil and English, in that order, as shown in this example for Dambulla. However, preferring to have Sinhala more prominently placed in the centre of their destination screen, the Tamil underneath was also correct but the English destination (now appearing on top) referred to the previous destination on the roll. The English destination was therefore guaranteed to be wrong. Since many drivers could not read English, they hadn't noticed. Since everybody else looked first for either Sinhala or Tamil, they were not troubled. Having learned from a driver how to adjust the roll, my problem was solved. For

the next two months, each morning after arriving at the bus station, I would ask a friendly driver to lend me his key and wind the screen destination to put Sinhala on top to see the right destination in all three languages.

The bus drivers got used to my antics and always laughed when they saw me in the mornings. Some probably thought this teenage English boy had a 'quaint habit' of rearranging the face of their bus *to see* where they were going. It is funny how one's forgotten infancy keeps cropping up as we meander through life. Meanwhile all the drivers at the central bus station made me very welcome. Those 'in the know' explained the reason of my 'quaintness' to other drivers who smiled broadly. A 'hearing person' would be less troubled as they would more naturally ask where the bus was going, and the destination sounds the same in all three languages.

Sometimes I went further afield and stayed the night in the home of a bus driver's family, or a policeman's house in the South before returning. With Kandy being a perfect hub, it was easy to visit most of the island in the ensuing weeks. At the weekends Bahu was free to travel with me.

One of my favourite daily trips was to watch the elephants bathe in the Mahaweli River at Katugastota. Everybody enjoyed themselves just like children throwing water and sponges in a giant bath; two species having such fun. My 'deaf-sight' savoured the way elephants loved to tease their mahouts with extra sprays.

During my many visits around Kandy, people often suggested extending my stay to include the highlight of the year in Sri Lanka, the elephant processions in the Kandy Perahera. About a hundred elephants would be dressed up for a ritual, they said, somewhat excitedly. The idea was very tempting but there would not be enough time sadly. I told them all that there was no doubt I would be back, not just for the Kandy Perahera but also because I loved their island so much. They had made me so welcome, they were so peaceful and generous, the climate and food so delicious, the scenery so green and the culture so rich.

When the time came to leave Sri Lanka, it was very hard to tear myself away.

The journey back to Cambridge began by the ferry to Rameshwaram. Except, this time the ferry was full of Tamils being forced home. An agreement had been made between the two governments to repatriate thousands of Tamils back to India every week. Many of them could not read or write. Sensing that help was at hand, they formed a long queue on the ferry deck asking me to help fill in their immigration forms. It was very sad for both of us as they shared their details. They didn't want to leave where they had been born.

From the south of India, my student train ticket took me through many towns up the east coast to Calcutta and Banaras. After a bus ride to visit Nepal, I continued by train across the north of India towards Pakistan. From there, I took a bus through the Khyber Pass and even more dramatic Kabul Gorge before arriving in Afghanistan's capital Kabul.

My reader will think I am hallucinating now and suspect something is being made up. But, it's true. I remember having coffee in a street café outside a branch of Marks and Spencer in Kabul, with girls in mini-skirts. Back then, in 1972, Afghanistan was still ruled by the King. There were effectively three irreconcilable societies. The King realised that there was no chance of them ever being reconciled, so he instructed them to leave each other alone. Broadly it worked. There was one section of society which was essentially Pashtun; then the Mujahedeen who believed that they had the right to slit the throats of non-believers; and finally a section of society which could have been transplanted from a café on the Champs Elysees in Paris. The extremes of society could not have been further apart, but there was little sense of discomfort about it. Instead, the masses of flies seemed more troubling.

After Kabul, I also remember arriving one evening at a small hotel in Kandahar. The owner asked me to give him warning before needing a bath so that he could light a log fire to warm the water. We had a chat and, having asked him about other travellers, he told me a group of six European tourists had been there the previous week. Naturally asking where they went, quite casually he replied that some Mujahedeen had come in the night and slit all their throats. Luckily my 'deaf-sight' helped me to determine that he had not approved. He was clearly on my side, but was not in a position to do anything. He had to accept something which could happen to tourists. I decided to trust him as I felt safe with him, although I sensed he needed to appear neutral in mentioning the subject in case he suffered consequences. There was no better choice really, as the alternative would have been to wander around town to see if there was another hotel, thereby drawing more attention to myself. Instinct is so valuable. I didn't have a great night's sleep, though. At first light, I had a bath rather quickly and set off for Herat. I wasn't going to hang around in Kandahar, which was the main area of the Mujahedeen.

After a brief visit to the expansive Mosque and market in Herat, my journey took me westwards and my memory is of being captivated by vast caravans of Bactrian camels near Mashhad in North Eastern Iran. Three weeks later, I was home just in time for the wedding of my second sister, Jenny, as promised many months earlier.

Back home in Cambridge enabled me to see all my slides, three rolls of film or just over a hundred pictures taken during six months. Just a picture a day on average; how different photography was back then. Not having been able to see any of the hundred pictures since embarking on the journey meant that I had not known they were all a little over exposed.

But they brought back such lovely memories such as this one of Bahu's morning shower in the Kandy hills.[1]

A few days after Jenny's wedding, there were still two months left before my Oxford studies were due to begin. Not wanting to waste the time, I

[1] Before leaving this chapter, let me thank my oldest friend for the kindness during my teenage years and for so much wisdom and friendship since. Bahu spent most of his working life in politics, always seeking to help the repressed. He stood, unsuccessfully, in the Presidential election of 2010. On my last visit a few years ago it was an honour to watch how much he was revered by the local population for all his efforts in Sri Lankan society. He suffered imprisonment on several occasions for his political views or for standing up for others.

went to Morocco. After touring many markets and lovely cities, my wandering continued east into Algeria.

After hitchhiking from Oran to Algiers, I decided to explore a little of the Sahara. It was easy to hitchhike six hundred kilometres down into the desert to a lovely town at Ghardaia with her fine narrow whitewashed streets. Having spent a few days in the intense heat, the desert seemed to be tempting me towards a deeper wandering. Reading about the southern oasis at Tamanrasset in the Ahaggar Mountains was pulling me very enticingly.

But, on reflection, a desert journey would perhaps be better in another year with more time. Instead of returning back to Algiers, I found I could hitchhike eastwards to Hassi Messaoud before turning north-east into Tunisia.

After a ferry to Sicily, I was home a week or so later.

Autumn brought the matter of Nuclear Physics at Oxford together with my sheepskin coat from Afghanistan which smelled too much when it rained.

Khartoum to El Aaiun

In the spring of 1973, during my first year at Oxford, I thought about travelling again in the long summer vacation. My thoughts were to visit somewhere new without wandering too much. After all, my best memory of 1972 was the long stay in Kandy. My choice was settled by volunteering to spend the whole summer teaching English and Mathematics at a school in Juba, South Sudan.

This chapter includes extracts (*in italics*) of my journal, *Khartoum to El Aaiun.*

After a flight to Cairo, some days in museums and pyramids, a mixture of trains and sailing dhows took me up the Nile to Luxor and the Valley of the Kings. A train took me to Aswan and then a paddle steamer to Wadi Halfa in Sudan.

We were packed for two days and two nights like sardines with no room aboard to lie down, even on deck. Attempts at sleep while sitting on the floor were the only option, but at least there was someone else's back to lean against.

Onwards to Khartoum was then nine hundred kilometres by train with a different discomfort; all the water jugs were empty more than twelve hours before we could find water again. Patience and enjoyable conversations with fellow travellers sustained me.

On arrival in Khartoum, the first task was to obtain my permit to visit Juba. The authorities advised me it was no longer possible to take up my voluntary appointment. Apparently violent 'troubles' of some kind had broken out and they would not let me go south.

This was a huge disappointment. I had been looking forward to a term with friendly African school children. But, it didn't make sense to just turn around with over three months until my second year at university began. Since there was no hurry, the thought came naturally to find a way back home overland, just as I had done from Sri Lanka. Staring at maps, and chatting in many cafés about the travelling conditions, suggested a route west to Kano in Nigeria, around 3,200 kilometres as the crow flies. There were neither crows nor roads but they told me there would be people going that way, surely. They said trucks went through Chad which was most of the way.

From Kano, I already knew there was a good road north across the Sahara through Niger and Algeria, even if over 3,000 kilometres. The frequency and ease with which trucks had taken me down to Ghardaia in Algeria the previous year reminded me of their stories of this road from the Mediterranean to Nigeria. My earlier wish to visit the mountain oasis of Tamanrasset was an exciting prospect. The Sahara crossing would be easy, I imagined. After all, I had already hitchhiked a quarter of the way across Algeria only nine months before. With over three months until my second year at Oxford was due to begin, the journey did not seem difficult. Also, the only visa required was for Nigeria. Remembering a kind Frenchman who had offered me a lift from Oran to Algiers, and his advice to take vitamin tablets, I bought some at a street stall in Khartoum. I felt equipped with my small bag, a sleeping bag and a map of Africa covering all the 6,500 kilometres ahead.

Looking back over my life, there is a trait which keeps coming up. A confidence that once a journey began it would be possible to figure a way out of whatever came. The key was to get going. The first step was the Nigerian Embassy. But they were very firm with a prominent notice stating that visas were only given to applicants 'in their home country'.

In spite of this, I filled in a form in duplicate which I then offered to the embassy clerk. My attention was immediately drawn to the rules by the clerk, but he decided to submit the papers and I was instructed to return the following morning, just in case. I left and had walked scarcely a hundred yards down the road when he came running after me, shouting that I should return. I finally heard him and he explained that the Ambassador requested to see me.

Somewhat surprised, I entered the room to be greeted warmly by a gentleman in full Nigerian dress. "I see you live in Cambridge, Mr Goodwin, I am pleased to meet you as I was a student at St. John's College." We sat and talked over a cup of sweet back tea, both equally nostalgic and then before I left he instructed the consul to make out a visa for me, gratis.

Feeling fully prepared and armed with the only visa needed, the journey home began.

There were however a series of unexpectedly daunting obstacles. There had been a drought in the Sahel for the previous seven years but the weather had 'broken' at last. Rivers flowing again broke bridges and made many tracks in the sand impassable to trucks. On arrival in Nigeria, the news that the border between Niger and Algeria had been closed to all travellers was devastating.[2] The only way north across the Sahara was now much further west by crossing through Mauretania. Additional detours were necessary to obtain visas for Mali and Senegal before heading north. This increased the overall distance to 10,215 kilometres between Khartoum and the Mediterranean. The bottle of 'vitamin tablets' turned out to be something else with the result that my health deteriorated while losing far too much weight.

There were a great many other challenges. This journey moulded me in many ways, and taught me a great deal. There are a number of lessons, looking back, which may have helped me with the eventual challenge of this book. My journal begins:

> *'with thanks to the nomads who adopted me like a long lost son,*
> *and to the many children who cheered me up in the more difficult times'.*

The map overleaf shows the route starting in Cairo, down to Khartoum before heading across Africa to Accra, Ghana and on to Dakar, Senegal, with a Sahara crossing in Mauritania.

---

[2] The most likely reason is that Algeria was nervous of security concerns while preparing for their first hosting of the Arab League summit, with the leaders of the first 17 member nations, later in the year.

In some respects the journey was like my silent years. On my return, someone asked me how I managed with all those different tribal languages. My spontaneous reply was, "It was just like my childhood. I didn't understand the words, but I understood everything."

My journal says: *I left Khartoum by train towards the south with a 4th class ticket to Kosti. It was hot, very hot, and the Arabs, squeezed between baggage and other travellers, were subdued with discomfort. I could not even find room to flick away the flies, wedged as I was between a lady of no mean stature and the window or grill. A fan was being frisked by a middle-aged lady on the same bench and I tried, with some success, to squeeze into a position whereby I could benefit from the draught. She smiled, reading my thought, and directed the air a little more in my direction. In spite of the congestion people continued to pile in and many wiser passengers were clearly waiting on the platform until just before departure. Inside was very quiet, the only voices coming from outside, but as the carriages lurched forward bringing a gentle and welcome breeze everybody started talking loudly. Surprisingly there did not seem any less room with all those jumping on-board as the train pulled out.*

As the suburbs turned to desert I decided there must be somewhere better to sit, after all, where had the 'wise ones' gone. It was not until I tried to move that I realised how tightly packed we were. I climbed carefully along the backs of the seats to a gap between carriages and stood with a foot on each buffer enjoying the wind from all directions. The train swayed and jolted so much that I had to hold on very tightly to maintain my footing which I nearly lost several times. With some assistance from a boy above me, I heaved myself up by stages onto the roof to find hundreds of pairs of eyes watching me. It was as if I had reached a new world and everybody made me instantly welcome.

Most sat chatting in small groups; a few dozed or prayed; some wandered up and down to greet friends and others to sell merchandise. Soon I was brought coffee and cakes as they gathered around me to ask my news and purpose. In particular, I made friends with two brothers, Mohammed and Ahmed, aged about twenty from El Obeid. I passed the time of day trying to improve my Arabic and listening to stories, only interrupted by the occasional telegraph wire forcing us to bend double as it passed…

…as it grew dark we had a final cup of coffee and then settled down to sleep under the stars, orientated parallel to the wooden sleepers under the rails to prevent us from falling off if we moved about in the night.

I had scarcely got down in Kosti before deciding it was a mistake. Why not continue further west with my new friends to El Obeid.

It did not take long for me to climb up again just before the train started to leave. They were not surprised, having not been able to imagine why I had got off in the first place. We spent the rest of the day talking about families, friends, and most importantly their camels whilst watching the occasional tree or shrub out of the corner of our eyes. Whenever the train passed near a village it would slow down, enabling the local inhabitants to run alongside offering cakes, coffee and kebabs in exchange for a few coins. We nearly always bought if only for something to do. Then the train would pick up speed, not a lot though, perhaps twenty miles an hour at most, but it took us into El Obeid in the morning after another night spent very happily on the roof.

I always enjoy arriving in a new town, seeing new faces and reading all the signs with interest. I wander about like a vagabond, smiling and waving to anybody or everybody and frequently stopping in cafés to talk with the old men, to drink karkadeh[3] *or to play backgammon. By contrast, when it is time to leave I creep out like a smuggler not wishing to say goodbye.*

Having found my feet in El Obeid, I explored how to make my way westwards. *The Sudanese railway south-west to Nyala was broken by floods and the sandy ground was impassable except by the largest of trucks. One or two trucks were however likely to depart for Al Fashir within the next twenty-four hours and so I had some lunch before seeking them out. The most reliable looking one intended to wend its way the following morning and having naively asked how long it might take, they replied laughing, "Perhaps two days, sometimes more than a week depending on the weather." It seemed a long time for only four hundred miles but then there was no road.*

The next morning, they told me the truck would not leave before lunch so my tour of the town continued. I met Mohammed and Ahmed in the street. They helped me choose some headgear to protect me from the sun. We found a targea and shar, which is rather like a Jewish skull cap with a two metre long white cotton scarf to wind around like a turban. Altogether it was much cooler than without.

After lunch, I boarded my transport. It was loaded to the top with boxes. The passengers, numbering more than twenty, had to sit on top of these. There was a three-inch thick metal bar down the length and in the middle, some four feet above the highest boxes. At first this seemed convenient to hold on to but I soon realised that it was the driver's sole contribution to our comfort being a ridge pole for a canvas sheet serving as a tent when it rained.

Almost immediately I took to two black men who were the mechanics and diggers in case the truck got stuck in mud or sand. They held on at the very back but I preferred the front above the driver's cab with my feet occasionally overhanging the windscreen. I was very comfortable there, able to enjoy the breeze and the view.

The track was quite good at first as we pulled out of El Obeid to waves from all the children and we made a reasonable, if bumpy speed.

Towards the evening it rained and our roof tent was pitched. It turned out to be very effective but there was not a lot of room underneath and everyone was falling over

---

[3] Karkadeh is a hibiscus tea, common in Egypt and Sudan.

everybody else in the darkness due to the uneven floor, or tops of boxes. As the truck swayed and reeled a few squeaks and groans ensued from the melee within but I managed to make myself tolerably comfortable and even to ignore the flying limbs to get some sleep...

The track became more difficult; every now and then the truck sank into the soft sand. The mechanics had to dig trenches and put metal 'sand-ladders' along the bottom to enable the truck to drive out. The truck would then try and maintain its speed to avoid sinking again while the mechanics had to run with the ladders and their shovels to catch up with us. It was very difficult for them but they were always grinning when they climbed back on board to start the whole process all over again. They did, however, have one consolation in that after a fixed term as labourers and mechanics they could enter into apprenticeships as drivers...

On the fifth day out of El Obeid life became very difficult; the truck had to follow one foot deep tracks like a tram and problems occurred whenever we met a truck coming in the opposite direction. The mechanics had to dig a 'siding' to let one truck move out of the way. It took more than four hours to cover half a mile. Finally the ground became firmer which took us into Al Fashir around five o'clock in the afternoon. I jumped down into a restaurant in the main market square for my first proper meal in five days; a delicious plate of rice, vegetables and kebabs.

Two hundred miles west of Al Fashir, about a thousand miles from Khartoum, lies Al Junaynah and the border between Darfur, Sudan, and Chad. Trucks were no longer going west because of the ground condition. Progress was only possible on foot, either human or animal. A group of nomads had taken me to the border but they decided to stop and wait for the water level to drop. We spent the afternoon preparing a feast of roasted goat and chickens before sleeping in a circle like the spokes of a wheel with our heads in the centre. Many other caravans stopped in the same place the following morning wondering when their camels would be able to wade through the river. When they all saw how high the river was, most decided to wait or turn back. Only one group were continuing westwards, so I followed them.

Crossing from Darfur, West Sudan to Chad with Zaghawa tribe, June 1973

After wading together through the river, their planned path began to veer too much towards the south for my westerly plans. They told me it was not far to Adré, the next village in Chad, and I could walk there easily alone. It wasn't even possible to miss, apparently, or so they said. Well, missing Adré was possible as my walk was much longer than expected. Eventually, in the afternoon, I found a small boy with a donkey and he led me into Adré from the other side of the village, which I had completely passed by walking too far to the south.

My debt to nomadic tribes is incalculable. They adopted me in a way which my culture had not. Not just in an ordinary superficial way, but with a more generous connection which was new to me. Their hospitality was so deep, offering all of what little they had, showing the richness of their wish to share their existence with a fellow traveller. The 'first hearing system', before noise began again as a seven-year-old, enabled me to communicate with them. My 'first language' of 'deaf-sight' enabled me to appreciate their welcome and feel safe. In a sense, whenever encountering someone with whom there was a common vocabulary, my noisy hearing predominated with lots of words. With no common language to exchange noises, we slipped into the language of my deaf years and understood each other perfectly. Reading my journal, there are some other details which I had forgotten:

I always made sure they realised how defenceless I was by not even carrying a small knife and by trusting them completely which in turn led them to accept me more quickly. A nomad told me how the Koran asks them to look after travellers, pilgrims, orphans, the poor and needy. He considered me all five. It was easy to feel their welcome. Many of them could speak English or French and they taught me to read and write Arabic in the sand.

The journey, despite the struggles, felt completely safe with these and neighbouring tribes. Perhaps the rains and the subsequent closure of the Algerian border enabled me to travel with people and tribes which I would otherwise never have met.

Looking back, there were just too many 'flukes', lucky encounters or synchronicities. There were so many occasions when someone saved me from disaster at a critical time. Or, is it possible that the 'deaf-sight' enabled me to see a safe path and to know who to trust. We will never know.

Hopefully, my entire journal might be published one day. Meanwhile, for the subject matter of this book, we will jump across Africa to Ghana and the beginning of the journey north. With the despair of extra distance and poor diet of my weeks on the road, I was becoming weaker and running out of funds. The expensive detour to Accra, through the west of Niger and Upper Volta (as she was then called) consumed much of my resources. The last straw was arriving in Accra and finding the embassy of Mali closed, having gone all the way down to the coast just for that visa. In a rash mini extravagance, I decided to spend some money on a taxi back to the hostel since everything seemed hopeless. It wasn't too rash as Accra had shared taxis and if there was room in the back they took more people…

A taxi pulled up with a middle-aged lady on the back seat and I climbed in beside her. After explaining my destination to the driver, the lady enquired of my purpose at the closed embassy. "I can help you," she exclaimed, "I am the personal assistant to the Ambassador. Come and see me at two o'clock this afternoon and I will prepare it for you in five minutes."

When I arrived back at the hostel, I met an Irishman called Noel of my age and we very soon established that we had almost similar resources and also intended to travel the same way.[4] *We decided to accompany each other and to set off the following day. It was a good thing that neither of us had any more money than the other so that we had no choice but to follow the cheapest route. Noel turned out to be a great success, having a repertoire of jokes and stories which kept us going through some very difficult periods in the desert when everything seemed lost. He would leave me to talk with the Bedouin (nomads) or the French officials, since he had not a word of Arabic or French, and to make the decisions, but every problem seemed lighter with his jest. The challenges sometimes even became enjoyable with his help.*

It felt so good to be heading northwards, at last in the right direction for going home. From the Gold Coast at Accra, Ghana to the West Coast of Africa at Dakar, Senegal was straightforward enough. Only a little anxiety troubled us on the way to the border with the Ivory Coast with a driver who had clearly had far too much whisky.

Once in Dakar, sitting on the beach and watching the waves, we considered a plan to get home. Noel enjoyed the fresh pineapples but my mouth was so ulcerated they were too painful for me to eat. My body was rejecting the vitamins that I needed to survive. Sometimes the mind or body rejects the life-raft, as if we have reached an abyss where the pain is too great to be able to reach a place of salvation, and without help we cannot make it through. Perhaps the pain would have been more easily bearable if I had known *why* it was necessary to force myself through. But when there is only pain, without the knowledge of *why*, it is too easy to remain stuck on the wrong side of the slippery slope.

Looking at the maps, there were not many options. We had to head north through the Mauritanian desert to Choum before continuing to the well at Bir Moghrein. But, from there the choice was almost an impossible one; either north-west towards El Aaiun in the Spanish Sahara or north-east towards the Algerian well of Tindouf. The journal explains:

Neither was easy nor appealing. Spanish Sahara was closed to British nationals, and therefore we would have to make an illegal entry. The route to Tindouf was the most

---

[4] We both had £40 with which to journey home from Ghana.

dangerous stretch of all Sahara tracks. The distance is about four hundred miles with only one well at Ain Ben Tili along the way. Navigation is difficult and finding that well was a matter of chance since it was so small and without trees. The 'road' is over a hundred miles wide as different drivers took different paths over the sand. Some prefer a more direct route, others prefer a less direct route but on firmer ground, and others wind all over the place to avoid the soft sand. We had learned that the 'traffic' was about one vehicle per week. We were told that the most recent Landrover had been unable to find the well at Ain Ben Tili; all twelve passengers had died. Two vehicles with nineteen people perished in the week before our possible attempt. We spent hours thinking about it, speaking with the Berbers to find out their choice but still could not decide. All the while Noel was a tremendous support with his never failing humour and cheer.

The only answer was to travel first to Bir Moghrein and find out more once we got there.

We crossed the Senegal River by canoe, which was faster than the ferry carrying a cargo of camels returning to the desert after the drought. We found easily a truck to take us to the Mauritanian capital, Nouakchott, which is very small and we did not realise we had arrived until the truck stopped at the main police station. Even in the 'city centre' the roads are just sand.

Whilst looking around, a Berber wearing a fine blue Djellaba came up to us very warmly. He insisted that we eat a couscous with him in a small restaurant before taking us to his house where all the children ran out to welcome us. He invited us for tea and requested we stay the night. Whilst having yet another sweet tea, we discussed our options of travelling north. He convinced us to consider the way to Tindouf really as a last resort; being so dangerous. The idea of an illegal entry to Spanish Sahara seemed the better option but we would still wait until speaking to others in Bir Moghrein.

In the very early morning our host directed us to a market on the outskirts of the capital through which ran the 'route' to Choum. But, in the market they said trucks can carry only one passenger by law and there was a police checkpoint about a mile down the road so no driver would pick us up before that.

The sun was rising fast and the heat even faster, so Noel did not appreciate the news of a walk of several miles. We had a final cup of tea in the market and then trudged out of town. We reached the police checkpoint and waved in good cheer as if we were out for a morning stroll. After another mile or so, once the police hut was hidden by a dune, there was no shade. However we saw a Bedouin tent not too far away and we walked over there. A small girl who was very shy and yet inquisitive brought us some goat's milk in a bowl and some tea. Her father came out to talk. I was so sorry to learn of how many animals the family had lost in the drought but he shrugged his shoulders saying he was confident the worst was over. The scant rains would be sufficient to provide food for his herd and that more rain was on the way. He asked whether I came from Egypt because of my Arabic accent. We spoke of the Nile and how lucky the Egyptians were to have such a river. It seemed so strange and such a long time since sailing up the Nile.

At half-past three, when the sun had passed his zenith, we heard the first truck of the day. There was plenty of time to say farewell and to thank him for his hospitality before walking back to the sand 'road'. The truck slowed down seeing my hand gestures. There was no doubt where either the truck or we were headed so he just asked us to climb in. He took us to Akjoujt, half way to Choum, where we stopped and slept on the floor in the police station as usual.

In the morning, the police advised us to walk a few miles east since some trucks drove directly from Nouakchott to Choum without coming into Akjoujt. We would have more chances there. Having walked first one way and then another until noticing a stretch that seemed darker, the 'road', we were joined by a Jordanian also waiting for a truck to pass.

A truck came by and took us to Atar where we again slept at the police station. While waiting for breakfast, we didn't talk, not liking the options ahead. Omelettes

Noel and 'the Jordanian' with my father's old 'white' naval bag, waiting for trucks towards Choum and the north. There was no shade for miles.

arrived covered in oil, but we were hungry enough for anything. A gentleman came towards us, pulling up a chair and inquiring our intended direction. He had expected us to say Choum and offered us a lift in his van which would leave in a few hours. It was not difficult to show our gratitude as he left. He promised to look around the town for us when he was ready to leave.

We visited the market and on the way out we bumped into him. He had already been to the police station to collect our bags. Everybody knows everything in these small towns.

The road to Choum was very different with a steady climb into hills. After weeks of travelling on the flat it seemed like a fairy story to be climbing several hundred feet into the sky and looking down on the vast open space. The view included all kinds of desert erosion and formations with mountains in one direction, dunes in the middle distance and unusually shaped boulders interspaced with a variety of scrub. Unfortunately the only signs of animals were carcasses in the sand, reduced to bones by the fierceness of the heat.

Shortly after the descent, our van developed a 'fault'. The driver did not seem to worry, just picking up a few tools as we all got out. A Syrian passenger with two small children invited us to join him for a glass of tea, obviously thinking the repair would not be simple. We crouched by one of the very few bushes for some shade. He produced a kettle from his bag as might have been produced by Aladdin, and started up a small fire with a few twigs. Out from beneath his djellaba he then produced two Lipton's tea bags on a string which he had been saving for just such a special occasion. It made our day. Second and third glasses followed before there was any sign of departure. We were in no hurry and we felt that we could not waste any of his brew.

Finally we re-boarded the van and raced along the sand flats, only broken by mirages. We spotted a large mirage; it seemed a little unusual as mirages are usually blue and this was grey, moreover this did not disappear as we approached. It became clear that this was real water so the rain of the last few days must have been very heavy. We stopped on the edge while everybody peered in as if not knowing what to do. Noel and

I knew however and within seconds had dived in for a swim, it being almost waist high. The top six inches of water was very hot and the bottom was like ice by comparison making the whole phenomenon doubly strange. Some of the other passengers joined in so we were rather a bedraggled and soaked bunch when the journey resumed.

In the evening we discovered that Choum is not really a town but only a bend in the railway line as a single track turns from south to west. Six huts mark the place to give the impression of a railway station of sorts. The train comes from the coast by Nouadhibou and continues up north to the mine at Fort Derrick where iron ore is loaded for the journey to the ships. Passengers, if any, are allowed to travel for free on any stretch, but between the mine and the port the train only stops at Choum. This is because the bend is also the only place where the line has double tracks to act as a passing place for full and empty trains.

As the sun fell into a dune and people began their evening prayers, a lady came out of one of the huts to offer Noel and I some supper. We followed her, squatted in the approved fashion, and waited patiently while she produced a meal of rice, mutton and even potatoes. This was excellent and more than satisfied our needs. We sat and talked over coffee as it grew dark; while the lady and her husband tried to give an impression of how big the train was, using all the words they could think of to describe length and other dimensions. Noel and I naively assumed this was only because the train appeared big to them.

We continued talking in the light of a petrol lamp until the rattle and rumble of the train could be heard just after midnight. The noise of shunting wagons seemed to continue for an eternity. When it stopped Noel and I climbed into the nearest wagon, empty apart from a floor of fine dust. It was late; we were both tired after a long day in the sun and rolled out our sleeping bags on the floor to sleep. At first it was quite comfortable, with a gentle rumbling as the train moved slowly, but as speed picked up everything started to rattle. Sleep became out of the question as the bumping and jolting threw us off the metal floor to come crashing down again covered in the dust which was also dancing on the floor. It was not long before lying on the floor became too much to bear. We stood up, leaning on the side of the wagon which came up to our shoulders. We could take the jolting in the legs by flexing a little, but we were too tired to stand up for long. There seemed no escape from the problem and we started to alternate between standing and lying with increasing frequency as we forgot how unbearable the other position was. Sitting on the floor had seemed to be the answer but my legs and buttocks went to sleep in a matter of seconds. We could not have climbed out without being left in the desert and no other wagon would have been different so we tried each position again, and again, until it nearly drove us mad.

Suddenly the sky became black and an echo abounded, the air became stifling and we both began to choke as if in a coal mine. We remembered that someone had told us of a tunnel somewhere, but could not remember how long it was. It was hysterically funny at first until the dust in the air forced us to keep our mouths shut….

The time when we only had to consider the jolting of the train seemed like a paradise lost. Then, as suddenly as the tunnel had come, it went leaving clear air and the beautiful sight of stars again. We took a number of deep breaths to clear our lungs and considered ourselves lucky in the original predicament. Placing all my clothes on a folded sleeping bag and lying on top, to soften the jolts, finally enabled sleep until dawn.

In the early light, I stood up. There were just a few heads looking out too. But, the train seemed to disappear into the dust over the horizon both in front of and behind us. What the lady had tried to describe was insufficient for this monster of a train.

It was such a relief to arrive at the mine. We were just glad to get off and none-the-less grateful for the free journey northwards. They told us it was the world's longest train with over two hundred wagons pulled by sixteen electrically synchronised engines. It was about three or four kilometres long apparently and we took them at their word.

All I wanted was to get going again to the trickiest part of our journey. Sometimes when there is a real danger ahead it is easier to go straight towards the fire rather than to hang about. I found a very pleasant gentleman intending to drive to Bir Moghrein at dusk. Yes, he would be delighted to have our company and would come and find us. At six, a Landrover turned up. There were two drivers, one for the accelerator, steering and clutch and one for the two gear sticks. They both kept their eyes skinned for patches of soft sand and occasionally we would swerve violently to avoid some. To enable the driver to pull very hard on the steering wheel his mate changed gear for him.

Whenever the vehicle showed signs of labouring in the sand, the remedy appeared quick as a flash from the pair up front.

Suddenly they stopped in the middle of nowhere. What had happened? Were we stuck? They descended for their last prayer of the day before driving all night. A small village appeared at dawn, which turned out to be Bir Moghrein herself. The drivers told me they had maintained their course by the stars and a sense of smell.

We had come to the place where we had to decide which way to turn. Sitting over coffee with a couple of Berbers, I picked their brains on the two directions. They told me last week some people had been refused entry at Tindouf and had to turn back. Another critical piece of information swayed me. The border officials for the Spanish Sahara were Berber and not Spanish. Trying to enter there illegally was my choice. Our luck continued with an offer of a ride by van to the border. I decided that, since we might be returning to Bir Moghrein, it was simplest not to get our passports stamped with an exit visa.

After lunch we climbed into the van and crept out of town by the least visible route, turning west after a while. Travelling at high speed across firm flat sand, we arrived at the border in just over an hour. The small building was not as noticeable as the beginning of a tarred road which we hadn't seen for so long. A customs official appeared from nowhere thus establishing he could only be local. He asked for our papers or passports which Noel and I had already passed to the driver. I could not help the rate at which my heart began to beat as the driver passed on our documents. Much discussion ensued between the driver and official but they had wandered off towards the hut, out of earshot. I half tried to watch what they were up to, but preferred not to know. It would have been much easier had I been talking to the officer myself. Then I noticed that he was reading the documents and so I watched his expression carefully when he came to ours. It was clear that he could not read mine as he held it upside down which, although not guaranteeing entry, at least suggested we would not have been better off even with a visa. It was therefore more dependent on what he had for breakfast and how he felt.

He looked up, coming towards the van and peering in. His eyes fell on me and he smiled with a greeting of 'Salaam Alaikum'. Things looked good and, being so dumbfounded, I almost forgot to reply 'alaikum as salaam'. He handed over the documents and beckoned us onwards with a courteous 'ma es salama'. Our driver then offered to take us to the nearest village. We climbed through some hills with many Bedouin tents and goats to Guelta which was the official frontier post and manned by Spanish troops. We were instructed to wait for the man in charge. The troops seemed friendly and pleased to meet someone new. The chief of customs turned out to have a very pleasant character and was nothing but helpful. We were issued with a 'salvo conductato' which meant that we were required to remain on our best behaviour for a maximum of three nights until we passed through the country. We celebrated with a large bottle of coke and a meal in the village restaurant before sleeping under a tree.

I woke several times in the night; it was so cold. By the morning, inside my sleeping bag and wearing every stitch of clothing with me, I was still shivering. Never had the Sahara felt so cold.

We found someone driving to El Aaiun on the coast which was an easy journey on a tarred road. Once there, we found a place for our best meal together since Accra; everything was so cheap, we could afford lobster and ice cream. Then, we walked towards the north of town in the direction of Morocco. After about a mile we came to the top of a hill and a police checkpoint; we sat on the ground, accepted a glass of water and rested against the wall. The police were similarly enthusiastic about activity and joined us on the sand for a chat about our journey and their life in the Sahara.

Despite my childhood, whenever away from home there was no shame and my nature was very gregarious. I enjoyed these conversations with new people in unknown places and always approached them so openheartedly. This time the conversation lasted several hours until the early evening.

A German couple arrived with a truck. They erected a very large tent next to the police station. Having explained they were driving to Nigeria, they offered us and several others a place inside their tent for the night. A French boy who was hitchhiking south and clearly on drugs was also there. The relief that the end of our journey was close lifted our spirits whilst sharing experiences of our route. We were all tired and agreed on sleep simultaneously.

I was woken very rudely at what seemed to be only a few minutes after I had gone to sleep but looking at my watch it was after three. A policeman was waking me and another was standing over me with a loaded gun aimed at my chest. The headlights of a Landrover lit up the entire tent. "Get up and come with us," a policeman shouted in Spanish. I jumped out of my sleeping bag. Noel was ordered to come too and he followed quickly seeing the rifle butt stuck in my back. It just did not seem possible that these were the policemen with whom we had been joking earlier. Once again I was reminded how easy it would be to vanish without trace.

I walked briskly the hundred or so yards to the checkpoint building as instructed. Upon entering I saw the French boy sitting in absolute terror, shaking like a leaf and as white as a sheet. He pointed at me and shouted, "C'est lui," with a very menacing look. I looked innocently around the room to find all eyes staring at mine and asked what had happened. A policeman replied in English, quite calmly, that I was accused of attempted murder. They boy shouted again that it was me. I was trying to kill him with a knife.

I stared incredulously and said that it was just ridiculous, I didn't even have a knife and why would I want to kill him. Besides, I was asleep and knew nothing of it. But this boy swore it was me and he looked sufficiently frightened for it to be true. I repeated that the whole story was nonsense and that they boy must have been having a bad dream, but he was well awake now and looked very convincing.

A policeman went to search my bag. Just after he left, I remembered that I did have a knife at the bottom of my bag, one which had been given to me by the Tuaregs in Niger. I felt cornered, surrounded by the stupid boy swearing at me, two soldiers with guns trained on me and the policeman who would soon discover my knife. Noel was the only one in the room who might have believed me, but I thought he looked convinced too. Suddenly, the French boy then accused Noel of helping me in the act. I was selfishly relieved to have someone on my side, and Noel was about to sound much more vehement in his refutation of the claim.

The policeman returned with my knife, and one from Noel's bag. I explained that I had forgotten all about it but could not have sounded very convincing. This policeman had however not realised that Noel was implicated too and I sensed some disbelief when he learned this new twist. He looked at me sympathetically and said the pair of us would be given a police escort to the border at dawn.

I felt initially extremely relieved and managed to joke with Noel that it would be a free lift and sooner than we could otherwise have hoped, but I began to wonder if we would really be taken to the border or just disposed of somewhere. Still, we were allowed to return to the tent to sleep and our 'victim' was guarded safely in the police station.

At dawn the police Landrover arrived as promised. We had a few minutes to gather the contents of our bags which had been scattered in the night in the search for the knife. Then Noel and I were bundled in the back, bags and all. The vehicle sped towards the north on a good road for about half an hour and then slowed down and made a sudden right turn towards some bushes. There were clearly no tracks; nothing as far as we could see which would warrant such a detour, except... Our thoughts were two frightening to contemplate. I looked at Noel and saw the same thought in his mind. Escape was useless even though jumping out the back would have been easy. We would not have survived a minute with the Landrover swinging around and the police aiming their rifles. We watched in fear as bushes brushed past while on an ever more extraordinary route. We were losing all sense of direction which provoked a new idea. It seemed that we were to be left in the middle of nowhere where we would just

die from the heat and lack of water; that way if we were found it would look as if we had got lost through our own stupidity whereas shooting us would look very messy, if we were ever found. Although I should have been more frightened by this prospect, I welcomed the chance to trust my wits rather than a firing squad. I began to look forward to the challenge of really fending for myself in the desert. I became impatient for the vehicle to stop so that I could start the 'adventure' but it carried on and suddenly hit the tarred road again.

After a few minutes we were asked to get out and the driver pointed to some huts in the distance. "That's Morocco," he said, "...walk." We did. The driver turned around and waved. Checking they had really driven away, we started walking. After half an hour or so, it was clear the driver was right. We saw some Moroccans sitting around the huts. A warm relief enveloped us as we greeted them.

Remembering the way we had spent all the previous afternoon in that friendly conversation with the police had probably saved our lives. The critical moment had come in a warm sympathetic glance, after he had found my knife, when the policeman and we had 'recognised each other again'. I communicated my vulnerability in him finding a knife which had been forgotten. No words were needed, trust and sympathy could be communicated anywhere in the world with a glance.

Inside the cover of my journal is a photograph which had been taken for future visa applications, dated Kano, Nigeria, 11th August 1973

A Tsetse Fly in Bedford

My doctor told me he very much doubted this weary and sick body would have survived more than three weeks longer in the Sahara. My mouth was full of ulcers. The first signs of scurvy and beriberi from a lack of vitamins, he said. For several weeks it was necessary to anaesthetise my mouth to relieve the pain before eating. But, with a good diet including much fruit and vegetables, my health quickly returned.

Back in Oxford, to start the second university year, my priority was how to repay some of the debt to those who had taken care of me in the Sahara. Magdalen College had a procedure whereby students were ranked by their awards before being able to choose lodgings in the College. Having started with the Mackinnon Scholarship for Mathematics, and subsequently been awarded a further Johnson Scholarship for Physics during my first year, it was my luck to have first choice of accommodation. Without hesitation, I had chosen a suite of three rooms overlooking St. Swithun's quadrangle. There was a bedroom with a large oak desk for studying; a small extra room; a large sitting room with stone fireplace and a sunny bay window with a bench seat. With this space, it was possible for me to offer free lessons in Mathematics and English to students from Africa and the Middle East. Having advertised in the Oxford Mail, several students came regularly for afternoon tea and tuition.

Mentioning that my very modest offer was a wish to repay some of the debt of gratitude for the nomadic hospitality which had sustained me during such a long African journey seemed perfectly natural to my 'students'. Among them was a boy my age, Nabhan Al Nimer, who came for the whole academic year. He was from Palestine, the West Bank of Jordan, and a real gentleman. His English was very good; we had great conversations and enjoyed each other's company.

The rooms in St. Swithun's were my first 'home from home'. My maternal grandmother Eva provided furnishings which had belonged to her husband, Henry Evans. These included beautiful fine silk Arab headdresses to hang on the sitting room wall, rugs and an inlaid coffee table from Damascus, tea glasses from the market in Jerusalem and a copy of my grandfather's letters to Eva before they were married, including postcards from Palestine. A small purse contained Henry's coins from the region.

One afternoon Nabhan's curiosity led me to share their story.

Henry and his twin sister Joan were born in 1890 at Bedford. My grandmother Eva, Henry and Joan were all in the same class at school from the age of 5. Actually Henry's twin sister, Joan, was my granny's best friend as a child. Tragically, Joan died at 16 from sleeping sickness. Knowing of sleeping sickness in Africa made me wonder what a tsetse fly had been doing in Bedford in 1906. There was no clue. But the loss of his twin sister drove Henry to study Medicine.

Henry also distinguished himself as a young sprinter. At the age of 18 he won the school championships for 100 yards before starting to train as a doctor. Although he was selected to run for Britain in the 100 and 200 metres at the 1912 Stockholm Olympics, he declined as he felt his medical service was more important.

Once the 1st World War broke out, he was sent to France as a doctor on the front lines. In the battle of the Somme he became isolated in a wood with his ambulance company and continued, for two days and nights, to treat the wounded under constant German shelling. He was awarded the Military Cross.

A little later, he contracted rheumatic fever and was invalided back to England. Once recovered, he was to be transferred to Egypt and Palestine. Henry was very keen on Eva but, being unsure of her response, held back and was cautious. Luckily, he came to visit Eva's family just before his posting to Palestine. Having discovered that the feelings between them were mutual, they corresponded until he returned three years later, hence the many letters. Times were different then, or were they? In matters of the heart it seems every generation has to learn. Eva writes that they were both reserved, and misunderstood the feelings they had for each other. It is clear that the letters somehow liberated them, and they could write more freely than they could speak. This reserve resonated with me, and made me feel more closely connected to an otherwise unknown Welsh grandfather.

The letters began during the Arab revolt, just after T.E. Lawrence's capture of Aqaba. Captain Henry had arrived in time to be present at General Allenby's liberation of Jerusalem, as was Lawrence, at the end of 1917. Henry wrote to Eva of his meeting with Lawrence of Arabia with great admiration. He remained in Palestine after the end of the war in charge of a hospital, only returning to England in 1920 when he became engaged to Eva and married quickly thereafter. My mother, Joan, was born in January 1923. She shares her name with Henry's lost twin and Eva's best friend who was so dear to both her parents. Then they had a son, Hugh, two years later who became my godfather and was a very important man in my life, particularly during my silent years when his warm looks were a life-raft for me.

Henry started a medical practice in Norfolk but caught pneumonia and died very soon afterwards, only two days following the first symptoms, in 1927 when my mother was only four. So, my only knowledge of him is through the letters to his family and to my granny, which I read for the first time during my second year at Oxford. I regret that we never met as we are, without doubt, kindred spirits. We agree on so many issues, it's quite uncanny. It is hardly surprising that Lawrence of Arabia remains my favourite film. My granny, Eva, with whom I spent a lot of time as a child, was my greatest inspiration for travelling and for my extensive wanderings as a teenager. Perhaps these letters inspired me to explore Palestine.

Nabhan was also fascinated with my grandfather's letters, particularly the description of Palestine in 1917 and a chance to see silk headdresses worn during the Arab revolt. At the following week's lesson, he surprised me with a gift of a Palestinian headdress to add to my collection. He then asked about my plans for the approaching summer. No idea was my reply. He suggested I come and visit him in the West Bank, at Nablus. He wrote his name on a little piece of paper, in Arabic, just his name and Nablus. No address or phone number. I can still see that piece of paper now, a little scrap torn out of the exercise book that he brought for his lesson notes. About the size of a playing card. The idea of visiting Palestine was very appealing. Was this because he was so charming, or was my grandfather calling me too? Had all these objects been waiting to push me? The region was a new part of the world for me so the matter was settled immediately. I have to admit though that I subsequently wondered if I would be able to find Nabhan with so little information. Was it like an American who invites one to visit them in Dallas and you wonder if they really mean it, or perhaps they were just being polite.

Thus began my next journey during the long university vacation in the summer of 1974 with a flight to Lebanon. Beirut wasn't calm at all. One evening on returning to my hostel there was a bullet hole through one of my shirts in the cupboard. That did not seem promising and spurred me to move on quickly to Baalbek and the temple of Jupiter. I hitchhiked to Damascus where the markets reminded me of Henry's rugs. One, which Eva had given me, was made from goats' wool and bore the crest of Guy's Hospital in London where my grandfather received his medical diplomas in 1913. Armenian refugees had made the gift and it was easy to imagine the care they must have received to have woven that wonderful rug especially for him. Although the market was very lively, otherwise Damascus had an uneasy feel about it. Probably it was because of the recent Middle Eastern war. There were eerie similarities. My grandfather had travelled from Beirut to Baalbek and then Damascus in March 1919, except he went by train. The bullets he had faced earlier were much more frequent and dangerous than the solitary hole in my shirt. But it felt as if I was following in his footsteps, or maybe he was guiding me.

Henry had written to Eva extensively about the markets, adding that, "...apart from Saladin's Tomb and St. Paul's House there is nothing famous to see in Damascus except the bazaars." This had struck him as strange. He wrote that, in this ancient city, half as old as time, so little had been left for future generations. He wondered whether it was because the city had never been fortified and therefore never withstood a siege. Six thousand years of merchants had seen everything pass through like the winds of wars and famines. It seemed to me that he might be right. After a couple of days there, my wandering took me on to Palmyra, Homs and other central Syrian towns. Many have just recently been destroyed by the 'Caliphate of Isis'. That part of the world seems to have never known peace throughout all recorded history.

Then, having passed by the Roman ruins of Jerash, I arrived at Amman in Jordan.

In those days the West Bank was considered part of Jordan so to visit one needed a permit from the Jordanian Home Office. Once there, they asked me the purpose of my visit to Nablus. "To visit a friend," I replied. They asked who? Replying Nabhan Al Nimer, they told me he wasn't there. That surprised me. Sensing my surprise, they added that he was still in Oxford and he wouldn't be home for another three weeks. That seemed even stranger as they clearly knew he was in Oxford and when he was coming back. It made me quite curious. I was sure they knew what they were talking about. Anyhow they wouldn't give me a permit until he got home three weeks later. It was very mysterious.

Well, not knowing what to do for three to four weeks I decided to visit Petra. Whilst hitch-hiking down there I was given a ride by Paul. He was about my age and was driving a brand new orange Volkswagen Passat which his mother had recently bought. She suggested he drive it around for a few months to reduce the Canadian import duty. So we travelled together like good friends. Let me show you a picture of him climbing the monuments in Petra. We had the place to ourselves, as there were few tourists in the months after the Yom Kippur war.

Petra; climbing the monuments for a better view with Paul, 1974

After driving around the south of Jordan, and having nothing better to do, we decided to drive to Kuwait. It seemed a good idea. We thought we would be able to take the car across the Persian Gulf and visit Persepolis and those places like Isfahan.

The direct route to Kuwait was straight across the Saudi Desert. We thought, why not. What would you expect of two boys our age with instructions to put mileage on a car with nowhere else to go? So, we went to the Saudi embassy in Amman to ask for a visa. They told us rather politely to come back in the morning for breakfast with the ambassador. That was apparently how it was done. So we came back the next day for breakfast. It was clearly also a first for the ambassador. He was not expecting to meet nineteen or twenty-year-olds who wanted to drive across the desert. He asked what we were up to and we replied 'just driving around and visiting'. It seemed reasonable to him and the visa was prepared by his consul as we chatted over coffee. A warm breakfast had been spread out and served in the nomadic tradition. Then we asked him how to find our way across the desert. Very casually, as if describing a shop around the corner, he told us to drive north-east in Jordan to a village; its name slips my mind now. Then we should turn right into the desert until we found the Jordanian border guards. After them, we were to turn left towards the North, and after a while we would find the Trans Arabian pipeline. He said we couldn't miss it. And once we found it he said we should keep it on our left and follow it all the way to Kuwait. There wasn't a road but the sand was quite firm beside the pipeline.

Looking back, maybe this sounds absurd. It was. We were very naïve. We didn't really know what we were doing. We decided to drive mostly in the night. We thought we could drive fast and get there in a matter of hours, so we set off in the early afternoon to make sure we found the pipeline before dark. We measured on the maps and found it was just over 750 miles, or something like that. We thought it would start to get cooler in the late afternoon and then we could share the driving through the night to arrive the following morning in Kuwait. We calculated that if we averaged 50 miles an hour it would mean arriving in Kuwait before it got too hot. So we decided we could do all that overnight. The idea is quite ridiculous, really, looking back. But at the time it seemed straightforward.

Well, we were completely mad, and very lucky. We didn't even take much spare water as we thought we wouldn't need much at night, or any food for that matter. Everything was fine at first. We found the Saudi border crossing in the village just like the ambassador had said. Soon enough we found the pipeline and we rattled along beside it at over sixty miles an hour on firm small stones and sand. But, after a couple of hours, and very suddenly, there was a loud bang and the car just stopped, dead. It felt as if we had hit an invisible wall or concrete block in the ground and the car slammed to a halt. We both jumped out immediately and saw that the back axle had separated from its fixings. The rear wheels and tyres had jammed into the wheel arches and chassis. It was a complete mess. We were both scared. It looked as if the car would never move again, as bad as a camel that had broken both his hind legs and wouldn't be able to get up or move another inch however hard he scratched with his forelegs. Luckily it was still light to see what was going on.

There weren't any other vehicles around. We didn't see anybody else. We hadn't seen another vehicle since we left Jordan. Just the empty desert and the comfort of the black pipeline like a giant handrail on our left. At least the direction was clear. The sand next to the pipeline was hardly a busy highway we had learned. We had no idea what to do. Being suddenly so nervous, I needed to pee and walked back three or four yards to relieve myself. At once, I saw a metal bolt in the sand. About six inches long and bent. I picked it up. We decided it must belong to our car. Neither of us were mechanics but we jacked the car up on some stones, freed up the axle and saw where the bolt belonged. It served to fasten a strut from the chassis keeping the axle in the middle of the wheel arches. We were able to hammer it straight and then bolt it back in. Just like that. I have a picture of us doing the repair, let me show you.

Car repair, next to Trans Arabian pipeline, Saudi Desert 1974

We found we could drive again. That smile from Paul as the car moved off smoothly will always remain with me. My relief was enveloping. But we were more careful after that. Not as fast as before and we agreed to set a maximum speed of about forty, or less if the ground was bumpy.

We took it in turns to drive for an hour while the other slept and maintained a constant speed. The drive was surprisingly calm, although we had to look out for any large stones or small rocks among the sand which might have jolted the axle and our recent repair-work. Looking keenly for rocks kept the mind occupied. We never saw another car or even a camel all night. As the sun started to rise it felt much safer. There is something about dawn that always rouses the spirits. We found a Saudi well surrounded by camels in the early morning. You can imagine how wonderful it feels to know you are back among animals and people. We were no longer on our own.

It was a beautiful sight. Soon after we found a normal asphalt road with a garage and could fill the car up with gas. That felt good. Even now, I still get a great feeling whenever a car has just been filled to the brim. It is the same feeling of relief. It's incredible to imagine it now, but it was sixpence a gallon. That's about four US cents a gallon. It can't have cost a lot, between one and two dollars to fill up the entire tank. When the garage owner saw we were young foreigners he waived the bill entirely. Just imagine that now.

A few hours later, we were in Kuwait city. They taught me a Kuwaiti expression. Let me write this in Arabic, since I can still remember:

إذا تعاركت سمكتان في البحر
فلابد أن يكون المسبّب إنجليزي

This means, "If two fish should fight in the sea, it must be caused by the English." Funny, but it's very serious at the same time. Sometimes we forget the trouble we British stirred up around the world, particularly in the Middle East. This is an expression that has always stuck with me. Often on my journeys, when meeting someone from that part of the world, I write it for them and surprise them. I think it must be a combination of their amusement or embarrassment at the phrase, combined with the irony that an Englishman has written it for them.

More than just sometimes, we English provoked a fight surreptitiously and then just stood there with a stiff upper lip and a pith helmet looking as if it was nothing to do with us. Perhaps we were just waiting for the fighters to ask us to be the referee as they were unaware of how we had provoked the problem to start with. It seems my nation has been 'poaching and game-keeping' all over the place.

Once in Kuwait, we went down to the port and quickly found a dhow that was willing to sail with our car across the Persian Gulf to Khorramshahr in Iran. A couple of years earlier, hitch-hiking back from India, I had spent time in North-eastern Iran at Mashhad which is an important Silk Road oasis. But I hadn't been to the south of Iran so it was a very exciting prospect for me. We drove on to visit Persepolis and Isfahan. Beautiful places. The southern cities are exquisite. The Persians have a wonderful history and culture. Not knowing the language, it was at least comforting that I could pronounce it since they use the Arabic alphabet essentially. Soon after Isfahan, though, I decided to go back to see if I could find Nabhan in Nablus. I wasn't giving up that easily. Or, something else was dragging me. Not by crossing the Saudi Desert again but the longer way round.

I left Paul with his car and hitch-hiked alone to Teheran. Then I continued west to the middle of Turkey before turning south towards Damascus and crossing Syria a second time. Arriving back in Amman two weeks later, I went immediately to the Jordanian Home Office to ask again for a permit. They asked the same questions. Why did I want to go there? To visit a friend. Who? Nabhan Al Nimer. But this time they replied: "Well, that's all right then. We will give you a permit." And they gave me the permit without any more questions. It was still intriguing and very mysterious though. How did they know?

Next, I took a bus to the Allenby Bridge, which is the crossing over the River Jordan to the West Bank. The border crossing was gruelling of a different kind. The Israeli officers went through everything. Even a bar of soap was cut in half to see what was inside. Luckily, not having much personal luggage, it didn't take me too long. So, after that, I caught a bus to Nablus. On the bus, I wondered if I would find him. Or even how to begin looking.

As I got down off the bus, I asked the first person I met, a young woman, if she could please help me find where Nabhan Al Nimer lived. I showed her the little piece of paper, but there was no need as she spoke excellent English. She said, "Yes! I will show you," and sounded as if she was certain. So we walked together and after a few blocks she pointed out his house. Knocking on the door; there he was. It was a relief after all my adventures and a very welcome rest with iced lemonade.

Nabhan Al Nimer, Nablus, summer 1974

It took a while to share all my adventures. He loved the story. But then, remembering the conversations in the Home Office in Amman, I asked him how everybody knew where he was. Rather sheepishly and humbly, he said: "Oh, my aunt is the Queen of Jordan. Queen Alia."[5]

---

[5] I subsequently learned that Nabhan's grandmother and Queen Alia's father are both from the Toukan family.

Oxford Finals and a Career

After my latest adventure in the Middle East, the task before me was to concentrate on the final examinations for my degree in the summer of 1975 as well as thinking what to do afterwards.

My tutor expected me to do well in the exams and I was offered a choice of fellowships. Oxford offered a fellowship in Astrophysics, and Cambridge offered a fellowship at the Scott Polar research Institute. But I could not really see myself as an academic somehow. The journeys with 'more grounded' peoples than the British 'how do you do culture' had made a much greater impression on me than nuclear particles. There was inevitability about my wish to be among friendlier cultures. This seemed a choice between the two hearing systems; like an arm-wrestle between a noisy but logical way along and a messier but warmer meandering closer to nature. There didn't seem a way to have both at the time.

Out of the blue, a 'flyer' came from the Foreign Office offering two year appointments in the 'colonies'. They had vacancies for six colonial officers; two in Hong Kong, two in the New Hebrides[6] and two in the Gilbert and Ellice Islands. An atlas was necessary to locate the Gilbert and Ellice Islands where the International Date Line crosses the Equator; the very centre of the Pacific Ocean.

Without hesitation, I applied to the Foreign Office and placed the Gilbert and Ellice Islands as my first choice. An interview was offered in King Charles Street, London. The room was enormous and the ceiling almost out of sight. A red carpet led through the middle to a large desk with three interviewers with a vacant chair opposite them for me. Nothing in the room seemed on a human scale. At first the questions were quite straightforward concerning my studies and interests. They

[6] Now Vanuatu.

asked me what degree I was expecting and my reply was very much hoping to get a 'first'. But then one of them asked a question which was worded and asked quite differently. They all looked at me more carefully as if there was a catch in the question.

"What makes you think you can survive on a small Pacific Atoll for two years?" I was surprised by the simplicity of their question, but responded quite spontaneously and without much thought. "I made a journey across the length and breadth of the Sahara. I imagine that the ratio of water or oasis to sand in the Sahara is quite similar to the ratio of sand or atoll in the Pacific to the amount of ocean. Perhaps the canoes of Pacific Islanders are similar to the camels in the Sahara. Maybe it will feel familiar." They looked at me and smiled.

Soon afterwards the Foreign Office offered me a 'junior position', class something or other, as a deputy something, at Tarawa in the Gilbert and Ellice Islands. The end of their sentence said all I needed to know. It didn't really matter what the actual job was or whether it was important. It mattered that there was no doubt my career would begin as an adventure. A few weeks later a course was provided, at Farnham Castle in Surrey, to help new colonial staff to 'acclimatise'. This was a little tedious and seemed more designed for people who had not 'really travelled' and didn't know how to pack. But there was one piece of advice which caught my attention immediately. They said we had about sixteen colonies, if I recall, and if any of them mentioned the word 'Independence' we should offer them a paper to sign to that effect immediately. That was more interesting; freedom for all.

The list of essential items to pack was rather precise. Luckily, back then, there was a shop called 'Tropicadilly' in Piccadilly which could provide the entire list as a colonial officer's outfitter. One afternoon, with my start-up allowance, it was easy to purchase the necessary numbers of white short-sleeve shirts, formal white shorts, a white leather belt, and long white socks. Garters were required as we couldn't let the socks down. White leather shoes were a novelty. Pith helmets were not on the list for the Pacific which was a relief. One suitcase was sufficient to pack everything for two years including my own double bed sheet. The latter turned out to be very handy for stringing between two palm trees and serving as a screen for a cinema on Tarawa.

Getting ready for the Pacific adventure was much more interesting than my upcoming exams but did not take up much time and overly distract me from exam revision. 1975 was an exciting time for nuclear particles, or at least for our discoveries about them. New sub-atomic particles were being discovered like a rash, particularly more 'mesons' and extra types of 'quark'. We already knew about 'up quarks', 'down quarks' and 'strange quarks' but then there was a 'charm quark' and a proposed 'bottom quark'. Their properties were redrawing the foundations of particle theory and made much of my university teaching outdated. This was going to be a challenge in the imminent exams.

When tired of reading about neutrons, quarks, mesons and leptons with their different charge and 'spin', there was an alternative entertainment to dream of the miniscule specks of land in the Pacific Ocean. The names of tiny islands like Butaritari, Maiana, Abemama, Nikunau and Arorae were much more highly charged for me. Clearly my heart had won over my mind.

After the final exams, my focus was entirely on the upcoming adventure to the Gilbert and Ellice Islands. Physics was fading from my mind. A dear friend, Robert Brydges, called me from Oxford with news of my first class Master's degree which made me smile before turning my attention back to flight plans. There was just one flight each week northwards to Tarawa from Fiji, and that took seven hours with a refuelling stop in the Ellice Islands. Fiji could be reached non-stop from Hawaii. Working backwards to London, thirty-six hours of flying time would consume a week on the way to reaching Tarawa. This was clearly going to be an adventure to the end of the world.

My heart was captivated by Arthur Grimble's book; *A Pattern of Islands.* Looking at my copy just now, there is a very British message inscribed inside: "After going down but before going out. Best wishes and a safe return, Father." There was no doubt that my career was to begin with a warmer tropical culture than the chilly and drizzly island of Britain.

The Gilbert and Ellice Islands

During the seven-hour flight north from Fiji my heart was bounding with excitement. The view from the window seat was an endless blue. At times the sky and sea appeared to merge. The gently rolling beautiful dark blue swell seemed so calm and friendly. By comparison the Atlantic looked colder and fiercer from the air. No islands appeared on the horizon in any direction until we landed after a few hours in Funafuti. She didn't look at first like a complete island; hardly more than a runway floating just above the water with a little sand each side. But we were allowed out to stretch our legs; so many lovely children watched and waved excitedly whilst holding on to the fence. After refuelling we hopped off to Tarawa. Surely she would be a bigger island?

My excitement on seeing Tarawa for the first time was tempered by how small she appeared – like a snake that had emerged from the depths to settle on the Pacific surface for a moment. From the air, it was clear that the runway was half the island's width which was a little scary. What would happen if the snake returned to the deep? Two hundred yards wide for two years worried me. But these thoughts evaporated on meeting the Gilbertese and their sweet greetings. A garland made me welcome.

The journey from the air-strip to my new house took over half an hour along a pristine coconut framed road made of coral reef mud interspaced by many friendly villages. How could anybody not be happy here? The waves from children with heavenly smiles melted every part of me.

And at least Tarawa was a long snake; there was some sense of stability in this speck of an island which took so long to drive along with the sea so close to the road on either side.

After a day to settle in and walk around, my work began. Assistant Under-Secretary at the Ministry of Local Government; whatever that meant. Well, Arthur Grimble had begun as a bottle washer's assistant too. My first task was explained; it was too extraordinary. Since September had just begun, my instructions were to set the budget for the following year; and for every island in the 'colony'.[7] To make this possible, the Government ship *Teraaka* had been scheduled to guide me. We would sail to each island, one after another, and spend the time needed on each stop. I had to pinch myself. This ultimate paradise of a task was apparently going to be my first 'work'.

The Secretary in the Ministry explained my challenge. He provided me with each island's budget for the current year; the expenses incurred so far; some indications of special cases where a larger 'project' might be needed for different reasons and whatever other advice he could think of. Not yet having any sense of the islands, I am not sure how much of his advice sunk in. But, being quite numerate, this was not daunting at all.

The Gilbertese captain told me how the *Teraaka* was originally built in Croatia for President Tito of Yugoslavia. Having been put up for sale, the Gilbert and Ellice Islands purchased her as a marine training vessel. One of the sources of income in the islands was repatriations by Gilbertese sailors working on long shipping routes; particularly on ships out of Hamburg, Germany. For all of these sailors, the *Teraaka* had been their training school. The captain and senior crew would spend each day teaching 'the ropes' to their new brood of recruits. He told me that it was not that important whether we spent one day or two in some of the

[7] This included the 16 larger inhabited islands of the Gilberts Group.

islands as this would not change his marine training plans. We could draft a plan together and make adjustments as we went along.

We set off, like a small cruise ship with only one passenger to stay the full course. There was a modest but comfortable cabin for me and the captain invited me for dine with him each evening in a splendid lounge. He was guided by the night stars or with his sextant by day and with 'dead reckoning' of the distances on his charts. In the morning we arrived at a new island which seemed even friendlier than the last. Or was I just enjoying everything more as the days went by? To visit all the islands took me a few weeks.

We were all lucky, back then. Cash was not really an issue. The Gilbert and Ellice Islands had one island, Ocean Island, which was full of phosphate; millions of years of accumulated bird droppings. By digging the island up, the colony earned millions of Australian Dollars per year. The entire Government budget was only 8 million. The remainder was invested on their behalf 'for the future'. My task was to check that each island's budget was reasonable or sensible. This was not a difficult task. It seemed to me that proportionality and fairness among the islands was important, as was the understanding of special circumstances.

As the *Teraaka* brought us to each new island, everybody ran down to the shore to greet her. Provisions and medicines were delivered from Tarawa together with the post. After the initial excitement and greetings, the elders met with me in an enormous thatched meeting house which seemed big enough to hold all the island's inhabitants. We talked. They explained their needs, their ideas, new projects and plans. I listened and made practical suggestions. After a few hours everything seemed eminently sensible to me; I could only encourage them and wish them well. We all agreed and enjoyed a feast.

The islands and people were so gorgeous, friendly and warm in every sense. It was heavenly. The society was so supportive and sustaining in every way. Memories of their joy and laughter still ripple through me, like soft waves and the constant sound of the sea.

During these ocean weeks, the captain's maps captivated me. He explained his course whilst spending time together on the bridge. We seemed so small in the enormity of the Pacific Ocean. As a child, the stars and galaxies had made me feel so insignificant, even more so while studying Physics at Oxford. In a different way, The Gilbert and Ellice

Maneaba, sacred meeting space for the entire village, Gilbert Islands 1975

Islands were vast, immense, and yet so tiny. From Banaba Island in the West to Caroline Island in the East is almost 4,000 kilometres. From Flint Island in the South to Teraina island in the North is about 2,000 kilometres. These 8 million square kilometres of ocean cover as much of the planet's surface as the continental United States. But there were so few specks of land, not much more than a sprinkling of dust really. Unlike my childhood feelings of insignificance and being lost, the love of the islanders made me sway as if in a hammock rocked by them.

Time seemed to disappear. The International Date Line ran through the middle, like a plumb line in the centre of a room, so not all islands were on the same day. But that didn't trouble anyone. Days of the week were not how local minds thought.

On my return to Tarawa the Ministry of Local Government was happy. Reports from the island elders suggested that next year's budget would be a success, the plans and suggestions all well received.

After a few months the British District Commissioner for Tarawa went on leave and decided not to return. This left a vacancy with about two years to independence and it was decided, to my surprise, to offer me the position. Apparently, the success of the island budget setting cruise had made a difference and given confidence to the powers that be.

This felt a great honour, but with a huge sense of responsibility and opportunity; a challenge to be grasped. The idea of serving such a role, at the age of just twenty-one, could never have been invented by my mind. It did not seem to be my place to be setting any direction so close to independence. The only possible course was to serve the local population and to help them achieve what they wanted. By being pragmatic, it would be easier to help them achieve more. I introduced myself by explaining this as my plan and began by consulting the elders in the different villages to learn their wishes. It was my good fortune to find an exceptional guide in Reuben Uatioa. Reuben was one of the founders of the Gilbertese National Party in 1965. Once the House of Representatives was formed in 1971, he was elected as the first 'Chief Member'. He was very wise as well as quietly progressive. He had tempered his impatience for rapid political progress so as to ensure the best form of Government post-independence. We became friends and it was always such a pleasure for me to go to his house to discuss what we should do next.

Reuben K Uatioa, 1976, Former Chief Member, House of Representatives

The first request of the island elders surprised me. They were concerned about wild dogs running up and down the island and asked me to do something about it. There had just been a tragedy of a pack of dogs running through a hospital in Fiji and taking a stillborn foetus, so this rumour sent chills up their spines. We brought in a new law that all dogs on the island had to be licensed, and a small round metal tag was commissioned from Australia. I still have one on my key ring, stating, "Gilbert Islands Dog".

We had a team that went up and down the island to capture every dog without a tag. They were impounded by the local council and kept for everyone to have a chance to retrieve their own. After a while the unclaimed dogs were put down. We planted more coconuts with a dog in each new pit. The elders were so relieved once the problem was solved, and the coconut trees did very well too. Afterwards many villagers realised how much their sleep had been disturbed by packs of dogs. The nights became quiet again.

I have such wonderful memories of my time in these islands. The pace of life was so gentle and calm, a true community where all the children were nourished, supported and encouraged. Their smiles are so genuine, whole and uplifting. Life centred around the village *maneaba* which was a sacred house and temple to the sun, serving as a sanctuary for everyone. Even in ancient times, with wars between chiefs, once someone reached a *maneaba* they could not be harmed. Arthur Grimble had also been District Officer Tarawa, but in 1916, exactly sixty years before me. He wrote how a young girl could run to the *maneaba* to protest a marriage suggested by her parents. Or a wife could protest some behaviour of her

Village house, 1975, Abaokoro Island

husband. The elders in the maneaba took care of everyone. If only our culture had such a safe place for young children to run to and be protected.

The Gilbertese have a creation myth of their world having been created by a giant spider, Nareau. Their ancestors came from the West, from a land called Matang, to where they would all return. The funeral practices were to help the deceased return to paradise. However sometimes they returned, being occasionally jealous and wanting to see what their descendants were up to. In the Gilbertese language a white man was called 'Imatang' which translates as 'from Matang', or from the land of the ancestors. This was an unexpected aid in my work.

Children of the Gilbert Islands, 1975

I remember being called on my radio by the head of police in Abaokoro, a small island to the north of where I lived. He was in distress as three prisoners were rioting in the small jail and he was alone to try and keep the situation under control. It was very early in my career and I had no idea what to do. But, I reassured him that I would come over to help him. It was a journey of a couple of hours by boat. I told him it would take about half an hour until my boat was readied and then I'd be on my way.

Just like my African journey, there was a confidence that, once on my way, a solution would be found, somehow. Well, a few minutes before setting off by boat, he called again on the radio saying that the prisoners had calmed down. There was no longer any need for me to come. I asked him how that had happened. He replied how he had told them, "The Imatang is coming." With that they all went quiet. I thought it was magic.

There were very few prisoners. Sometimes the small jails were empty. In the local culture the main taboo was theft. This was one of their more serious crimes, even worse than murder. In my understanding of their beliefs, murder never happened unless someone was drunk and incapacitated on fermented coconut juice. On the other hand theft was always a deliberate act. They had no need for it. They had a word *bubuti*, meaning a form of special request. If you asked somebody for something, using the word *bubuti*, then the other was obliged to give you what you asked. In this way possessions were passed around. They felt that anyone could have asked openly for what they needed, and it would have been given. So it was much worse just to take something. It broke all the cultural rules.

In the rare instances of murder, the prisoners used to help out and build during the day. They would walk along through the village with their large machetes whilst a solitary policeman led them with a truncheon. The sight tickled me. Nobody feared a sober murderer; they could even babysit if needed.

The Gilbertese 'family unit' was the *kaainga* which we can translate as a hamlet or village with up to a hundred islanders. Much was done communally which enabled the most effective distribution of roles among the members. Children were sometimes more collectively brought up by the generation of grandparents. This left the middle generation free to build houses out of coconut beams and pandanus thatch, and to fish. There were no orphans as the village would take care of all the children. Although a few Christian missionaries had arrived on some of the islands from the 1850s onwards, their influence on the culture varied enormously, particularly with respect to sexual relations. Both men and women were freely in charge of their bodies and sexuality. If two people were attracted they could just follow their feelings immediately, and then resume whatever they were doing afterwards. In 1919 a Protestant missionary had sought a ban on Gilbertese dances because they were 'too sexual'. Arthur Grimble had been asked to write a report on the situation. He replied, "Making love is the national pastime. It is not believed that there exist a hundred virgins over sixteen in the whole group. Of these the vast majority will be the daughters of the Pagan chieftains in the North."[8] The Church's wish for a ban was declined.

I sometimes teased the girls by suggesting they were lesbians by day, while their village men were out fishing and heterosexual by night. Some girls seemed to have very little to do during the day, apart from either playing cards or playing with each other. Likewise, some of the men enjoyed relations with each other while they were away at sea. There was no stigma or comment about sexuality. One went with the feelings as they arose, quite naturally. As Grimble had suggested, this was definitely a national pastime.

There was jealousy sometimes, but rarely. They were very open about all their feelings which seemed to limit any jealousy. However, I can remember my cook, Teimaua, sometimes cutting her thighs with a kitchen knife to relieve the jealous feelings when she missed a man she favoured.

Speaking of Teimaua, she was a lovely cook although limited by ingredients. There were many varieties of fish, but only one type of chicken, rice, fried plantains, pawpaw and the local root vegetable babai. Every six weeks or so a ship arrived from Australia and brought many surprises with her. Suddenly the local store was filled for a few days with items we wondered how we had managed without. Like Maraschino cherries complete with toothpicks to snare them. Once, Teimaua came back with a shallow plate-sized tin saying Fray Bentos steak and kidney pie. She liked the picture on the front. At the time my attention was rather absorbed by writing up my journey from Khartoum to El Aaiun, having brought the maps of the Sahara and my notes. Somehow the two journeys were still connected by my interview in that giant hall. Teimaua interrupted to ask how to cook the pie. Luckily the instructions were printed on the bottom of the tin which I repeated to her. She went back to the kitchen satisfied and leant against the door for a smoke whilst I was totally absorbed in my Saharan struggles. Suddenly there was an explosion. Teimaua shrieked and fled. I rushed down to the kitchen to find steak and kidney pie everywhere. The door of the oven was off its hinges and Teimaua vanished. My heart sank as it dawned on me that I hadn't explained how to open the tin. It took several days before she felt

---

[8] *Tungaru Traditions*, Arthur Grimble, Edited by H.E. Maude.

safe to return. After that, we went back to locally produced food as less dangerous.

I remember her educating me on the culture one evening as if it was yesterday. I used to receive a week's supply of the airmail edition of *The Times* on the weekly flight from Fiji. Since there was no television or radio, or telephone even, it did not trouble me during two years on Tarawa to be reading my daily newspaper exactly one week late. The copies were individually rolled inside a blue band so the headlines were not visible. Just the date was marked on the address label to enable me to organise them all for reading the following week. The dining room table looked out towards casuarina and frangipani trees with the ocean surf providing rhythmic music. My evening ritual of Teimaua's cooking together with *The Times* and the ocean view was calm and lovely. After dinner, I had been trying to explain to Teimaua what was going on in the world, but she didn't seem very impressed. Instead she suddenly asked: "What are you going to do on your own all this time? What kind of girls do you like?" Although somewhat taken aback by the directness of her question, imagining a light-hearted change in the conversation to something she understood, I described the kind of girl I liked. She said she knew someone in the village like that. She was going to fetch her. Twenty minutes later she reappeared in the garden and introduced her. Just like that. Our feelings were mutual, although I was initially a little nervous of the sexual freedom she enjoyed easily. She had no inhibitions. I had no idea the culture was like that.

Once Teimaua had alerted me to the local freedom of sexuality, I found a lovely girlfriend called Tebabana. She was so full of love and joy. Life was different from then. I think my British reserve scared her from time to time and I had to persuade her to be patient with me. If she was busy one evening because she was singing in the choir, she might offer to send one of her girlfriends to make sure I did not stray outside of her network, but I told her there was no need. This was quite a common approach among the girls to keep tabs on men they liked; a special kind of spider's web with silky lines.

The medical structure in the islands consisted of local nurses mostly. With increasing population growth, birth control was made available with a three monthly hormone injection. The village nurses kept track of when the women were due for their booster. We were lucky on the Gilbert Islands as there was very little tourism. I kept a log and counted only seventeen tourists during my two years there. Usually they came as a couple on a yacht crossing the ocean, or something like that. We did not have much risk of new disease.

I don't remember sensing any repression of women in the Gilbert Islands. There was also negligible domestic violence. It seemed that the ability to divorce immediately by either party was a factor, as was the cultural acceptance of freedom in this respect. There were many safety valves to avoid sexual pressures. These were controlled by women who always had to give permission. For example, once married, a man could also sleep with his mother-in-law or his wife's sisters if his wife agreed. A bride could not sleep with her husband's brothers, but following her mother-in-law's permission she could sleep with her mother-in-law's brothers. Different islands had variations on the rules, but they seemed designed to release any sexual tensions by providing safety valves. It was not my place to comment here; only to observe how the system worked for them.

Gilbertese dance, 1976, also in the maneaba

The local dance, including many bird movements, was very beautiful to watch. Birds guided them to fishing grounds, and to find their way home. Just imagine trying to find a speck of land a few hundred yards wide in such a vast ocean without the guidance of flights of birds.

By far the most important sport was canoe racing. Every Saturday there would be a race with many canoes, and they were fast. Captain Cook had remarked in the 1770s how they would scuttle around his ship at high speed. Cook didn't know that it would take until 1942 for the Australians to design a catamaran which could overtake a Gilbertese canoe. These little islands had produced the world's fastest sailing boat, probably for millennia. With the excitement of local races, boat construction was shrouded in secrecy. Their design was fascinating. Having often admired different canoes, I decided to be rash and approach a possible builder.

Te-iti-n-Ueaua was born on Abaiang Island, in 1910 or thereabouts, he couldn't remember exactly when. His grandfather had also been a canoe builder. From birth Ueaua was both deaf and dumb and therefore spent much of his time in and around the house while his brothers were out fishing. He watched his grandfather building canoes, learning the basic carpentry required, but not the closely guarded secrets associated with really fast canoes. Once he was a teenager, his grandfather decided that the time had come to pass on some of the accumulated family knowledge of canoes. After all, he was getting old and someone would have to maintain the family tradition. The story, as told by Ueaua's grandson Tooto, is that his great great grandfather was a very cautious man and chose Ueaua to learn the art because of his disabilities and to guard the secrets.

When I first met Ueaua in 1975 he had built 38 canoes. He was sitting in the shade of a pawpaw tree watching one of his fastest creations racing around Bikeman Islet in Tarawa lagoon. I told him that of all the canoes, his looked the most beautiful, resplendent in their black and red lines. After translation into sign language by Tooto, his face lit up in a broad smile. We conversed for a while, all the time watching each other closely. I asked if he would be willing to build me a canoe. He smiled again, explaining through Tooto that he was very old and not as strong as he used to be, nor was his sight as good, but he might just make one more canoe. He asked me to come back in a few days so that he could have time to decide. Looking back, maybe there was a connection which was never mentioned between us. Perhaps we had both known somewhere how we shared something from our childhood challenges. We definitely trusted each other. Some months later, I trusted him with my life. My father had also wondered during my deaf years whether my future could be as a carpenter. At least, that is what he told me as a teenager.

When I came back to look for Ueaua a few days later, he was already out looking for wood for his 39th and last canoe. He had gone up to Bonriki village with another grandson, Keakea, to look for a suitable branch of a tree to use for the bows, known as *Te mango*. Keakea would point to a branch and Ueaua would shake his head, bending his arm to show it was too straight. Another would be crooked, or too young or too old, too thin or too thick, until at last a perfect one was found and then, after asking permission and leaving some tobacco for the spirits, the desired four-foot-long branch was carefully cut off the tree and taken home.

Before any building started, Ueaua and Keakea built a small shelter behind their house. Keakea's wife weaved coconut fronds into a curtain so no-one could spy. During the first several weeks whilst the hull was built, no visitors were allowed near the back of the house. To make sure no-one crept in during the night, Ueaua slept next to the canoe throughout her construction. However, the family allowed me to watch the building progress.

Once she was fully decked out, she was very fast. My instructions were that no other Gilbertese family could sail on her. Other Imatangs were fine because they wouldn't understand the secrets. But, if I wanted a local crew member, I had to come back to Ueaua and borrow someone. This was fascinating and fun. Ueaua would look at the wind and the swell, he would savour the air and then decide which of his grandsons or great nephews would go with me that day. Sometimes he said two were needed because of the gusts.

Occasionally a younger one was sent in addition to bail out water because it would become choppy later. Ueaua was always right. I imagined he had all his relatives lined up in his mind like brass weights and knew the exact combination needed for every journey. We had a race most weekends and his canoe performed quite well, even winning sometimes.

1976 canoe racing with Tooto Kabwebwenibeia on the outrigger

Some months later, it was necessary for me to sail to Abaokoro Island. Before leaving Ueaua's village of Nanikai, he told me to promise him that I would not steer. He had set the mast to guide me there. To a western yachtsman this would not make sense. But the design of a Gilbertese canoe has the mast a few inches from the bows as in the picture just above. The hull is slightly twisted to move absolutely straight counterbalancing the outrigger. The direction of the canoe can be set by tilting the mast off the vertical, either towards or away from the wind. Since the wind direction was so reliable, a navigator can tilt the mast just enough to counter the wind and swell and thus aim for a particular course. This was not uncommon in the islands as the winds were so predictable. Some islands had navigation stones showing how to set the sails to reach other islands. I knew how the principle worked, and the physics made sense to me, but I hadn't depended on it thus far. To resist any temptation to steer, Ueaua asked me to remove the steering oar and to place it on deck. I trusted him and agreed. But once south Tarawa disappeared from view beneath the horizon, I became suddenly anxious. There was no view of land anywhere. I was desperate to steer despite my promise. While touching the oar and considering putting her in the rowlocks, a different fear came to me. Which way would I steer, as I knew nothing of my course? Realising that I might steer too much one

Ueaua's grandson Tooto who taught me to sail, and the District Officer, 1976

way, or the other, I might then be in an even greater panic from wondering whether my steering was right. Trusting Ueaua was the only option which felt manageable. Maybe an hour or so later, Abaokoro came into view with similar relief to driving off after the car repair alongside the Trans Arabian Pipeline, except this time Ueaua was sure of my path even if I had no clue.

Sailing became a large part of my life. At the end of my tour of service in the Islands, the canoe came back to London with me, shipped in a large Toblerone shaped crate to unpack and reassemble. She is now on display in the National Maritime museum at Falmouth, Cornwall, having moved down there after her prominence in the Captain Cook exhibition at the Greenwich Museum. I had given them my drawings of her construction with no glue, no nails, no screws and only stitching holding her together. A few years afterwards, some of the coconut stitching had disintegrated. The museum had no idea how to repair her. Luckily, Tooto sent me two sacks of coconut string and my memory enabled her to be rebuilt.

I will always be grateful to my deaf and dumb canoe builder for such a large contribution to my life in the Pacific, especially for saving me with his navigation skills and choices of family members as crew. Ueaua was an unusually true friend.

Knowing myself to be the last English District Officer before independence, I threw myself into every challenge. My love of the islanders was matched by sensitivity to their environment. In 1976, we set up a nature reserve on the uninhabited Vostok Island, which is the only peat island in the Pacific. Then we hired Roger Perry from the Galápagos Islands to set up a nature reserve on Christmas Island, much to the approval of the World Wildlife Fund. A solution was found to the problem of refuse disposal, reclaiming a stagnant bay and building houses on the top of compacted refuse covered by coral sand. This solved a need for more housing while at the same time stopping the practice of dumping waste at sea. With pragmatism, combined with local wisdom, we solved many problems using solutions with local materials. We went out of our way to avoid plastic, imports and pollution.

Just in case my reader searches for these islands in an atlas; the spelling has changed even if the pronunciation has not. The Gilbertese language was not written until the first missionaries arrived around 1850. They only use thirteen letters from our alphabet. Thus, *Kiribati* is the phonetic way to write *Gilberts*. They use K for G, R for L, and Ti for S as in the middle of the English word 'station'. *Kiribati* is pronounced as *Kirribass*, or when softened becomes Gilberts. In the same way, Christmas Island, 2,000 kilometres south of Hawaii, is written as *Kiritimati*, and pronounced *Kirissmass*. Learning Gilbertese is also a fond memory, enhanced by their giant smiles in my struggles. Words are constructed from others quite easily. The word *man* pronounced *maan* means an animal or messenger. *Kiba* is 'to fly'. So *manikiba* means animal or messenger to fly, which is a bird. Since *wa* is a sailing canoe, *wanikiba*, is then 'a canoe to fly' or an aeroplane. It's lovely.

We planted a botanical garden, as a memorial, at the site of the beachhead of the battle of Tarawa. We collected all the different plants from the central Pacific to commemorate the site where so many American marines tragically fell, about one thousand seven hundred men in all; the second largest losses for the Marines after Guadalcanal. Some years after independence, it was moving and surprising to meet someone who had recently visited the memorial. He described the plants and mentioned that it was known as 'Mark's garden.'

My love of nature since my silent years drew me to make a photographic record of the different birds. One journey was to South Tabiteuea, with a nearby uninhabited islet well known for birdlife. A fisherman and his young son offered to sail me over there. The Russian Zenit E was still travelling with me since the trip to India, but my camera had been enhanced with an extra 200 mm lens. After a few pictures, the fisherman, watching my strange postures with this silver and black metal object in front of my face, asked me what I was doing. "It brings bird closer" was the best response manageable in my rudimentary Gilbertese. He looked very perplexed and told his son to help me. The young boy asked which bird needed to come closer. I pointed quietly. He then walked over to her, picked her up and put her back on a branch next to me. My smile made them both laugh. The noddy just sat there, with her wings drooped the way the boy had placed them, looking nonplussed and apparently unperturbed by a novel way of flying from one branch to another. I showed them both how the noddy looked through my long lens but was unable to explain the eventual outcome of a 'photograph'. Whilst curious, his son found it was much easier to fetch the different birds for me. With an absence of predators, the birds were unafraid of being picked up by a gentle boy, except of course the migrating birds that 'apparently' knew better from travelling to far off and dangerous lands.

Drooping Noddy on branch after a 'manned' flight.
South Tabiteuea, Gilbert Islands, 1977.

In early 1976 a conference began to be planned in Apia, Western Samoa for all countries involved in the Pacific and titled, 'The Apia Convention on Conservation of Nature in the South Pacific'. Knowing of my keen interest in the Pacific flora and fauna, the Foreign Office asked me to attend. This didn't surprise me as I had assumed there would be a British delegation. I remembered how the Foreign Office had recommended

Roger Perry to me for the nature reserve on Christmas Island, so it was not unreasonable for them to include me. From time to time, as the conference approached, I was sent a telex from London reminding me to protect some other bird species like a lesser spotted warbler. All these notes were carefully taken with me. The first surprise which followed was a different one. They were not sending anybody else. I was supposed, at the age of twenty-two, to represent Her Majesty's Government as well as all our Pacific dependent territories in this matter.

On arrival in Apia, I was met by a smart black car sporting the Union Jack fluttering on its front wing which felt rather grand. After greeting the Prime Minister of Samoa, we were taken to their Parliament building for the conference. I suddenly realised that the UK delegation, which was only me, was dwarfed by a dozen representatives from each of France, USA, Japan, Australia, New Zealand and all major countries involved in the Pacific as well as smaller delegations from the independent islands. They all had lawyers, experts and everything. Never mind, I would find a way through this somehow.

Discussions were initially very heated against France over their nuclear testing; much shouting and fury. The French retaliated by citing the Australian treatment of Aborigines. As the discussions became ever more awkward, it became clear to me that we were not going to be able to speak about the lesser spotted warbler. Instead, I concentrated on a line more in keeping with the emerging independent states, like the Cook Islands. I make it look as if I was offering entirely my own independent views, but I was often recycling the views of smaller islands in my own particular style once I understood the merits of their wishes.

Embarrassingly, the Prime Minister of the Cook Islands became so grateful for my support that he reminded the audience the story of how they originally became a colony. He explained that some ships with a French flag appeared close by and they had no idea what to do. But, a local lady missionary instructed them to find some coloured cloth and they were able to create a Union Jack which they hoisted on a coconut tree. The French ships did not come ashore. Every time another ship came they repeated the process. After a while they decided to write to Queen Victoria to ask if they could become a British colony. Apparently they waited years but did not get a reply. Their letter was forwarded to New Zealand to check them out and so they became a New Zealand colony instead. The irony is that the Maori had come through the Cook

Islands so it should have been the other way around. But his punchline was to conclude by saying he would like to donate one of the uninhabited Cook Islands to me personally. I went quite red with embarrassment and did not know how to reply, so said nothing. Luckily the subject never came up again. It was, in any case, some light relief amongst the fiercer arguments flying around.

As the week wore on, it suddenly dawned on me that we were likely to be able to agree on a treaty. The British Foreign Office had not led me to anticipate signing something. It was just a conference they had said. In anxious haste, I prepared a brief for the Foreign Secretary, James Callaghan, and sent this in code from the New Zealand High Commission in Apia.

I waited anxiously for a reply. The signing ceremony approached and still there was no word from the Foreign Office, even after thirty-six hours. So, faced with a choice, it seemed there would be a greater potential scandal if the UK was the only power not to sign the treaty. I decided to sign on behalf of the British Government and all our dependent Pacific territories on Monday 12th July 1976. Initially I had thought to wear a suit for the treaty signing. But, as we were getting ready, I noticed that the independent islands were wearing their traditional dress. I changed into Gilbertese national dress; a white shirt with a long dark red skirt that came half way down my calves, a fine belt and bare feet. This was the formal Gilbertese attire for a signing ceremony. I used to have it with me when travelling in case of a need to be more respectfully attired. The French delegation was offended and excluded me from their photograph but the other Pacific Islands appreciated me as if one of them.

Actually the British Foreign Office never replied. Years later I met James Callaghan who had risen to Prime Minister and later retired. Having reminded him, he replied, "Ah yes, I remember that. Your telex came in on a Saturday and nobody saw it in time. We presumed you had probably signed it."

In addition to the very wise and gentle support offered by my experienced political mentor, Reuben K Uatioa, a much younger politician became a good friend for different reasons. Ieremia Tabai was only three years older than me, and was elected as the Member of Parliament for the island of Nonouti (pronounced 'no-nose') at the age of twenty-four. Soon after my appointment as District Officer, Ieremia became Leader of the Opposition in Parliament. We would speak about the future of the islands like brothers, except that we agreed on everything unlike normal brothers. Our conversations covered every ambit of the culture and environment. During the early run-up towards independence we spoke often about his campaign. The choice for their first President was between a much older man who believed in Westernisation, Central Government and the islands' first defence budget on the one hand; or a young Ieremia who was in tune with the needs of the islanders, who could listen and communicate well, didn't want to waste money on guns and believed in their ancient traditions. My reader will not have difficulty in sensing my choice. After the sadness of my departure from this Garden of Eden, tears of joy came back to me when Ieremia was elected Chief Minister a year later and subsequently became their first President.

Two years among these wonderful people in an exceptional natural environment are unforgettable. The idea that my experience was collecting clues to help with the task of this book never entered my mind. But, in retrospect, their offering is both huge and priceless.

I went back to the Gilbert Islands a year ago after a gap of over forty years. The first message on stepping off the flight was that Ieremia was waiting to see me. We spoke like we used to in our early twenties, except that this time he could also help me with the challenges of this book.

A CHILLY OPTION

Returning to Britain after two years was quite a shock. There was an option to return to the Gilbert Islands but, having already prepared my local successor, this idea seemed awkward despite my love for the islanders. The Foreign Office offered me a position in the Falkland Islands, but this didn't make sense to me either. Nothing could match my experience of the Pacific, and the idea of continuing to serve in 'colonies' didn't seem right any more.

Instead, I decided to do something completely different. Whilst waiting for ideas, there was a notice in *The Times* for a management position. Having applied for an interview, I discovered they were an American consulting company. The idea of hiring a British colonial officer tickled them. They offered me a position as a trainee consultant starting the following Monday. Not having anything else to do, and with their assurance that I could leave at once if it didn't work out, I decided 'why not, for a while'.

Actually the 'why not, for a while' experiment lasted seven years until becoming Director General of the European division at the age of twenty-nine. One of my clients was the British company, Tate & Lyle, who refined cane sugar. The consultancy work with them was not going well. I decided to ask for a meeting with the Chairman, Neil Shaw, and told him that I was going to 'fire him'. Obviously, working for an American company had affected my speech somewhat from the gentle tones in Pacific Islands. We had to stop really; his colleagues did nothing we suggested and yet they paid our bill every week. It was going pear shaped and was bad for my reputation. Neil thanked me; he was very surprised but did not resist and seemed to respect the clarity.

Soon afterwards, I was transferred to the USA. A few months later Neil Shaw called me, out of the blue. He said, "Why don't you give up consulting and do a proper job?" After asking what he had in mind, he continued, "We have four sugar plantations which we manage but they are not profitable, so we need someone to make them viable or get out of the business." Having asked where they were, he said, "In Swaziland, Zambia, Belize and Jamaica." Without hesitation, I knew it was a perfect offer and the right moment.

The idea of returning to tropical lands and helping in a more virtuous way was irresistible. A link with Africa pulled me back like a giant magnet. The offer had also come at a very important time in my life. In New York, I had met my future wife, Tertia, and was ready to settle down and start a family. I wanted to return to London and luckily she was very happy to come with me. We were married on the *Queen Elizabeth 2* on the way home, with a Bishop from North Dakota guiding us on the ceremony and watched by Rod Stewart in the bar. The ship was heaving in the rough seas and Rod with a friend were the only others not hiding in their cabins. He did not like flying whereas we chose to go by sea to bring all Tertia's art and her cat, Merlyn, who we could feed with turkey regularly along the way. Thus, at the age of twenty-nine, the next chapter in my career began as a 'tropical farmer'.

Tropical Farming

There are several debts owed to Neil Shaw. The first was when he decided to have me 'assessed' to make sure he wasn't making a mistake in appointing a twenty-something-year-old to oversee this responsibility. A whole morning's 'psychological assessment' with Bill Acker in the New York Athletic Club caused me to think about myself. Nothing like that had happened before. Bill was razor sharp and his report seemed to have seen right through me. The idea which spawned was how my crawling around since infancy, with an insatiable curiosity, had never thought about venturing on a deeper journey into the depths of my own mind.

The second debt was when Neil noticed, early on, my difficulty with speaking in public. He told me this needed to be overcome in order to be more successful. He didn't know why it was hard for me, but he saw it. Then he sent me the name of an Irish public speaking champion who gave personal coaching. I sought him out. He taught in a basement next to Trafalgar Square, rather like the basement in the film '*The King's Speech*' or was that even the same place? I wish I could remember his name, but this was more than thirty-five years ago. I remember everything he taught me though.

The first question he asked was: "Why do the Irish tell better jokes than the English?"

At first, I assumed this was a joke. But his face told me otherwise. Having no idea; he said it was because they understood the importance of proper nouns. For example, an Englishman telling a joke would say, "There was this man walking down a street," whereas an Irishman telling the same story would say, "Timothy O'Leary was walking down Trinity Street." Just the addition of proper nouns changed the whole feeling of the sentence.

To prove his point he gave me a copy of that morning's *Financial Times* about a session of the European Parliament, and a transcript of the actual discussion which had taken place. It was my homework to compare them. Highlighting the actual text whenever the newspaper article referred to something, it quickly became clear that the only points of the speech which caught the journalist's attention included paragraphs with proper nouns.

That was fascinating. Then he taught me that he always spent a third of his speech preparation time understanding the audience. Who were they? What were their ages and interests? Why were they coming? And so on. That made sense. He taught so many simple guidelines which enabled me to erect some scaffolding and to have confidence while speaking in public. He explained his different way to prepare a speech: to start by imagining the lecture hall; to imagine that just as he had finished speaking, someone sneaked into the back of the room, discovered they had missed everything, and asked someone else what they had missed. He said he would start by writing down how he would want that person at the back to reply.

One of his most valuable lessons was to share his golden rule. A speech should always start with something that had *moved* me since waking that morning and which could be connected to both my audience and subject matter. Then it would be true, emotionally true to me, fresh and connected with the audience.

Looking back now, my memory of the choice of word 'scaffolding' is interesting. On the one hand, we can erect scaffolding in front of a building to give a completely different impression and to be successful. On the other hand, the building inside might not have changed. Sometimes the scaffolding is there for fundamental repairs to the building. At other times, only to paint the window frames. Whilst valuing the scaffolding, I knew the building hadn't been repaired. This is an important clue for the next part of this book.

From a deep embarrassment of my voice as a small child – except in another language which somehow by-passed the shame like my nine-year-old French lessons – over time I learned to feel gratified while speaking in public. Just a few years ago, Hermes had a conference in Paris at the Grand Palais. There were about two hundred heads of supply chain and manufacturing from all over the world and they wanted an outside speaker. Someone suggested asking me.

As I was walking down the Champs Elysees, on my way to the Grand Palais this morning, thinking about my speech to Hermes, I suddenly saw a Visa card on the sidewalk right in front of me. My first thought was to ignore it, seeing that I didn't know what to do with it and I didn't want to be late. But then I looked around, and there was nobody else there. It was opposite the door of Tommy Hilfiger. So, on second thought, I thought I should pick it up as a gesture. I went into Tommy Hilfiger and told the sales assistant that I had found it outside. They thanked me and said that they would keep it in the drawer. But I said, no don't do that, how would the owner know that you had it in your drawer. Why don't you telephone Visa and tell them that someone left their card and they could pick it up; they might come in and you might get another sale.

This was how my speech to Hermes began, in French, adding how my talk was about what else they could do to find another customer. It is not possible to convey the energy with which I told this true story as it was fresh then, and it isn't now. But the audience was gripped by the energy with which I began. They spoke about it a lot among themselves over coffee, being sure the story had been made up by a very good public speaker. The truth of course was that the speaker was a former deaf child who had a deep shame of his voice, but who had been coached how to overcome the fears. Perhaps speaking in French also made a difference to my energy. The coaching has helped me ever since, and pleasure comes because the response is the opposite of my childhood fears. But, like many actors, the gratification doesn't repair the building.

We should get back onto the track of the chapter; tropical farming with many other hidden clues. On joining Tate & Lyle, there was really not much which was needed from me initially. That was lucky as my only knowledge of sugar was of having a sweet tooth; particularly for Tate & Lyle's Golden Syrup. We had truly excellent managers, with John Ranger in Swaziland, David Tate in Zambia and Mickey Browne in Belize. They knew so much more than me, and my role could only be to support them at the quarterly board meetings. In Jamaica we had just begun an interim assignment to look at how we might be able to help rebuild the sugar industry, and this was also going well. Some of my predecessors had already taken the necessary steps to make the division profitable which were coming to fruition.

This gave a perfect platform to reflect and determine my responsibility, just like the beginning of my time in the Gilbert Islands. There were many similarities in my way of approaching both roles. The foundations were built on a love of indigenous people, having been adopted by nomads in the Sahara and swayed in a warm hammock between coconut trees by the Gilbertese. These peoples offered so much which my culture had not provided for me. On my visits to the Royal Swaziland Sugar estate at Simunye, on the lowveld in eastern Eswatini, the Chairman of the Board was a local Swazi Chief. He was so dignified in his loin cloth while sporting a red feather in his short hair. He knew how uncomfortable we became in the heat and insisted we keep the air-conditioning on even though he was covered in goose pimples. Looking at his smiles was my way of thanking him while reminding myself of my inferiority. We all admired John Ranger's excellent management, particularly when the sugar yields were among the best in the world.

In the cases of Swaziland, Zambia and Jamaica, the sugar industry belonged to their Government with a few minority investors including Tate & Lyle. Our role was to manage on the Government's behalf for a fee which was determined by performance. In the case of Belize, the sugar industry was a cooperative owned by all the local farmers. The Belize Sugar Industry estimated the sugar price at the beginning of the season and paid the farmers by weight of sugar cane delivered. At the end of the season, any profit was divided among the farmers according to their deliveries. This seemed such an elegant model for providing services to agriculture in the developing world, and in harmony with my feelings of helping the Gilbertese.

Looking back, perhaps my life course was easily influenced by coincidence of events. Just before leaving New York, Tertia's sister Shawn had shown me some of her work on the Hunger Project which was published a year or two later as; *Ending Hunger; an idea whose time has come.* In those years, there were the most horrific stories of African children dying from hunger. Almost every night on television there were ghastly scenes, particularly of Ethiopian famine.

Knowing that Africa and other tropical lands were suffering so badly, and that my help was not really needed in these four sugar industries, created a different opportunity. If we could be so successful in those countries, why not expand the model? Just like throwing myself into every challenge in the Gilbert Islands to help them, what could be better than helping food production in the developing world? The logical first step was to talk with the only other major provider of such services, a division of the Booker Company. They were managing sugar industries with a similar approach in Kenya, Sri Lanka, Papua New Guinea, and Somalia.

Booker and Tate & Lyle knew each other very well. One developed the Tate Gallery and the other a prize for fiction. They both had a long history of sugar production in the West Indies. The Booker family was there first. Three Booker brothers left Liverpool in 1782 and set up a farm in Guyana on the Demerara River. They shipped a light brown sugar back to Liverpool called 'Demerara' after their farm, hence the name still used in England for this type of sugar. James Cook set up his engineering works in Scotland in 1788 to produce services to the West Indies; in time his company became the earliest part of Tate & Lyle.

Knowing from my interview with Neil Shaw that the four sugar industries were not 'core' to Tate & Lyle, nor sufficiently profitable to be of great interest, enabled discussions with Booker. They had a similar view which led quickly to a merger of their tropical farming businesses into a new company, Booker Tate.

With an openness to learn and trust those with more wisdom; whether they be Saharan nomads – others on my travels through India, Ceylon and the Middle East – Gilbertese elders, especially Reuben K Uatioa and my canoe builder Ueaua; it was natural to seek a mentor for this next chapter. The choice was extremely easy and he was very keen; Lord Jellicoe was my instant answer, George the 2nd Earl Jellicoe, KBE, DSO, MC, PC, FRS, FRGS.[9] He was already a Director of Tate & Lyle and had been particularly interested in my plans.

George had such a distinguished and extraordinary war record. He had a career in the Foreign Service before becoming leader of the House of Lords and served on Her Majesty's Most Honourable Privy Council. He had little to prove to anyone. Thus he could approach the challenge of Booker Tate like a wise grandfather and give me plenty of advice. He was an exemplary coordinator, never letting a subject at a board meeting conclude without ensuring he had everyone's views. And he was such a kind team-worker; he used to write a hand written thank you note in response to all the thank you letters he received. We made a very effective pair when

---

[9] Page of Honour to King George VI at his Coronation on 12 May 1937, Distinguished Service Order 1942, Military Cross 1944, Légion d'honneur, France 1945, Croix de Guerre, France 1945, Greek Order of Honour 1950, Greek War Cross 1950, Privy Counsellor 1963, Knight Commander of the Order of the British Empire 1986, Fellow of the Royal Society.

travelling overseas. George almost always managed to get an audience with the President of the countries where we farmed, or sought to help. It was my good fortune that George was around with similar values in the "late afternoon and evening of his life," as he often used to say.

Together we developed a Booker Tate philosophy. We shouldn't want to own vast tracts of land in someone else's country; that was not a sensible desire. On the contrary we should prefer either local interests or even the Government to own the land while we managed the production in their best interests. A further advantage was that we would not need much capital. The plan was to offer to take a very small equity stake as a gesture of goodwill and commitment if the owner desired while agreeing a contract to manage with our fees based on improvements to the farm performance.

The Booker managers had already seen the merit of branching out beyond sugar. In Papua New Guinea they managed a cattle ranch, a poultry processing plant and twenty thousand crocodiles. In Kenya they were involved in the poultry industry, known as Kenchic. In many countries we subsequently diversified beyond sugar into cotton, tea, coffee, sisal, forestry, oil palm, cocoa and rice. Building on our local construction expertise we were able to support tourism and other industries. The business grew very quickly.

Following David Tate's successful management of Zambia Sugar, we were asked to manage their tea industry at Kawamba, in addition to the coffee industry. On our first joint visit to Zambia, Lord Jellicoe was invited to lunch with President Kenneth Kaunda or KK as he was known, at State House. The invitation was extended to David Tate and me. After a very splendid meal, KK invited us into his drawing room for coffee, which he served. With the coffee pot in hand, reminding us of his gratitude for our efforts managing Zambia Coffee, he turned to me and asked, "How do you take your coffee, Mark?" to which I replied very quickly, "White please." Suddenly I felt very ashamed for the remark which could be taken as insensitive. But KK took it in his stride, and with a wink he replied, "Oh do you? I take mine white, but without milk," and we all laughed.

Our business model created a virtuous circle. We could draw on the best plantation managers as well as specialists in agriculture, irrigation, soils and crop diseases to support the farms. The results meant that development banks were very keen to lend money to large farms if we managed them. As a consequence, we could easily finance further development through loans. Our philosophy was attractive to many governments as they could finance and develop their food production more easily so long as we were the manager. Booker Tate became the largest provider of management services to agriculture in the developing world.

Soon after joining Tate & Lyle and having innocently asked our agricultural experts where in the world, if they had complete freedom, they would build a new large sugar estate, they all said Ethiopia. On asking why, they explained a number of factors. First of all the soil in the highlands is excellent, but the altitude generates bright sunshine in the day and cooler nights. The cool nights make the sugar cane much sweeter than a humid environment like the Caribbean. The yield of sugar per hectare would be much higher in the Ethiopian highlands. There was an abundance of water for irrigation from the Finchaa River which runs into the Blue Nile. Above all, the Ethiopians were among the best managers and engineers in Africa. They had a great culture, history and education system. Even though no other reason was needed, there was such a shortage of sugar in Ethiopia that everything we could grow was desperately needed. Listening to this, and remembering *The Hunger Project*, made the idea of Finchaa Sugar in Ethiopia one of our foremost objectives.

The facts on the ground, of a communist government under General Mengistu, were not a sufficient deterrence for someone with my perseverance in Africa. We were all determined to build a beautiful and vast farm, a grand project irrespective of the politics. Our first step was to make a model; we found that we needed about $260 million for development. In the context of Ethiopia in 1985 this was a huge amount.

The amount was immense because, in addition to a factory, there was a need for infrastructure: housing, irrigation, roads, and schools; like building a town of around a hundred square miles. The total area of the farm was planned to cover 270 square miles. To put this in perspective, the largest sugar estate in Africa we managed was called Mumias on the north shore of Lake Victoria. It was about half as big as Greater London in area, with 400 kilometres of our own roads and twelve schools. 34,000 families produced sugar cane for the farm. President Moi used to call it the largest source of Kenyan shillings after the bank of Kenya. This reminds me; Booker Tate won an award for the Mumias estate as the best sustainable development project in Africa. James Callaghan presented the award which I received on behalf of the company, and it was on that occasion that I asked him about the South Pacific treaty signed in Samoa while he had been Foreign Secretary.

At first glance it did not look possible to raise that kind of money for a project in Ethiopia despite all the other merits. But, my instincts were always to embark on a journey and see what happened, a similar approach to the challenge of this book. We were not going to be deterred. A colleague, Peter Cheshire, was asked to work full time on the development of the scheme. We identified the potential suppliers of all the equipment and asked if their Governments would supply a loan on more favourable terms to Ethiopia. Many countries like Sweden, Australia, Yugoslavia, and the UK, were happy to do this. Once we sensed the plan might be feasible, Peter presented the idea, with a scale model of the farm, to the Ethiopian Government. President Mengistu told us that if we could raise the money then we could build and manage the farm.

It took Peter a couple of years, but his team raised the entire $260 million at an overall interest rate of about half a per-cent. For the countries involved, it was also a perfect use of their aid money as we were building something needed for the future as well as generating significant employment. Most countries gave their aid as an almost interest free loan in return for the equipment supply. Of course once we presented this to the Ethiopian Government they were delighted and we started construction.

We had been building for two or three years when the civil war broke out between the Government and the Tigrean army. The Mengistu Government ordered us to leave the country. This was an obstacle as challenging as the closure of the Algerian border to a nineteen-year-old. There had to be a way around. Finchaa sugar was my most important task. Luckily the British Foreign Office was well aware of Booker Tate's involvement in Africa and this farm in Ethiopia in particular. On approaching them for help, their response was the complete opposite to my telex from Samoa. They were 'on it' at once. Within two days they had arranged for me to meet a General of the Tigrean army at a 'safe house' in Clapham, South London; quite astonishing. My estimation of the Foreign Office went up enormously.

I showed him our model of the farm and explained how we had raised the money. I implored him to help because of how much this farm meant to us, adding that it was not my business as it belonged to the Government of Ethiopia and through them to the people of Ethiopia who needed the sugar. So whoever was in Government would be our client. He was very interested. He changed the subject to share with me his maps of Ethiopia. He showed his plans for the advance to Addis Ababa and how long he expected it would take to win the civil war. He spoke quite openly as if he could trust me completely. As we finished the meeting he shook my hand warmly and promised to protect the farm.

A few weeks later he telephoned my office near Oxford. He said he was calling from 'our' farm, where his troops were resting on their journey. He added there was no need to worry about anything, everything would be preserved. An extraordinary telephone call – one couldn't make up a story like this. Well, he was true to his word. The Tigrean army was extremely disciplined and once the Government changed we went back to the farm. We discovered that we had lost one vehicle and four blankets during the short visit of the rebel army. So we were able to complete the construction of the farm.

Finchaa Sugar courtesy of Booker Tate

From time to time I look up the Finchaa Sugar Estate on their website and see how they performed in the previous harvest. They seem to be going well. The factory capacity is now 4,000 tonnes of sugar per day and the farm extends to 270 square miles. It appears that the factory is still expanding, which is how it should be as one of the best places in the world to grow sugar. The Ethiopians are such wonderful people. I will always remember driving up to the farm with Lord Jellicoe and seeing what seemed to be almost a Biblical land. There were horses covered with tapestry saddles, tassels and a vivid impression of richness from the soil.

Sadly, Ethiopia was not the only civil war which challenged us. As Africa's largest farmer during the 1980s, many of the farms we managed suffered violent struggles. It seemed these civil wars were indirectly a consequence of the Reykjavik summit between Reagan and Gorbachev in 1986, that maybe Reagan pointed out to Gorbachev how many African leaders only survived because they were supported by either Russia or America against the other, and they should stop this as a mark of a new relationship. The idea, if true, was wonderful, but the reality was completely different and unmanaged. They should have undertaken to help a transition to a new generation of leaders rather than simply pull the rug out from under the ones who were there. Mengistu in Ethiopia lost his Russian support and fell. Next door in Somalia, President Siad Barre lost his American support and fell. Ethiopia possessed the ability to retain order. But in Somalia the opposite happened as the country fell apart. Global powers don't seem able to learn here.

Somalia has still not recovered. Booker Tate was also the largest farmer there, managing a fine sugar estate alongside the Juba River. Not long after the Reykjavik summit, the rumblings of resistance to the Somali Government were audible. These escalated until the banking system collapsed with a purely cash economy. Then hyper-inflation accelerated to the point where buyers arrived with wheelbarrows and trucks of cash. The farm operated with a 20-tonne container of banknotes in the local police station. Soon the cash economy failed due to the rampant high inflation and the Somali Government then had to pay wages using sugar as currency. Booker Tate was desperate to save this farm despite the economic crisis, as she was one of the few functioning industries in Somalia. Lord Jellicoe and I went together to see how we could help. President Barre gave each of us a camel in gratitude for our efforts. But the Government soon fell in the civil war. Even with no government in Mogadishu, we still tried to keep the farm running for the benefit of the local population by trading molasses out of the port of Kismayo for foreign spares. We survived many months after the fall of the Government until the farm was destroyed in the subsequent fighting. There is nothing left now.

The Ethiopians, with supporting infrastructure, were able to work through chaos. In the case of the Finchaa farm, we could be open with both sides. That proved impossible in Somalia. I remember meeting one of the Somali farm managers begging on the street in Nairobi a year after we were forced to abandon the farm. It was so sad and such a tragic waste.

In Uganda, after the atrocities of the Idi Amin and Obote years, a resistance army led by Yoweri Museveni was finally victorious in January 1986 and Museveni became President. Booker Tate made a quick visit to the sugar estates to see what help they needed. Very soon afterwards we were able to get an audience with President Museveni during his first overseas visit to Rome. He was very sharp, a razor mind, as well as charming. I asked his permission to become involved in rebuilding the Kinyara sugar estate, telling him it would not take long to restart because we had found out that only the number three boiler was damaged in the civil war. With a broad grin and a twinkle in his eyes he looked straight at me and replied, "Yes, I know. I blew up that boiler myself." He was very open to our help and we started the repairs in 1987.

Having been challenged in Africa as a teenager, and believing in these kind people, it was easy for me to help them through difficulties. I never forgot the help they gave me during my long journey of 1973, how they had fed me and guided me.

Booker Tate was asked at the end of the 1980s to take over the management of the Guyana Sugar Industry, Guysuco, and we signed a management contract in early 1990. The industry was in serious decline with production having fallen by half from 324,000 tonnes in 1978 to 168,000 tonnes annually in 1988. Since 85% of all sugar was exported this was the largest source of foreign exchange and the fall in production thus had a dramatic effect on the economy of Guyana generally. The industry was often on strike. I cannot remember exactly what provoked the strikes but I recall several of them, smaller strikes of several weeks each. After each strike, fewer agricultural workers returned to work. We decided to find out why. As it turned out, some of the striking employees went out fishing and discovered that they could earn more with a few fish than when they were being paid to work. So there was no point in returning to work.

There only seemed to be one answer. We needed to pay the workers more to save an industry which was a third of Guyana's economy. Since so much of the revenue was exported, it dawned on me that we had to devalue the currency drastically from about 33 Guyanese $ (G$) to 45G$ to the US dollar. Only then could the company afford the plantation workers a decent local wage.

Although relatively young at the time, there seemed no other solution apart from giving up the sugar industry, so I presented the proposal to the President of Guyana, Desmond Hoyte. He was very open and saw the merits of the proposition immediately. He asked me to travel with his Minister of Finance to Washington to present this proposed devaluation to the IMF and the World Bank. Because of Booker Tate's reputation, together we were able to get agreement to this and to secure a loan enabling us to rebuild the sugar industry and the economy generally. It was a tipping point in the history of Guyana.

This wonderful memory remains with me. It was a case of doing what was right for the country, and quickly. Luckily, the President was a clear and logical thinker. So everything worked out and, following the devaluation and improved management, the sugar production in Guyana doubled between 1990 and 1999. This proved very instrumental in saving the overall economy. I felt so lucky that these opportunities had crossed my path, and that it was possible to grasp them. There were many other stories as Booker Tate grew to manage perhaps ninety farms. In the end, it was the civil wars which 'got to me' and precipitated my leaving the industry. My experiences in the Gilbert Islands, together with helping tropical farming, are the parts of my career where my heart was most open. These times also provided many of the signposts for my quest to find the source of a psychic river.

Mentors

Michael Meade reminded me of Homer's Odyssey; how Odysseus and Penelope's son Telemachus had been taught to sail and navigate through personal dilemmas by Mentor. Thus the name Mentor has stayed with us for an elder who imparts wisdom as we ramble through life.

As my reader will continue to discover, there have been a great many who have taught me how to navigate obstacles. Some might think this tendency to look for guidance as a virtue. But, there may be an alternative origin. In my infancy and childhood, there was no doubt that something was going on which was 'beyond me'. Having heard normally until the age of fifteen months, I knew in my bones that a dimension was missing during my silent years. Whilst able to see what was going on, there was always a need for someone to communicate with me what hadn't been heard; a face to *look up to*. These 'mentors' could show me what had been hidden by my envelopment in silence.

My godfather Hugh was one of the first; his looks were like a life raft to me; a look like an arm reaching down to comfort me whilst about to sleep in the attic 'lookout' of his house facing the sea.

During my early wanderings, particularly in Africa, many nomads mentored me. Two elders in Darfur made a small leather pouch containing hand written surahs from the Koran for me to wear as protection on my journey across the Sahara. Having treasured this small Sacred Pouch and never taken her off, the Pacific Ocean salinity finally dissolved and swallowed this amulet. Although so sad, this felt a fitting reminder of how my protection in the vastness of a deep blue ocean with so little land had begun in the vastness of the dark yellow Sahara with so little water.

In the Pacific, Reuben and Ueaua were very different mentors, but there was never any doubt how much my life and contribution had depended on them. The success of Booker Tate would not have been possible without George Jellicoe's kind tutoring of my development towards leading an organisation. These mentors all arrived at critical times.

But, in my case, it seems that my relationship to mentors is a reminder of how our infancy keeps cropping up as we meander through life. Grasping for a *face to look up to* enabling an extra dimension had been as natural as wearing shoes. Just like it was natural to want to see clearly the face of Ceylonese buses to find my way. As the Mayans say, "There is no such thing as a man's past because he carries it with him all the time."

CONSTRUCTS IN THE MIND

In the discussions with Meredith, my initial interest had been how his research at Henley Management School had led him to determine successful 'team roles'. But there was another surprise. He had other research called the Personality Preference Questionnaire, or PPQ, which had not been published and which was much more interesting for me.

His research at Henley began with detailed observations and recording of the role played by each member of a team as a game unfolded. Observations had led to the 'Belbin model'. This had made me wonder if my observations of different cultures could lead somewhere and might have contributed to spawning my own writing. It dawned on me that the Henley recording was 'conscious' whereas my watching since a child had been 'instinctual' even if honed by experience. A little like the migratory birds off South Tabiteuea having learned to be wary whereas the innocent birds could be easily picked up. Clearly, there were different ways of observing because of what else we pick up.

Meredith led me to see which parts of my life were influenced more by my nature, and which by my experience or nurture. He would throw in some knowledge or a different angle which sent the conversation into more interesting territory. We usually began each session with a tour of his garden, inspecting the plants and enjoying everything in bloom before settling on the sumptuous sofa with some Lapsang Souchong tea. A tall Aboriginal statue of a Mimi watched over us in the delicious spring warmth enhanced by the invention of glass. Conservatories can become very warm in spring and early summer. This reminded me of tropical farming days.

I had been looking forward to a more detailed conversation on the PPQ for some time. This seemed likely to be a very fascinating instrument. I wondered how it would compare with the report written by Bill Acker using his 'psychological instruments' in the New York Athletic Club. Meredith explained how the PPQ grew out of 'construct theory' which was a new idea for me. We recorded our conversation:

Mark: "What is construct theory?"

Meredith: "I'll tell you first how it came to me. We had a laboratory just as you had in physics. The equipment included a tachistoscope. Have you heard of a tachistoscope?"

Mark: "No. I can't say I have."

Meredith: "Well, a tachistoscope has an eyepiece. You're looking at a card and then you get a momentary flash. You have to say what you see. What they do is to adjust the timing of the flashed object progressively until you can see something. Of course, if you had a long exposure, you'd see everything quite accurately. With this instrument you only have a minimal glance but you can see enough to say, 'Oh, yes, I think I saw that,' and then you say what it is."

Mark: "What might it have been, for example?"

Meredith: "It might have been an animal, a man with an animal, or something of that sort, nothing very extraordinary."

Mark: "And what is the point?"

Meredith: "Well, the point is that several people will see the same flash but they see completely different things. So, what they're seeing is something within their preconceptions. What it's doing is reflecting their mind to some extent of how they see the world. That is a construct. Everybody has these constructs, so the exercise purely triggers these constructs."

Mark: "So, based on your constructs, it affects what you see?"

Meredith: "Yes. It shows that people come with preconceptions of the world. When they look at the world, they see entirely different things. I wanted something that would help me elicit constructs. That was how I made the Personal Preference Questionnaire or PPQ."

We agreed the easiest way for me to understand would be to take the test and find out what my constructs were. The test didn't take long and left me with a mixture of curiosity, anxiety and excitement. Meredith promised to evaluate my responses, and see what they meant, before we met again.

I did not want to start the next meeting by immediately asking for my PPQ results. I felt sure the subject would come up if Meredith had found time to review my answers. None-the-less, I did wonder what the test results might reveal. What he might have learned about my constructs was therefore 'suspended in the air' as we began the next chapter of our discussions.

Meredith: "We should pause to reflect that scientific research has proven that the majority of behaviour is genetic."

Mark: "Yes, and no. I am interested by the research on the behaviour of twins raised apart, including identical twins. One such research is the Minnesota twin study. Even though the findings point to the strong influence of genetics, the family still shaped the personality tendencies. For example, a family might make a timid child either more or less so but would be unlikely to make the child brave. The overall conclusion is that many, but not all, of our behavioural traits are significantly determined by genes."

Meredith: "What did they find as particularly genetic?"

Mark: "Among the traits found to be most strongly determined by genetics were leadership and, surprisingly, traditionalism or obedience to authority. David Lykken, a psychologist in the Minnesota project, was surprised that the tendency to believe in traditional values and the strict enforcement of rules was more an inherited than learned trait. In fact, they found it is one of traits with the strongest genetic influence. Another highly inherited trait, though one not commonly thought of as part of personality, was the capacity for becoming rapt in an aesthetic experience such as a concert."

Meredith: "That is very interesting."

Mark: "They also found that a sense of well-being and zest for life; alienation; vulnerability or resistance to stress, and fearfulness or risk-seeking were also strongly determined by genetics. More recent studies comparing identical and fraternal twins show that identical twins are much more similar to each other on crime and aggression than fraternal twins. Identical twins separated at birth are surprisingly similar with respect to antisocial personality."

Meredith: "What did they find as more influenced by the environment than genetics?"

Mark: "They found that the need for personal intimacy appeared the least determined by genetics among the traits tested; about two-thirds of that tendency was found to depend on the environment and experience. People high in this trait have a strong desire for emotionally intense relationships; those low in the trait tend to be loners who keep their troubles to themselves. This is very interesting to me as it highlights the importance of the environment in terms of the quality of relationship with others. I can speak about my experience as a deaf child."

Meredith: "I can imagine that you have a clear insight for this subject."

Mark: "Indeed, with some lessons which might help those struggling with autism or introversion. Interestingly, it is shamans who are the most helpful in this area since the blockage can be very deep."

Meredith explained to me how he had grouped constructs into a number of categories, such as determination or courage and so on. He was then able to compare the test results with an interviewee's actual behaviour. Their constructs had matched their behaviour. He found that the way one 'sees the world' affects how one behaves. When he shared my results, he pointed out two extremes. Firstly, he had a 'tribal construct' which he called 'clan' and on which I scored absolutely zero. This made sense and perhaps explained why there was never a strong pull for me to stay with an organisation just because it was familiar; I had 'moved on' regularly throughout my career.

On the other extreme, Meredith found that my strongest drives were ethics or values. He suggested, "Knowing your test result, I could have predicted the ethical way in which you approached your early career as a young man in the Gilbert Islands. Values underlie your respect for primordial society; I suspect they knew they could trust you."

His findings made so much sense, in retrospect, and reminded me of a tea estate which Booker Tate started in the late 1980s on the Baram River which runs into the China Sea from the Kelabit Highlands in mid-eastern Borneo. Our local manager in Malaysia was Mike Waring who had a background as a tea planter. We had often spoken together with maddening frustration about the destruction of primordial Borneo societies like the Penan tribe or the Kayan and Kenyah tribes. The Penan were the only truly nomadic people left in Sarawak and amongst the last of the world's hunter-gatherers in Asia, still using blow pipes. They had a traditional society where the children all stayed together in a long house

Tribal village elders, Baram River, Borneo, 1988

like a child's dormitory under the supervision of the grandparent generation.

The village system had started to break down through the invasion of logging camps which encroached on the tribes and hired their younger generation to work. Suddenly men in their twenties had cash, glaring tee shirts and financial power which the village elders could not match. We felt it would be better if they had a different evolution with a collective cash society initially. We helped them to start a tea plantation by transferring the existing village hierarchy of elders onto the management of their own tea plantation. In this way the whole village continued to work together rather than a few being selected to go off to the logging camps. I wondered what happened to them while remembering how Mike and I had struggled to protect their primordial society against the deforestation.

Meredith's 'psychological instrument' changed a number of thoughts around my motivation. Together with the earlier realisation that his research was founded upon observations was perhaps one of the triggers to reflect and reassemble the observations from my life. Sometimes several forces combine to alter the path of our lives. Reconsidering my way of watching opened me up to the wishes of the octopus with the specific subject of self-destruction. It is time to explore, and delve into, aspects of the construction of mind. Most of the pieces of the puzzle were already there, but they needed to be realigned to make sense and to create a picture which could be understood.

Introduction to Part Two

The challenge is to understand the mind when, in reality, much of the mind cannot be understood. We are all unique in so many different ways. Each of us has a genetic mix which is unique. The spirit which infused our conception is unique. Each of our journeys in the womb is unique. Our birthing experience is unique. Whilst we might argue that the culture we land upon is similar to the experience of some others, the effect of every other aspect of our existence being unique means that we will all have a unique relationship to the culture of our arrival. We have to accept, therefore, that we cannot make a 'template' to explain different minds.

Robin Skynner taught me that the English word 'understand' meant to 'stand under'. In this sense, the word could be thought of as 'experiencing from underneath'. Like standing in the rain. Whilst crossing Africa, from the Nile to Senegal in 1973, some of the tribes told me that it had not rained for seven years. During the long walks and rides, it occurred to me how hard it would be to describe rain to a seven-year-old child who had never experienced anything but blue skies. My imagination sought metaphors to explain the feeling of being 'rained upon'. Nothing seemed able to prepare such a child for the first time of their life when suddenly the sky went very dark and water poured down.

A few years previously, I had been surprised by a telephone call from Bahu while he was at Darwin College. He was almost breathless with excitement. He begged of me: "What is happening? The sky is all full of white butterflies." It took me a few seconds to realise, looking out of the window, that his childhood in Ceylon had not prepared him for the experience of a rare winter snowfall in Cambridge.

The analogy with the weather is deliberate. Our early relationship with culture takes place before consciousness. Then, we did not yet have the mental apparatus to understand what was happening. To a small child, the states of distress, despair, shame, terror and sorrow are experienced like violent storms coming from all directions and completely enveloping. Even with parents who are not violent, a small sensitive child might feel lightning and thunder in the family looks.

There is a catch 22 with our minds. To understand them we would need to get underneath them. And what could we use to observe them apart from our own mind? Could this be why so many philosophers tell us how hard it is to 'observe ourselves'? Michael Meade reminds us that the word 'religion' comes from 're' meaning 'again' and 'legere' meaning 'bind together'. Perhaps, the parts that need to be 'bound together again' are parts of our own mind.

It is not easy to find self-understanding insight without the presence of somebody else's mind. Together with another, we can explore the relationships within different parts of our minds. For many of those in despair, it is the absence of the 'other' mind which is so critical. In some cases, it is an aspect of our self-destruction that inhibits the assistance of the second mind. We need to explore why this remains so, and from whence it could have appeared that the lifeboat of our salvation became rejected.

My material is based significantly on what others helped me to find in my own mind. But, my research includes a detailed observation of many cultures around the world – where they are similar and how they differ, using the keen eyes of a deaf child. It is my hope that my reader will find enough of value, or connection, to sustain them through this part of the book. There is much joy on the road; we won't let a fear of self-destruction take us over.

The questions with which the book began are:

> How does an individual mind become 'poisoned' by a self-destructive tendency? How is the source hidden, and harboured, in a part of the mind which is 'out of reach' or 'unknown to us' so we cannot simply 'deal' with it?
>
> How did our environment or culture develop in such a way that this 'poison' became thrust so deep into our children's minds?

The approach must be scientific and Darwinian. However, we can learn from many illustrious people who have sought answers to these questions through the ages. We have, in addition, a pair of important clues:

> We know that self-destruction cannot be genetic or our species would not be here.
>
> We know that death cannot be the greatest fear, or suicide would not be possible.

Before we embark, let me stress there is no wish to cause any offence to any religion. The conflict between religions misses the point. We share this moment in which our mortal existences coincide on earth. When we meet a dear friend and enjoy their company, we don't argue about whether they arrived by air, whether by train or sea. What matters is that they are here now. By which route they came is irrelevant. Some believe in creationism, that God put them here. Some believe in genetics, or a 'selfish gene' which has evolved to make them as they are. There are many different beliefs, but what difference does it make? We are here now, and it is the here and now that matters. There is absolutely no value in arguing about the way we got here. We can discuss it if we want, but why fight about it. This book wants to share some experiences of the journey, as if among friends, without any disrespect to the journey of others.

Sources and Stepping Stones

To gain effective insight into one's own mind requires the support of another mind. It would not have been possible for me without the guidance from a number of marvellous guides. Our paths had crossed for a reason, and my gratitude is immense as they all arrived at critical times.

Jeremy Russell

Returning from over two years in Kiribati to my native island of Britain was quite a jolt. And that was not just the blustery weather after the warmth of the South Pacific. Once acclimatised, I found a small studio in Petty France, St. James; a couple of hundred yards from Buckingham Palace and next to the passport office which seemed very appropriate. Three years later, after Sunday lunch with my sister Jenny, her husband Peter and their boys in Greenwich, Peter showed me his architectural plans for a house conversion. An apartment with a terrace in a London garden square looked gorgeous on his plans. Since it was still in the design phase, it was possible to make an offer to purchase directly from the developers which was affordable with a mortgage.

This was how my first proper London apartment was in Redcliffe Square. Having established myself there, and needing a local doctor, my new neighbour recommended Dr Noel Russell at Paultons Square, just off the Kings Road. This was a family practice. Noel was almost retired and his son, Jeremy Russell, thus became my GP for almost all of my working life.

Jeremy was an exceptional doctor. He was very wise, gentle, and kind. Unlike most doctors who expected me to make my way upstairs once he was free, Jeremy always came down after his previous appointment to greet his next patient. Even years later, after a knee operation which made the stairs harder for him, he continued this warm courtesy.

The most common reason for visits to Jeremy concerned my anxiety, which had been a part of my life for as long as my memory. It was only the degree of anxiety that varied. Ever since childhood my natural state was anxious, biting my nails to the quick whenever my mouth or fingers weren't otherwise occupied. Every now and again the foothills of anxiety turned into mountain ranges with peaks of fear. The only variable was the strength of the storm, and the viciousness of the wind.

My stiff upper lip did me a great disservice in explaining to Jeremy that it was only an occasional problem, asking for help to catch an anxiety attack 'in the bud'. He prescribed me an anti-anxiety medication for occasional use. But, thinking about it now, it is clear that my mind did not make the connection with the way that my anxiety faded in climbing the stairs behind him. Sitting across from Jeremy's desk, as he smiled to greet me, the sun came out briefly between two storm clouds and almost made me forget what had triggered the surgery appointment. So overwhelming was my terror of this fear provoking monster within me that even the trusted Jeremy could not be told of the full extent.

At times, a full-on panic attack immobilised me. A cowering retreat, chased by the fear, cornered me in a bathroom cubicle. At least the toilet doors at Heathrow reached closer to the ground than their American cousins giving a little more secrecy. Jeremy had said that the anxiety tablet worked more quickly if sucked slowly. The memory of his words comforted me while waiting for the tablet to get the 'upper hand' on a fear which was too strong for me. Half-an-hour maybe until it was possible to emerge. Looking around it didn't seem that anyone else had seen my recent difficulty.

It was like being in a war of anxiety with demons – constantly having to keep watch over myself, not being sure which side the fear would rise from next. At the same time, it seemed vital to ration myself to no more than one and a half tranquiliser tablets per day to protect against a fear of becoming dependent on medication. It was a vicious circle, desperately wanting relief from anxiety but fearing dependency on a drug to cure it. There was nobody who could be trusted with the subject; the idea of a shared discussion brought immediately the fear of completely falling apart.

In my anxiety cave, chewing over possibilities as to the fear's origins, it was hard to identify any root cause. The only clue was that, whenever enraged, it became worse.

Sometimes at night suicidal fears enveloped me, but, gritting my teeth it was possible to will myself to sleep and avoid a fear whose origin seemed a riddle which couldn't be solved. None-the-less, sometimes a thought of what the fear might be gave temporary relief. Finding a coat hook to hang it on, or finding some outside situation to transfer it to, made its management more potentially feasible. The worst times were nights when a terror enveloped me that I would not be able to prevent myself from killing myself – that there was a part of me which wanted to kill me and that I was powerless to protect myself in order to prevent a suicide.

One of Jeremy's virtues was to know the best person to ask whenever a medical problem might benefit from specialist attention. When it was finally possible for me to share something of the extent of my distress, Jeremy was very supportive and recommended Dr Robin Skynner without hesitation. He was sure that Robin would know what to do, or recommend the best course of treatment.

Robin Skynner

The first possible appointment with Robin was six weeks later. Surprisingly there was no fear before the meeting. Perhaps, it wasn't possible to imagine a worse situation than my internal struggles and therefore a new approach could only be an improvement.

Robin was sitting in the middle of the room on an upright chair, with me facing him from a large low soft armchair. He had a clipboard and a form on it, and started taking down details on my name, address and then he asked, "You're married?"

"Yes."

"Then I've got the wrong form," and he got up and left to get another form. "So why isn't your wife here?"

"She couldn't come; she's in the States."

He continued very insistently; "Why did you come alone?"

It was surprisingly easy to answer all of his questions about my family, my childhood and my marriage. At one point after mentioning that I hadn't been myself, Robin picked up on it. "You weren't yourself?"

"I wasn't how I usually am."

"You were depressed?"

"No, I don't get depressed; I get anxiety attacks and palpitations." All the while avoiding Robin's eyes, and instead looking all over the room while he continued to make notes.

"How did you handle it?"

"Well, I kept calm and kept my feelings to myself."

"Stiff upper lip?"

"Yes, that's it."

"Very soon after our marriage, something frightened me."

"Something frightened you?"

"What?"

"I don't know, but it made me withdraw."

"Withdraw? How do you mean?"

"Well, I drew back from her. I know it's mostly my fault, but I don't see it."

As my first session with a therapist drew to a close, Robin rose from his chair and at once reached out his hand in a very warm handshake. It seemed like a giant leap towards my recovery. It had never been possible for me to share anything so freely about my situation or inner thoughts before. Yet it was so easy to talk to him. Nobody had told me what a relief it was to share what was on my mind. More importantly, he gave me hope with simple explanations, sharing that the problem in my marriage was because we both "had problems with independence and distance."

Following this session, Robin was able to see my wife and me jointly until he had a space in one of his couples' groups. He explained that groups were better and faster, which appealed to my impatience.

Anthony Storr suggests there are two conditions for the patient to recover; the first that he has someone with whom he can journey, and the second that he has a model to make sense of his distress.[10] Robin provided both in abundance. His book *Families and how to survive them*, written jointly with John Cleese, provided a very helpful framework. Unlike the stereotypical psychotherapist, Robin was very active in therapy groups. His frequent explanations of what he saw going on between couples was very important for me to make sense of my own distress. He frequently jumped into challenging situations with spouses to illustrate a better role model.

Having realised that virtually all feelings eluded me, and having asked him for help in finding them, he brightened up, was extremely active and obliging. Every time I tried to get close to a feeling all that came out were thoughts, and Robin pushed me back, saying this was just repeating the same old behaviour. "Stop thinking, stop thinking," he said. This wasn't possible for me. He leant back in his chair, stretched out his legs and started shaking his feet in a very irritated manner. It took me several days to be aware of my irritation then. Sometimes he mimicked my struggle which was very effective in helping me. When a fellow group member was grieving, he quickly and in an irritated way shoved the box of tissues in their direction, whilst looking at me. It helped me to see the struggle with my feelings. Once when my mind wandered off, which was my standard response to avoiding an emotion, he got up and went over to a radiator under the window and fiddled with it. It was unnecessary and too deliberate for me to believe that he had done it for any other reason than to point out my 'getting up and wandering off with my mind'.

The early sessions with Robin were a journey to find lost feelings and emotions, like an African safari to find lost animals. All the while my anxiety reduced progressively as it became clear how many of my fears related to feelings which were unknown or uncomfortable for me. Robin was the affectionate elephant in the room. Nothing perturbed him. He was able to support everybody with everything, as if he had seen everything before.

It comforted me to think of an elephant as affection, since this described so well the fear of finding her. How could a young boy, never having met an elephant, imagine from the size of the dung-heaps and the devastation of uprooted trees that such a beast could be kind?

---

[10] Anthony Storr, *The Concept of Cure.*

Around this time, while visiting Ethiopia to review the progress on the development of the Finchaa sugar estate, it was fun to explore which animals might represent different feelings. A hunter, Wobeshet, suggested that the elephant also represented joy, playfulness, security and trust, all the hallmarks of affection, because his size meant that so little defence was needed. The rhinoceros was anger but he was also aggressive and foolhardy. The lion was pride, power, laziness, self-confidence and majesty. The horned goat was sexuality. The hyena represented gluttony and cowardice. The leopard was ferocity, cruelty, greed, viciousness, stealth and selfishness. Wobeshet shared with me that unlike a lion that never killed for pleasure, the leopard was capable of really vicious attacks driven neither by defence nor hunger. The gazelle was grace, timidity and shyness. That a hunter could explain all the human feelings in other animals helped me in some unknown way.

Robin used many metaphors to help us, his group members. Without his descriptions, it would not have been possible to learn how my sudden and sharp withdrawal could be felt like the flipside of violence and potentially provoke someone else to aggression. He referred to Voltaire's Candide with the French Admiral looking through a telescope saying "How far off the English Admiral appeared," to which his assistant replied that "He must appear equally far off to the English then." It struck me as obvious and profound. In a relationship, the distance apart must be similarly felt by both sides even if the reason for the distance might be quite different.

In terms of anxiety, Robin described a car, driving down a slippery mountainside road with poor brakes. He said my response was to climb over into the back seat to try and get further from the fear. But, no longer having my hands on the steering wheel and thus having no control, the resulting anxiety became worse than the original fear. He suggested becoming more present, to get back into the driving seat and then respond to whatever came around the next curve. Sometimes, when alone and anxious, it helped me to give myself a gentle slap on the thigh to become more present.

Another man in the couples' group described feeling a barrier whenever he tried to reach his wife, like a fence he couldn't cross. Robin suggested, "She wants you to get through whatever it is and to be tender on the other side." She nodded her agreement. My thought was perhaps the fence was 'elephant spoor'. Watching the difficulties of others in a group, chewing and digesting my observations and then looking to find the same phenomenon or difficulty in myself was the most valuable aspect of therapy groups for me. Robin kept me motivated and full of hope with a gentle comment one evening: "The part of you which frightens you the most might be the part of you which you love the most when you find it." Even now the thought of these words helps.

It is not possible to express the full depth of my gratitude to Robin, and his groups, for the assistance provided as my first therapist. He will always be remembered as a very loving and wise man, with the gift of finding many different paths and simple metaphors to help others journey towards themselves.

Before his retirement Robin shared with me how he had wondered in the beginning if my challenge was being autistic or suffering from Asperger's. As we smiled together, it was a measure of how far we had come on the excavation of my difficulties during my silent years.

Robert Bly, Michael Meade and James Hillman

Robert Bly opened a new chapter in my life with his ground-breaking book *Iron John*. Bly says that a man needs his anger to cut himself off from his self-pity, and that struck a deep chord. Robin had said to me: "You won't be able to reach your feelings of affection until you have reached your anger." Thus it tempted me to join a men's weekend in Dorset facilitated by Michael Meade and James Hillman.

Michael is a renowned storyteller and made a powerful impression while drumming with his rendering of the Brothers Grimm tale of *The Six Servants*. As a hundred men shared their feelings and experience to enrich Michael's account of the story, so many aspects of my struggles were aroused. Whereas my work so far seemed to have been to find feelings in myself, the work with a hundred men helped me to find myself inside a group feeling. Michael used to say that, in ancient times the Greeks went to the temple of Mars to be in the feeling of Mars. When a hundred men felt enraged, it was a new experience for me to be inside the temple of Mars, totally enveloped but safe.

The weekend taught me constructs of a King and Princes in the mind. That, to the eldest Prince, the feeling is felt as being inside, but to the young prince the feeling is experienced as all around him, enclosing him.

Our language makes it clear from which part of the mind we are speaking. One cries, but the other is *in tears.* One loves but the other is *in love.*

When a hundred men grieve together and the room is filled with grief, the feeling is different. There is no doubt that the emotion is bigger than all of us individually. The frightening animals are around us but shared.

During that first weekend, there was a conflict between the British organisers of the event and many of the men attending. The organisers all decided to stand down. Feeling the future of this work to be at risk, two of us stood up at once to offer to organise in the future, Richard Olivier and myself.

Richard had experienced more men's work and suggested that it might help me to attend an initiation weekend, following sacred American Indian traditions. This was a brilliant idea of his and subsequently made me feel a foot taller. It led to the courage to find and purchase my first house and garden with a large mortgage.

For the next two decades and more, it was my privilege to host the teachers who came over from America to lead subsequent men's weekends. Having such wonderful teachers and their partners stay regularly in my house was a new form of therapy for me. Writing this, there is a lovely picture to the left of the front window, painted by Michael's wife, Erica Meade, showing the view from the window as it was then. My daughter Alika still remembers how Erica always brought her favourite 'pink lady' apples.

Michael had many lovely expressions: "Animals don't trouble themselves with future grief, because that's not the grief that's coming." It was a timely reminder of how our minds manufacture most of the possible outcomes to be anxious about. But of course what actually comes is something else we have not thought about. James reminded us of an unforgettable paradox: "The most beautiful moments in our life are when we are out of control, and yet we spend the rest of our life trying to stay in control."

It was also invaluable to have started in the men's weekend workshops while still attending Robin's groups. The strong feelings evoked in the men's work could be properly and safely processed in a small therapy group.

The value of the European fairy tales was brought to my attention, particularly *The Six Servants* and *A Tale of One Who Travelled to Learn What Shivering Meant.*[11] The tales provide a forum in which the heart and mind can meet. James Hillman shared with us that Freud had found nothing which was not in the Greek myths. But then, as a Jungian, he would say that wouldn't he? James had many brilliant insights and was the complement to Michael's comfort in helping others with anger and aggression.

Lionel Kreeger and Claude Pigott

Following Robin's retirement and having taken up a new appointment based between Paris and London, my inner journey continued in both cities. Lionel Kreeger took over responsibility for my therapy group in London and agreed it was permissible for me to attend occasionally. Meanwhile, having been referred to Claude Pigott in Paris, an individual analysis began at the same time. Looking back, this was very valuable. The different approaches enabled me to make richer discoveries. If someone asked my advice on this now, it would be to share both openly as the techniques reach us from different perspectives.

The analysis with Claude was a totally new experience. In the first session he enquired about my dreams but none were remembered. This was a great disappointment for me and had to be rectified. Apparently it was necessary to buy a beautiful notebook and a new pen especially for the dream-world, placed beside my bed. Whenever a dream was remembered, he must be written in the same light of the dreamtime as a brighter light could chase him from memory. Quite quickly the dreams flowed like a torrent, sometimes more than five a night. The most exciting discovery was how some dreams were clearly a subsequent chapter from a dream episode a few days earlier, as if pieces of a giant jigsaw puzzle had been delivered in the night for me to arrange; it was simply a question of putting them together once there were enough pieces to play with. Without Claude's support and guidance they would have been indecipherable.

Once, Claude had to cancel our following session. It felt wild driving back to Neuilly down the Boulevard Maillot beside the Bois de Boulogne, a combination of wildness and thin air, which Claude later

---

[11] Both tales in the Brothers Grimm.

suggested was because he'd cancelled the last session. It didn't take long to connect this to the fear of losing Mother. Apparently, one of the qualities of rage is to transfer the fear of loss. We talked about it at length. So that was why a parent might become enraged on finding a child thought to have been lost. The reminder of how close they had come to losing their child had made them selfishly transfer that fear using rage.

For some months the subject evoked by my dreams was death. When Claude asked me about my feelings during the dream, he was able to guide me that the calmness suggested the images of death were about loss, and separation, but not death itself.

One evening, we were talking about the fear of death and why this was still interfering with my life. Claude had said, "It's not so simple. Sometimes people are ready to die, like a soldier in battle who feels that he is going to die as a hero, but just imagine if you felt that you were going to die because of some violence from the person in the world you loved the most. What could be worse than dying at the hands of the person you loved?"

It took a while for the penny to drop. More importantly, one does not need a violent mother to experience this fear. In a very sensitive child, even the sudden withdrawal of mother can provoke the same fear. Looking back, the realisation that this monster was the fear of dying at the hands of mother was liberating. From that evening onwards, my nails were never bitten again.

Bringing the subject to my London therapy group, Lionel was not surprised and simply asked, "How did you get there?" Soon after, having left Paris and returned to London full time, Lionel became my regular source of support in the ongoing journey. His patience despite my resistance to getting healthier was quite extraordinary. This is another lesson for those of us with deeper afflictions; to understand the extent to which we are sometimes fighting our salvation. This is one of the hardest lessons to learn, that we are our own worst enemy and that our self-destruction can be well hidden from us. It reminded me of my journey across the Sahara in 1973. Well knowing that there were unlikely to be many fruits on the journey, I had purchased a bottle of vitamin pills. However, unknown to me they were fakes and useless. As the weeks turned into months my weight dropped and my mouth became ulcerated. Finally arriving at Dakar in Senegal and although surrounded by fresh pineapples they stung my ulcerated mouth so much that I couldn't eat them. Unknown to me, the solution to sickness caused by vitamin shortage was out of reach because of the pain of the cure. Sometimes in therapy it is the same, the pain makes us avoid the cure. This is how it was for me; therapists had to survive my constant attempts to frustrate the help they offered. But this was not visible to me. It felt, on the contrary, as if all the right therapeutic vitamins were being consumed.

Out of the blue one day, Lionel told his group members a personal story. Apparently he had almost lost a leg a few years previously because of a thrombosis. Many Harley street doctors had come to the same conclusion that he needed an amputation. As a last resort before surgery, Lionel had gone to see an expert in autogenic meditation to see if his affliction might be helped. Like a miracle, this was quickly successful. He recommended to all of us in the group to try this method. In brief, the mind is taught to repeat in words the sensations commonly experienced by others in deep calm or hypnotic states. By repeating these feelings in words the idea is that it helps one to become calmer. Many of us tried the same course with varying results.

There was a separate learning for me here, in the encouragement to try many different paths. Just as Robin had encouraged my involvement in the men's movement, Lionel had encouraged the analysis with Claude. My other teachers were also so open-minded. This empowered me to find my own path. At the same time, it made me wary of therapists who swore by their own 'therapeutic modality'; like my wariness of preachers who swore by only one religion. Just as the expression, "It takes a village to raise a child," so a variety of solutions towards psychic health might be empowering. It was a useful reminder that we are all responsible for our own journey towards salvation.

There is much more to write about in my learnings from both Lionel and Claude. Because of my silent years a unique team of therapists had been necessary to assist me to begin the climb out of the well of unexpressed feelings and fears. Without them my life would have remained forever dark with clouds full of dread, consternation, horror, despair and tribulation. They helped me to find a path which led towards light and the dispersion of the darkest clouds.

Malidoma Somé

The year following my first men's conference, Michael Meade returned to lead a ritual weekend with a Dagara shaman, Malidoma Somé. This was a new phenomenon for most of us. With Michael and Malidoma drumming together all night it took us into another state of consciousness. Having shared with Malidoma the experience of losing my hearing at the age of fifteen months, he looked at me and said simply: "Yes, it was your first achievement." That comment hung on a special coat-hook of my mind for another twenty years before becoming clear he was right.

Malidoma seemed to be operating in a different dimension. But, surprisingly and deliciously, we understood each other immediately. As if we could communicate better in silence. We spoke about this twenty years later, just a few months ago in the middle of another discussion which we were recording:

Mark: "This reminds me of the many times you were in my house, the number of conversations we had without words, just looking at you and understanding things."

Malidoma: "I know, because it was always intense. I always remember that. Intense because we'd never stop talking."

Mark: "Even when we were silent."

Malidoma: "That's right and whether it is verbal or silent it was always going on, oh boy. Great, great."

It might surprise my reader to discover that a deaf child can communicate in this way. But, perhaps this is the way we all communicate with others in the world before our culture overwrites this skill with the conscious cultural language. Like, "In the beginning there was a common language" or "In the beginning was the word?"[12]

Malidoma is a wonderful teacher, and he returned to stay a few times with his lovely wife Sobonfu. Sobonfu was initiated as a Dagara shaman when she was a small girl aged 4. My first impression of her was to be totally overwhelmed. Never having met such a wondrous spiritual femininity, my initial reaction was to retreat into the next room and eat junk food hurriedly. It took time to be able to digest the spirit she brought with her.

---

[12] Book of Genesis and Gospel of John.

Malidoma and Sobonfu led several workshops, both individually and as a couple. We all learned so much from them. Very sadly, Sobonfu passed in the last year. She will always be remembered for the brightness of her spiritual teachings, her aliveness and generosity.

Malidoma's biography is titled: *Of Water and the Spirit.* This reminded me of the Gospel of John and of the guidance suggesting we must be reborn "of water and of the Spirit".[13] The question was among one of the last conversations in Paris with Claude. Malidoma had appeared at just the time to take the subject onwards.

That evening with Claude, I had seen a sparkle in his eye and quashed it suddenly with an inappropriate remark. At the following session we spoke of it, with my wondering whether his sparkle had been quashed because of my being frightened of life itself. That was it. A fear of life, and yet as a child my little sister had nicknamed me Marklesparkle because of my sparkle. So there was another fear alongside the fear of death; it was also the fear of life and light. Could this be a fear of the tunnel of death because of a fear of the sparkle of light at the end of it? When Claude continued that love and life were the same thing, it seemed that everything fell into place and some steps towards the real journey could begin.

Michael Meade had said that "One only starts to get the true benefits of therapy when one turns one's head from looking back at one's childhood to looking forward towards one's death."

James Hillman had told us this message is underlined in the story of Lot's wife, that because she was unable to stop looking back she became a pillar of salt.[14] James suggested that the metaphor of salt describes a heart preserved like meat for another day when the tears of grief can wash off the salts to let the heart be offered afresh. It made me wonder if the days when my heart was tight and my chest had felt constricted were the days of trying to look away from death, and the heart becoming as a pillar of salt. Very salty tears are perhaps needed to clear such days.

In the recent conversation with Malidoma which we recorded, and during the discussion about our speaking together in silence, the subject of my deafness came up again, twenty years after his first comment.

---

[13] The Gospel of John 3.

[14] Genesis 19:26.

Mark: "You might not remember but I was deaf as a child. I didn't know if you remembered that."

Malidoma: "No."

Mark: "Because I lost my hearing when I was 15 months old and I had complete silence from 15 months till I was seven years old, and then my hearing started to recover between seven and 13. I didn't hear normally till I was 13. What you said to me; I shall never forget this, you said to me during one ritual, you said my deafness was my first achievement."

Malidoma: "I said that?"

Mark: "You did."

Malidoma: "No, that was a spirit coming through."

Mark: "And I often wondered what the hell you meant by it."

Malidoma: "Oh my God."

Mark: "My deafness was my first achievement. I thought that was a very interesting comment because I have sometimes wondered to what extent I did it to myself."

Malidoma: "Yes, because on the basis of what we have been discussing so far I can see why it is something you may have done to yourself in order to protect something very critical that later on became the juice of your life. I don't know, but I'm suspecting you just don't go deaf and then out of the blue get your hearing back without major surgery, or hearing aid, or something that would be compensatory to the recovery. So there is some kind, I like to call it mythological initiative associated with that, something that is done in the other world that would translate into a muting, like you press a button in the other world and in this world you mute everything out, allowing the devolvement of another hearing which then when it came into effect was sound and grounded enough to unmute the button from this world, and from then on the noises of this world never distracted you from the fundamental focus. You never missed a mark. Otherwise, the definition of distraction in this world is essentially noisy. It is noise. That's what distracts people from the other. The noise of silence is more conducive to a soul journey than the noises of this world, and so most likely it was something that I could see at that time."

We spoke about it for a while. It became clear to both of us that my deafness had been 'self-inflicted'. Subsequently, the extent to which some autistic or withdrawn children may have shrunk into themselves became clearer to me. It takes one to know one. This is a subject we will return to.

Martín Prechtel

During the mid-1990s, Robert Bly decided he would come over from Minnesota to lead one of the men's movement weekend retreats in Dorset. He was going to come with someone we had not heard of so far, a Mayan shaman from Guatemala, Martín Prechtel.

My only experience of shamans had been the fascinating and delightful work with Malidoma and Sobonfu. My heart was therefore fully open to another shaman, particularly one who came with the highest recommendations from Robert Bly. The day duly came when Martín was to arrive and stay at my house for ten days.

The doorbell rang. Upon opening was revealed a giant turquoise macaw, with flowing golden hair shining against the backdrop of the dark leaves of my neighbour's tree of heaven. Dripping silver earrings glinting in the early morning sun, with long feathers everywhere, stood before me. There was even an extra black bag of feathers. A wondrous sight; clearly a treat was in store.

Mark: "Are you hungry?"

Martín: "Yes."

Mark: "Then let's drop your bags and we'll go out to eat."

Martín came downstairs with his bags and, having dropped them, we immediately set off for lunch. As he had just arrived from the USA, the thought came to my mind to take him to a burger joint, the Big Easy on the Kings Road. Leaving the garden gate, Martín said: "You walk ahead. I am going to walk five paces behind you."

Mark: "Why are you going to walk behind me?"

Martín: "To see how you walk."

Mark: "Why do you want to see how I walk?"

Martín: "To learn everything about you."

Mark: "Ok then." But no sooner than saying it, the discovery was how hard it was to walk normally when every step was being mirrored by a giant parrot. It wasn't possible to resist the temptation to look over my shoulder every few steps. And there in a perfect mirror was my last step. The springiness in the stride, the haughtiness, the determination and every aspect was me for sure. This tickled me and left me to walk on normally until we arrived at lunch. Not wishing to waste any of his discoveries, and being certain he knew everything already, we hadn't even introduced ourselves before I started a conversation brazenly:

Mark: "I am struggling with my daughter, she is always angry with me."

Martín: "Of course. She is trying to find your anger. She will not feel safe until she sees the edge of yours. That's why she is angry."

We looked at the menu and ordered lunch while Martín's words sank in. He was right that the edge of my anger had still not been found, and it seemed very reasonable that my daughter would feel safer once this was reached.

But then Martín continued: "Your house is full of animal spirits." This came as a complete surprise, and whilst looking at him with puzzlement he continued: "It's full of the spirits of exotic animals that were looked after." This was a complete mystery to me. Once we had finished lunch and walked home, Martín wanted to take a nap. Being suddenly without him, and full of excitement, I went immediately next door to tell my neighbours Alex and Maria Kroll. They were not surprised at all. Maria told me that when they had bought their house in 1953, mine had been owned by two retired lady vets. She remembered hearing the sound of lion cubs in the basement at night. Alex nodded his agreement. Apparently the lady vets had regularly, in their retirement, taken in small exotic animals and looked after them until they could be returned. Our jaws dropped as it was just too unfathomable. It couldn't be explained and yet there it was. Martín had somehow sensed in just a minute or two something which was unknown to me and had taken place forty years previously.

Returning to my house, and sitting in the kitchen while Martín continued his nap was like being a four-year-old waiting on Christmas morning. Not wanting to wake my father up but knowing that no gift could be received until he woke.

Thus began a very special friendship with a truly extraordinary person. My luck in finding Martín and having him to stay in my house was hard to believe. Every minute was clearly going to be an adventure.

The weekend workshop with Robert Bly and Martín gave birth to another unexplainable experience. We were about ninety men in the audience, arranged in three concentric circles listening to Robert, when suddenly the man on my right suffered a psychotic episode. At once, Martín got up and walked to the corner of the room with a white feather. He danced with the feather while facing the corner, and apparently looking away from us behind the man on my right. In a direct line of sight both were clearly visible at the same time. Suddenly it became clear to me that Martín's dance was in perfect harmony with the psychosis which was unfolding next to me. Not a gesture in one varied from the other. In a few minutes Martín's dance slowed, as did my neighbour, and then all was calm again as Martín returned to his seat next to Robert Bly. Watching the unfolding dance with the white feather held me spellbound. This was like something from a different dimension beyond my reach. As if a part of me had woken to observe something beyond the comprehension of my mind. There was no space for doubts concerning Martín's gifts from that moment onwards. My trust was complete and unwavering.

At the end of the ten-day visit, just before Martín set off for home, we discussed the men's work in general. It had been my wish to start doing mixed rituals instead of weekends with men, and Martín was very keen on this idea. The change was not supported by my fellow organisers of the UK men's movement and so we decided to split. They continued to organise the men's work, while my time was devoted to organising and supporting Martín's work with a mixed audience. Instead of workshops every year, he decided to lead a mixed group named: *New Sap in the Old Tree*. The greater good fortune for me was that the group met every three months and thus Martín came to stay at my house for ten days every quarter. We became good friends, and my debt to him escalated.

Having known Martín for longer than all my other teachers, and since he has probably stayed about a hundred nights at my house in London over the years, my reader will not be surprised by the extent to which his teaching has empowered me. So many of 'my ideas' came from his mouth, or more frequently 'from his looks', over such a long period that my few references to his specific guidance will never represent the extent of his help.

Sometimes, he brought his guitar to London. One evening we all sat around the large oval kitchen table after dinner with Martín strumming while my sister Ann recited one of her poems. The music was so delicious for my cats that they frantically seemed to be trying to climb into his big toe. One of Ann's later poems has traces of those warm and sweet evenings with Martín. With her permission, we will read it here now:

My Blue Hen by Ann Gray

I sing to my blue hen. I fold her wings
against my body. The fox has had her lover,
stealing through the rough grass,
the washed sky. I tell her, I am the blue heron
the hyacinth macaw. We have
a whispered conversation in French. I tell her
the horse, the ox, the lion, are all in the stars
at different times in our lives. I tell her there are
things even the sea can't do, like come in when
it's going out. I tell her my heart is a kayak
on wild water, a coffin, and a ship in full sail.
I tell her there is no present time,
an entire field of dandelions will give her
a thousand different answers. I tell her
a dog can be a lighthouse, a zebra finch can
dream its song, vibrate its throat while sleeping.
I tell her how the Mayan midwife sings each child
into its own safe song. Tonight, the moon holds back
the dark. I snag my hair on the plum trees. I tell her
I could've been a tree, if you'd held me here long enough.
I stroke her neck. She makes a bubbling sound,
her song of eggs and feathers. I tell her you were
a high note, a summer lightning storm of a man.

Martín is still my teacher now, twenty-something years later. And, just like the continued visits with Malidoma as he comes to London, through my silent language it is possible to converse constantly, whole paragraphs in a single glance. Martín never spoke about his arrival at my house until, six months ago at a public talk, he mentioned the first time he had stayed in London. He remembered that his room had smelled of lion cubs. What he didn't mention at this talk was the extra details; he hadn't just smelled lion cubs, he had also correctly smelled they had been 'looked after' together with other exotic animals.

Michael Meade had also shared with me how he had seen Malidoma sense things which had happened a generation before. So there is something going on which our conscious minds cannot grasp, but shamans can.

Hopefully my reader can understand something of my good fortune to have received guidance from such a delicious mix of marvellous teachers during the last thirty-five years. Hence the range of ideas in upcoming chapters as much of what they taught can be shared.

'DEAF-SIGHT' AND 'BLIND-HEARING'

This chapter is a mystery to me. Hopefully by the end it may also be a mystery to my reader.

As a child, learning to lip-read was quite natural during my silent state. With my sisters having helped me to talk early it took a while for my speech to degrade. Thus many other cues which a 'hearing person' might hear became instead visible to me. These included the full array of body language, gesture, emotional cues in the eyes and other signs. It never occurred to me that others could not see, and read, all that too. Why would it? They never noticed that they heard what appeared visible to me.

Since my childhood and formative years were so visual, it was normal for me to teach using images, cartoons and metaphor which could be more easily pictured in the recipient's mind. In the early 1990s, while teaching Japanese production methods to machinists at a factory in Cheltenham, I used many of my favourite images. Almost every one of my sentences as a new slide appeared began with, "As you can see..."

It seemed the session had begun well. Everybody seemed to enjoy it and learned a lot. Certainly they laughed at my images and cartoons. During the first coffee break everybody went to get some coffee, or stretch their legs, or smoke while the next hour or two of slides were organised by me. Almost ready, I suddenly became aware that one of the machinists hadn't moved from his chair. We were the only two left in the room. So it was quite natural to go and talk to him. Having wondered why he hadn't left like the others, Adam explained that he was blind. At first this filled me with shame. How had it happened that nobody had told me? How awful it must have sounded, and how insensitive, for a teacher to begin almost every sentence with, "As you can see." But my second reaction was to be fascinated. It wasn't sufficient just to take this new knowledge into account as the workshop continued. We focused on it at my instigation. After all, none of them had pointed out the error of my language and they all knew Adam was blind. Perhaps it was necessary to share my shame. In any event we made a lot of discoveries together.

We learned that there were over three hundred employees in the factory and Adam knew every one of them by their footsteps. When they were about four feet away he would greet each of them by name. Then the maintenance crew shared how his machine never broke down. He would call them over to mention a sprocket that sounded worn, or a vibration suggesting something out of alignment. Following his guidance, they checked and adjusted; his machine ran better than all the others which were operated by people who could see.

The subject gripped me, because of its significance as the loss of a different sense. This reminded me again how my brother-in-law, Peter, had lost his sight for almost a year as an eighteen-year-old. He became subsequently terrified of losing his hearing because he had relied on sound entirely to communicate with his family during that blind year. By contrast, my fear was of losing my sight as it was my only means of communication during my silent years. Neither of us feared losing the sense we had already lost once.

While the blind may use their hearing to see, my sight seemingly enabled me to hear. We have to remember that it is not eyes that see, but the brain that sees. Perhaps it is the same way with hearing. Our minds process the sensual inputs in different and complementary ways. Birds and dolphins find their way when temporarily blindfolded by using other senses.

As some of the blind walk with a stick, they hear more than a hearing person can imagine. The taps of the stick set off a sound which echoes differently from a stone wall, than from a door, or windows, or the approaching corner of the building. It seems almost as if they can see the building through the sound echoes. Before we think that this is extraordinary, let's not forget that many other animals do the same. It is natural for bats and dolphins. Perhaps this gift is still hard-wired but the seeing person lets the skill atrophy away, being replaced by their 'superior sense'. Research at the University of Montreal suggests that a blind person's brain can 're-wire' to use the visual cortex with signals based on sound and touch. But, if that is surprising, what about Erik

Weihenmayer who went blind when he was 13 years old? He can climb rock faces using 'BrainPort' technology which enables him 'to see with his tongue'. Wearing a camera on his helmet, technology converts light into electrical impulses in his mouth stimulating his tongue instead of his retina. With more tactile nerve endings than any other part of the body except the lips, he can find his way up almost vertical rock faces.[15]

For most 'seeing' people, the idea that the blind can hear more acutely seems very easy to grasp. For some reason it is easy to accept that there is quite a spectrum of different hearing abilities. Somehow it seems normal that the blind can make up for their loss of sight in another way.

But the mystery for me is why it is so hard for 'hearing' people to imagine that the deaf see more. Think about it for a moment. Why shouldn't it be similar? Why are 'hearing' people so threatened by this idea? Why is it hard to imagine that others might be able to see more?

Having learned to lip-read by myself, to take in all the other visual cues unconsciously, led to a few consequences for me. Without doubt it has often made me make choices which would not otherwise have been made. Some remembered ones can be shared, but others might have been seemingly so natural that there was nothing unusual to suggest worthiness of remembering.

When, as a thirteen-year-old, my 'confirmation' lessons in the Church of England began and a similar phenomenon happened. It wasn't possible for me to continue as the voice didn't seem to be coming from the priest's body. Returning home for Sunday lunch I announced that I would not be confirmed. When asked why not, my excuse that 'the priest didn't understand the bible' was accepted. My father never pushed me to continue, for which he has my gratitude.

Earlier, having wondered about the American Indian comment: "The white man speaks with forked tongue," made me wonder if they see what some of the deaf might also see? What about our youngest children? Do they have this extra sight before they acquire the language of our culture? It is said that a child 'knows that their parent is lying' by the age of fifteen months. Do they pick up the mismatch between the two languages this early?

Could this also be why it is so threatening for some hearing people to imagine that the deaf see more? Because to admit this might imply that

---

[15] Discover magazine July 2008.

there is a dimension which we are ignoring, or deliberately keeping hidden from our everyday mind?

The Montreal research found the brain can 're-wire' by using inputs from sound and touch to reach the visual cortex, so maybe other 're-wirings' are possible. Perhaps other sensory facilities can be 'gifted' to a different sense when the inputs cannot otherwise be properly used. For example, I have very little acoustic memory. It took until almost my twenty-first birthday to be able to distinguish between my three sisters on the telephone. Even now, they always introduce themselves when calling as, "This is your big sister;" "It's your middle or little sister." The habit has not been broken. It seems as if my visual memory has taken over some of the space which would normally have been reserved for acoustic memory.

Dr. Sophie Forster, of the University of Sussex, discovered that our sense of smell is very sensitive to our level of 'mind focus'. That, when our mind is 'busy on a task', our sense of smell can disappear. However, it seems to me that this idea is not so threatening to the hearing and seeing folk. Somehow the sense of smell has been downgraded by our culture. But, this is not the case for our animal friends as we shall see, or for shamans.

However, as Neil Shubin says, despite the stunning variety of photoreceptor organs, every animal uses the same kind of light-capturing molecule. Insects, humans, clams and scallops all use opsins to be able to see.[16] Thus there exists one of the bases for a 'common language' between species.

For now, we can leave this question of 'deaf-sight' and 'blind-hearing' as a mystery and return to the matter later. In the meantime let me share one of life's ironies. Whilst training to be a psychotherapist, my first patient was blind. She will never fathom what I saw, just as I will never be able to imagine what she heard in my voice. Could we both have smelled our way at times?

---

[16] Neil Shubin, *Your Inner Fish.*

The Minds of Birds

Some of our friends, the birds, have a brain weighing barely a gram, a raisin really. But the contents of the raisin are extraordinary. The bird has no flying lessons but manages, in her first fall from the nest, as if she had been taught for a life-time. She must know what she needs to eat as well as what to avoid. The raisin contains an entire botanical and zoological encyclopaedia. She must also know how and where to search for the food she needs. There was no time in the nest for this learning. The birds of the Pacific Ocean begin with a programming to include the skill of finding their fish, penetrating the water with the right angle, speed and enough force to catch their prey as well as to emerge without drowning. Ascending from the water, she must have the ability to navigate her way back home.

Except for the frigate birds of course; they are different. Desiring fish but having a wingspan so wide that it is almost impossible to take off from the ocean when wet is not a good genetic set up for a sea-fish diet. Unless the fish fly out of the water first, it is hard to catch them. We often watched frigates flying high in Kiribati, well above the other birds, swooping down to dislodge a fish caught by a smaller bird and then accelerating down to catch his lunch before the fish dropped back into the ocean.[17] This is how the frigate bird eats ocean fish without touching the ocean or soaking his wings, and why he shares his name with another of high speed and manoeuvrability, the frigate ship. Having the largest wing area compared to their body weight in the bird family makes them perfectly designed for piracy. Like buccaneers all over the world, they can harass other birds until they vomit up their stomach contents in flight to be caught and eaten again by the frigates. Thus an unsuccessful hunting expedition by a smaller bird may force her to give up what she ate earlier

[17] Kiribati is how The Gilbert Islands are now written in their local language.

– like a pirate stealing the contents of the hull from a smaller hunter with both living for another day. Also, like pirates, the frigates stay out at sea longer than other birds. They catnap in a glide or whilst enjoying an updraft, harass others for food while awake, and spend an extraordinary time between their feet touching land. Over two months between landings is not such a big deal for a frigate bird. Perhaps the size of the Pacific Ocean caused them to evolve such a continuous airborne ability.

Some migratory birds fly over sixty thousand kilometres in a year, yet they can still find where they started from. What is just as extraordinary is the distance in one flight for some. Bar-tailed godwits fly more than eleven thousand kilometres between Alaska and New Zealand, the longest Pacific crossing, without landing. Obviously they don't need as much time as we do worrying about what to pack for the journey. But pack they must, even if this entails substantial changes in diet to increase body fat as well as meticulously cleaning up their feathers before the trip. Again, this was not taught in the nest. Then the birds must know their calls, their courtship rituals, how and where to build their nests as well as the knack of finding suitable materials so the wind doesn't rip them apart.

It is fitting that we should include the Galápagos Islands, where the mind of Charles Darwin underwent a metamorphosis observing the birds. Having wanted to visit these islands for many years, my luck was to find Fabrizio Prado. Fabrizio is a wonderful teacher and delicate photographer. He was born on the Galápagos Islands.

Some birds are so delicate; they can almost walk on water like insects. By contrast the frigate bird would be 'in a soup' if he tried. Should we be surprised that the favourite colours of the pirates are the black and red of the male frigate bird? Or that the buccaneers scare first and then empty out the holds of another ship. The frigate bird is not a killer of birds which hunt in the ocean; that would reduce the number of raids he could make in the future. On the contrary, the more birds that are scared of him and surrender easily their uneaten catch, or the contents of their stomach, the better. Just like pirates everywhere. The fear facilitates the frigate's task and makes lunch possible. From beneath the water, a fear of giant tuna scares smaller flying fish to leap out of the ocean. The frigate swoops and with a long hooked bill catches them when the tuna cannot. Thus the long hooked bill is a common theme among pirates.

Pictures by Fabrizio Prado; born on the Galápagos as was the male frigate bird below

Our friends, the birds, have quite an array of instinctual intelligences already imprinted before hatching on the 'hard-drive of their raisin'. Intelligences for flight; navigation; migration preparation;[18] migration routes;[19] botany and zoology; protection against predators; locating and catching nourishment; nest planning with where and when to build; nest architecture, foraging for materials and construction; courting; nurture of young; defence; calls and communication with other birds amongst many other gifts. To refer, in a derogatory way, to a 'bird-brain' is clearly quite absurd.

The more interesting question for us is why the Victorians should have felt that 'instincts' are somehow derogatory, or taboo, even if fascinating.

Other cultures think differently about birds. Kiribati would not have been inhabited three thousand years ago without the navigation of birds. The Pacific Ocean, covering 161 million square kilometres (km²), makes up a third of our planet's surface. But, excluding the larger countries of the Pacific Rim, the land mass is only 89,000 km². Of this, most is in the far South-west: Solomon Islands, New Caledonia, Fiji, and Vanuatu. Apart from these, the specks of land which remain are spread at the rate of one square kilometre of land for every 14,000 km² of ocean. Since most of the islands are coral atolls without hills, the horizon swallows an island after just 12 miles. To find an atoll, the 1 in every 14,000, the navigator must pass within 12 miles of her. In 1975 the flight to Kiribati from Fiji took seven hours, refuelling at Funafuti in the Ellice Islands. Once, when the radio mast was damaged, the plane had to turn back to Fiji as the risk of not finding Funafuti was too great. No wonder the Kiribati islanders revere birds, covering their arms with tufts of feathers for a dance.

Arthur Grimble kept detailed notes of the navigational assistance provided by birds. He writes, *The traveller knows that he is nearly in sight of the north end of Abaiang, but has fallen away to westward, when he sees numerous terns flying in pairs, of which one bird continually revolves about the other.*[20]

Perhaps the birds can make us wonder about some of our paradigms, particularly concerning our 'birth gifts'. First, though, we could learn a

---

[18] Some double their body-fat in the weeks before migration. Godwits grow new feathers for the flight as well as fluffing and washing more.

[19] To be able to migrate such distances, some birds fly at specific higher altitudes to catch the right winds.

[20] *Tungaru Traditions*, Arthur Grimble, edited by H.E. Maude.

Ready for a dance ceremony based on bird movements, Tarawa, Kiribati, 1975

little more about birds. We might discover that we have missed answers because we have been asking the wrong questions.

Bird brains don't stop their development at hatching. They have an advantage over us in being able to develop more neurons when needed. Obviously they have a different programming because of the criticality of extra weight affecting flight performance. Their neurons are much more tightly packed. Charles University in Prague found that birds had twice the number of neurons per gram of brain compared with ours. Could this help their speed of decision making which needs to be so much faster whilst in three dimensional flight? We could perhaps distinguish their pure instincts as separate from a 'hatching intelligence' which has been subsequently enhanced by exposure to the environment.

Dr Nathan Emery has written a beautiful book containing glorious pictures: *Bird Brain. An Exploration of Avian Intelligence.* His careful, well researched, and detailed exposition of the talent of birds shows how much we under-estimate them.

Jennifer Ackerman informs us in her book: *the Genius of Birds* how there are *...birds that can count and manage simple arithmetic, make and collect different tools for specific uses, dance to our music, understand physics, remember the past and plan for the future, invent novel solutions to new problems, copy each other's behaviour, mimic songs and calls to advantage, understand cause and effect in others, find their way to a place thousands of miles away they have never been to before, or anticipate the arrival of a distant storm.*

Jennifer goes on to explain their social skills so eloquently: *They breed in colonies, bathe in groups, roost in congregations, forage in flocks. They argue. They cheat. They deceive and manipulate. They kidnap. They divorce. They display a strong sense of fairness. They give gifts. They play keep-away and tug-of-war with twigs, strands of Spanish moss, bits of gauze. They pilfer from their neighbours. They warn their young away from strangers. They tease. They share. They cultivate social networks. They vie for status. They kiss to console one another. They teach their young. They blackmail their parents. They summon witnesses to the death of a peer. They may even grieve.*

It is humbling how much we under-estimated them. Apparently New Caledonian Crows have greater cognitive ability than the great apes.

Emery writes that Western scrub jays seem to grasp what others know. If a jay is aware of another bird watching while he hides his food then he may return later when alone and move the food cache somewhere else. But it is only those jays with a history of pilfering from others that do this. For the innocent the idea of hiding food does not occur. Perhaps, then, hiding is not a pure instinct. Southern African Drongos have a special talent, to learn and mimic alarm calls of other birds and meerkats to steal their food during the ongoing distraction.

Birds develop good memories to learn from the past and an ability to plan for the future. As Fabrizio Prado showed me on the Galápagos Islands, some finches trim twigs to the perfect length to be able to dig out tasty insects. Sometimes they use a very sharp thorn, like a fork, to impale a grub. Surely they learnt this from their environment? Birds have to be able to measure in order to build a nest. But the Galápagos Islands are an exception when it comes to nesting, since the absence of predators means most birds don't construct nests there. They simply deposit their eggs on the ground, and ignore humans. Just like the black Noddy picked up on the islet of South Tabiteuea and rearranged for his photo-shoot with me.

Birdcalls are inherited and on the 'hard drive', whereas songs are learned, usually from an elder male. This helps us to see how the programming for calls is there at hatching, but can be adapted for a song. Without instinctual intelligence and programming we would not have our 'conscious intelligence'. After all, it is upon the foundations of instinctual intelligence and brain circuitry that all other intelligence is built. Rather like my dependence on the programming of Microsoft Word on this computer to be able to share thoughts with my reader.

In Japan, some crows apparently place nuts on roads at traffic junctions, wait for cars to drive over them, and then quickly retrieve the crushed contents while the traffic lights change. If the process proves unsuccessful, the crows may move the nuts for future attempts as the lights change.

Some birds, like the Jays, store seeds and nuts in a very large number of hiding places. Later they can find them, even after months. They seem to recall the 'sell by date' on their cache to know what to consume first. Emery explains that their evolution includes an increase in size of the hippocampus, precisely to aid in remembering locations. He describes how earlier scientists overlooked the existence of a bird's forebrain because theirs is organised differently from ours.

Ancient and indigenous people knew about ravens and crows, not from dissecting bird brains but just by being with them and watching. They have a special place in many of our ancient stories. Aesop knew what the crow could work out, dropping rocks in the pitcher to drink as the water level rose, or so he wrote some 2,600 years ago. Crows recognise human faces and can remember them for up to three years apparently.

A number of metaphors including the birds may help the journey to understand our minds, particularly with links to my culture – the Indo-European mind of North-West Europe, where we are more like a flock of individual minds. In Asia, the family is more important than the individual, and other metaphors help more. My reference to 'my Indo-European existence' is motivated by the observation that other cultures have different paradigms and we make a huge mistake in assuming their thinking is the same.

Considering how much is already 'printed on the hard drive' of the bird's raisin before the eggshell cracks, why did it take us so long to discover multiple intelligences in the human mind? Just imagine that our brain may weigh 400 times that of a bird when we are born. And yet, it seems that some 'advanced' cultures treat the brain of an infant as if a blank sheet at birth.

Perhaps our ancestors knew, and we forgot. The Greek philosophers brought to Rome the idea of 'aptitudes', 'aptus' in Latin, for our gifts at birth. A birth gift which was modified by experience in our early environment was called a 'trait', from the Latin 'tractus'. Then there is that specific mixture which motivates us, from 'motivus' in Latin. Each of these ingredients in our minds was called a 'talentum'. The plural is 'talenta' which became our English word 'talent'. Talent is thus the combination of our gifts at birth, the mixed effect of the early environment on these gifts, and our drives. The word education derives from the Latin 'ex ducere' which means 'to lead out' and suggests helping our young children by 'leading out their talent'. In our Indo-European culture we do mostly the opposite. We stuff their minds with what we want to put in there, like overfeeding a goose with so much corn that her liver becomes bloated and can only be served as Foie Gras.

My previous paradigm was that most of my mind developed from my schooling and experiences, all under my conscious control. The amount of mind, which began with me at birth, had been severely devalued both by my conscious mind and my culture's mind. This seemed one of my first corrective lessons from the birds. Perhaps absorbing my culture's devaluation of my indigenous mind was a way of learning self-destruction by default. The question is therefore whether we are asking the wrong question, having massively under-estimated the abilities of birds. Instead of being concerned with how much 'cognitive intelligence' the birds have, why were the Victorians so derogatory about our animal instincts? Why is the animal in us so feared?

We know that our minds are made from elements of nature and nurture; why are we so scared of the nature component? Are we really scared of our nature? If so, why could that be, and where could this have come from? Is the fear of the part of us which is natural connected with self-destruction? Are we worried that the natural instinctual part of our mind might not be controllable if let out?

A smart bird might well ask, through that piercing eye, why some of their neighbours, the human species, have so much difficulty with their human instincts – much more difficulty than the bird does with her cognitive intelligence. They have given us a very useful clue to take forward on the journey.

The birds have another teaching for us in the matter of self-destruction. Suppose the bird was caught, and put in a cage. Of the instinctual intelligences, what will she still need?

- Her intelligence for challenging flights will scarcely be needed with so little variety of possible movements inside the cage.

Soon, all motion will be so repetitive that her flight instincts will atrophy...

- Her navigation, migration and migration preparation programming will not be needed at all. Some birds in captivity do continue for a while to adapt their diet as if about to go on their annual migration, but that will atrophy too...
- Her vast knowledge of botany and zoology will be quickly forgotten as she will be regularly fed without choosing anymore...
- Her special skills of hunting, locating or catching nourishing food will no longer be required...
- Her protection against predators will no longer be required as predators can no longer get in to her cage, just as she cannot get out, but it will take a long time for her to feel safer from the lack of such predators…
- The need to plan for her nests, including foraging and construction materials will vanish away…
- Courting skills might still be used from time to time, unless only two of the same species are sharing the aviary. Thus much less preening will be required…
- The song and communication with other birds may however still be used, if there is still something to sing about as the captive days and nights go by…
- Of course, she will still nurture her young, but this is almost all she has left of millions of years of evolution on her raisin…

Most of the birds' instinctual intelligence disappears or progressively atrophies in captivity. Millions of years of evolution or divine construction squashed into a trash can. Could her frustration make her destructive? Just like my destructiveness as a small boy? We cannot ignore that many 'civilised' cultures have done the same to our minds. The 'progress' of the last ten thousand years has caused much of our instinctual and intuitive abilities to atrophy, or become hidden almost out of reach. In a sense, we may be living in captivity without realising it.

Both Nathan Emery and Jennifer Ackerman refer to the 2002 Oxford University experiment conducted by Alex Kacelnik and his team. A New

Caledonian crow, Betty, was challenged to find a way to retrieve a tasty piece of lamb's heart from a small bucket inside a vertical plastic tube. Betty 'blew away the experimenters' by bending a straight piece of wire to make a hook to pull up the little bucket. However, my question is a different one. Would she have done that if she had been in the wild? Can the fact that she was in captivity be considered to have made a difference to her mind? In captivity there are such a large number of neural circuits – with programmes of instinctual intelligence – which are all going to waste. There are plenty of spare neurons and circuits to come up with all kinds of ideas and insights. What shall we make of that?

Is it possible that, out of the boredom of captivity, the bird might instead develop new tricks to keep their owners entertained, perhaps for exciting rewards like a portion of lamb heart?

Some species of animals, particularly the African hunters, find it really hard to locate their own nature when released into the wild again after only a few generations of captivity. Many die before they can relocate their survival instincts. After millions of years of careful design or evolution, the atrophied aspects of such instincts cannot be instantly switched back on. Significant effort is required to let such intuitive and instinctual behaviour return. Perhaps this is what many of our religions are referring to in the idea of 'rebirth'. Are they referring to re-accessing the part of us which makes us 'whole' or 'Holy'?

These light blue sky pieces of the jigsaw puzzle of our minds need to be carefully placed on the table in plain view as we move on to seek other pieces.

Bird Navigation

There is one aspect of the genius of birds which warrants a chapter all of his own. The way that birds, among other animals, can find their way home is so extraordinary.

Jennifer Ackerman writes that birds have their own internal positioning systems, like our GPS, which may be global. When migratory birds were captured near the Eastern shore of USA, flown over two thousand miles west in boxes, and released from the West coast, they were able to make a course correction to aim for the original destination. A similar experiment north of Kaliningrad, Russia, involved capturing migrating warblers. Half of them had their trigeminal nerves cut. This nerve runs from the beak to the brain and may transmit magnetic information from iron in the beak. Having then released the warblers about a thousand kilometres east of the point of capture, those with intact trigeminal nerves reoriented themselves by correcting their course whereas the others remained on the same direction as if they had not been displaced to the east. It seems convincing that the beak contains an ability to recognise the earth's magnetic field.[21]

Jon Hagstrum has suggested that natural infrasonic signals or low frequency noises in the atmosphere may be part of the birds' mapping system.

In Floriano Papi's research on Tuscan pigeons, when they had severed olfactory nerves (so they could not smell) the pigeons never returned. My first reaction was maybe they were smarter – why would one fly back to someone who conducts such an experiment? But birds clearly have a 'smell map'. Birds were taken from the Azores and put on a cargo ship to Lisbon. Some had been fitted with small magnetic bars that scrambled their magnetic sense; others had their nostrils washed with zinc sulphate,

---

[21] Jennifer Ackerman, *The Genius of Birds.*

temporarily obliterating their sense of smell. They were released hundreds of miles from their breeding island. The ones with mixed-up magnetics found their way back, but those with neutralised noses were completely confused and meandered around the ocean for weeks. Some never returned.[22]

Research has shown that birds use a combination of innate programming while sensing, which can be a combination of sight, smell, temperature, pressure, magnetic signals and ultrasonic or infrasonic sound waves. As well, they learn from experience in earlier flights by recording their senses during a journey based on the inputs from several systems. Apparently they can also calibrate their compasses with the sun and stars daily. As such they are able to develop much greater accuracy from the use of several systems in unison.

Birds have several navigation systems which operate independently – like boy scouts with a map, a GPS device, a compass, a sextant, a barometer, a thermometer, camera recorders to store images of a journey for later retrieval, a set of instructions of how far and when to fly, a list of what to look for, with extra sensors picking up smells and retrieving signals such as infrasound waves. Sight is a bonus among their instruments, but may only be used for fine tuning at the end of their journey after other systems have guided them close enough. Unlike the Boy Scout who would have needed a satchel or duffel bag for all his devices, the bird has the devices miniaturised with the processors hard-wired into their raisin. More importantly the birds teach us something more, like a 'sixth sense' that is continually reading and comparing data from all the other inputs to generate 'integrated' navigation. An unconscious confidence comes from mutual confirmation between their different guidance systems.

For most of the time, while our bird is on a migration she is much too far above sights for individual recognition. The complexity and brilliance of the bird navigation systems are quite extraordinary – even more extraordinary to realise that these systems are all pre-stored on their raisin. But then, considering the distances they travel and their ability to find their way home again, perhaps we should not be so surprised. Apparently, homing pigeons can get within a mile or so of their home even if blindfolded; sight is only needed for the last few hundred yards. The Kiribati dances express their gratitude for these bird gifts on which their culture was dependent.

---

[22] Jennifer Ackerman, *The Genius of Birds.*

Many creatures make extraordinary annual journeys, including the looping 1,800 mile mass migrations of blue wildebeest in East Africa. Their sound is as impressive as the sight of rising dust between them all. In 1991, Lord Jellicoe was with me on a tour of the East African agro-industries managed by Booker Tate. After visiting Kagera Sugar near to the Tanzania – Uganda border, we chartered a small plane to take us to Dar es Salaam for lunch with President Nyerere. The pilot was trained by the Air Force and was happy with my request for the extra loops and turns to follow the wildebeest in the Serengeti.

Tanzania used to be the world's largest producer of sisal for cordage. We were keen to provide Booker Tate's assistance even though we had never grown sisal before, but there were too many headwinds, particularly the lower price of nylon as a substitute. Despite an ability to produce more it was not possible to compete with nylon, and Tanzania's largest industry, 'green gold', which employed over a million was becalmed.

Returning to animals, the record migratory run on the hoof is held by the movement of caribou running almost 3,000 miles across North America.

Land migrations are not in the same league as those in the air or the sea. After all, the wildebeest have somehow beaten down paths and unchanging sights to guide them. In some respects the journey has more definite signposts and 'landmarks'. Perhaps there are very distinctive smells from years and years of hooves on the same pieces of land. Like the discoveries made in the 1960s by Iain Douglas-Hamilton of elephant trails twelve feet wide and thousands of years old deep within African forests.[23] There do not seem to be such 'air-marks' or 'sea-marks' for the creatures of air and water to follow. If there ever were any, they would have been regularly blown or washed away. Or are our paradigms mistaken? Perhaps the 'air and sea marks' exist but are beyond our comprehension. This makes the genius of the air and sea creatures to be of a different order. It is not just the distances, but their ability to find their way back home even if sometimes alone or separated from the flock. Could this be why our creation myth has the fifth day devoted to development of creatures of the sea and the air, separately from all other beasts on land?

Some of the migrations which stand out include humpback whales tracked over 5,000 miles between Costa Rica and Antarctica – the

---

[23] Carl Safina, *Beyond Words – What Animals Think and Feel.*

longest migration of any mammal. But a female great white shark was recorded swimming almost 7,000 miles from South Africa to Western Australia and back within nine months. A female leatherback turtle was similarly followed on a journey of 12,700 miles from her Indonesian breeding ground to feed off the US Pacific coast.

However, the land and sea migration records pale by airborne standards. Painted lady butterflies travel from the desert of North Africa to the Arctic Circle on a round trip of over 9,000 miles. The annual journey of a bar-tailed godwit is about 18,500 miles.[24] The figure of eight route of the sooty shearwater exceeds 40,000 miles a year between breeding grounds in New Zealand and feeding sites in Alaska.

Arctic terns might be the record holders with their flights from the Farne Islands off the English Northumberland coast to Antarctica, extending the record-breaking migration to 59,600 miles. Thus the arctic terns witness midsummer in both hemispheres while travelling outside their breeding season.

We didn't see the arctic terns in Kiribati, but one of the most beautiful visitors was the fairy tern with her gossamer wings.

Fairy tern, Tarawa, Kiribati, 1975

This makes me wonder whether our human 'sixth sense' could be an unconscious confirmation resulting from the combined signals from our five known senses. But there is more. Could there be a 'seventh sense', or something beyond the reach of our consciousness, which is pulling the strings based on everything developing from without and within. Something which cannot be understood because it is underneath everything else? Something which is so natural that we cannot find her or get under her to 'understand'?

Migratory birds are seemingly hatched with an outline of their first migration. Their innate directions give them a distance or time to fly, a magnetic direction and altitude. Perhaps it is not the altitude they are guided towards but a particular pressure they are seeking which defines

---

[24] US Geological Survey biologist Lee Tibbetts: This journey is completed in three non-stop flights over the course of about 20 days of flying.

their altitude. Thus, they may not have hatched with maps but their innate clock, compass programme and other senses enable them to develop a map right from their first flight. There is a German word for migratory restlessness, *Zugunruhe.*[25] It was found that captive birds in a round cage primarily jump or flutter in their migratory direction. When the magnetic field is artificially turned horizontally, in the absence of celestial clues, the birds reorient to follow the magnetic field.

One of the biggest differences between birds and Indo-European humans seems to be that birds trust their instructions (intuition and instinct) and get on with it. As they make their first journeys they are able to record their sights, smells, sounds, temperatures and pressures as if creating a mental map to make future migrations easier. Of course, in many cases they will have more experienced migratory cousins to follow. But the research shows a bird can be very accurate even when alone.

The part of our brain which stores these kinds of memories is the hippocampus; recording what happened and where, which is rather essential for success as well as to avoid danger. Birds are the same. The more a bird is dependent on navigational memory, the more the hippocampus develops. MRI scanning finds the same with the London black cab drivers who spend two years learning the knowledge of London's streets. Compared to the London bus drivers, the black cab drivers have more grey matter and a bigger hippocampus – just like birds that need 'the knowledge' to survive. The birds teach us how a part of the brain is 'elastic' and can be exercised and stretched to a greater capacity to meet specific and definite needs.

Unlike our laptop computers which have a rather precisely defined memory space, it seems that animal and human brains are flexible to enable adaptation to their usage. The greatest hippocampus relative to bodyweight belongs to the hummingbird who remembers individual flowers as well as the time needed to replenish pollen before the next feeding. The research with birds also neatly squashes the sexist assumptions on brain memory and spatial senses. When a gender role requires greater memory, that gender's hippocampus exceeds the average. In the case of cowbirds, only the females locate, monitor and revisit the nests they parasitize.[26] Hence, there should be no surprise that the female cowbird develops superior spatial ability to the male.

---

[25] Kramer, 1949.

[26] Jennifer Ackerman.

Although not related directly to navigation, but a necessary trait to explain the extraordinary migrations, Jennifer Ackerman explains that birds experience the same cycles of slow-wave sleep and rapid eye movement (REM) that we do. However, in addition, they can modulate deep sleep by opening one eye, limiting the slow-wave sleep to half of the brain while keeping the other half alert, perhaps to navigate while sleeping in flight, or to watch for predators. Could this help explain the original design and evolution of the two brain hemispheres?

In the very moving story of Saroo Brierley, *A Long Way Home,* which was adapted into the 2016 film *Lion*, he seemed to navigate his way home eventually just as a bird does. At the age of five, he travelled with his elder brother by train to Burhanpur. They became separated and Saroo tried to find his way alone but wound up instead at Howrah railway station in Calcutta which is almost a thousand miles away. He survived by scavenging on the streets whilst also venturing on trains to look for his home. But all trains seemed to bring him back to Howrah. Unable to find his way home, he was taken to a centre for abandoned children. From there he became adopted by an Australian family and moved to Tasmania.

Twenty-five years later he sought to find his home village. He had a sense of how far he had lived from Howrah railway station. As a bird would, he looked at the earth from above, using Google Earth. He remembered the texture of the sound of the towns near his home. He remembered topographical features such as the hills and a fountain near the train tracks where he used to play. Just like the birds, when one sense told him the direction was wrong he searched another. As time went by, he eventually found several signs that matched his memory, the distance, the topography, the phonetic sounds of the village names, the landmarks. Then a part of his mind which operates like a conformational vortex indicating that all the senses are resonating to agree led him intuitively and quickly towards his home. Without Google Earth he might never have found his way home.

The birds would have approached the homing problem in a similar way, and much quicker, by trusting their raisin full of independent navigation systems. They would not have needed to wait twenty-five years to access Google Earth as all thc information was on their raisin before hatching. Jennifer Ackerman writes that homing pigeons do not take the same direct route home even when making a regular journey. On each occasion they take a slightly different route until their guidance systems are coordinated. Their method of navigation is a triumph of integration without any evidence that any one sensory system is dominant. A form of motivation increases with the resonance generated by confirmation from more than one source of navigational clues.

Many of us have had an experience of the warm vortex towards confirmation from independent sensory systems. Maybe we call this a sixth sense. Or we find her overnight by letting our unconscious do the work while our conscious mind cannot interfere. Could falling in love have similar properties of allowing us to fall into a warm pool at the centre of the vortex by trusting what our senses are guiding us towards?

While watching the film, *Lion*, another aspect struck me very strongly. In the retelling of Saroo's story, as played by the actor Dev Patel, Saroo had retained his childlike intuition and instincts as to whom he could trust. He saw at once as a five-year-old when an adult's intentions were not destined towards kindness. Watching this part of the film reminded me of the similarity of my childhood instincts, and the uncanny accuracy in interpreting the actions of others.

In summary, the 'raisin' of the bird can digest and process information about landmarks and air-marks – distances, spatial relations, memories, sights, temperatures, pressures, sounds and infra-sounds as well as smells – all without 'thinking'; combined with a compass and sextant for the sun and stars as well as reading the earth's magnetic field.

This all makes perfect sense. Our friends the birds and fishes would not be able to navigate home with only rigid navigational systems which did not take into account the changing strength of the winds and currents. They must be taking other sensory information into account in order to adjust their course to the changes in circumstance, particularly when we consider the medium in which they travel.

In the next chapter, my journey explores learnings from ocean creatures.

Ocean Creatures

The octopus somehow guided me to explore what his fellow creatures had to say. Salmon remember the way back to their spawning stream after five years in the ocean. Turtles return to the same beach where they hatched. They all have an innate way to 'get home'.

It has been suggested that sea creatures are using the earth's magnetic field for guidance, but more recent research indicates they also have several other navigational systems. For salmon, magnetic detection is just one part of their navigational skill. Fish can use their sense of smell to help them locate the exact stream of their birth.[27] Some have proposed that salmon release pheromones on their way out to sea which they can detect on their way home; like leaving a trail of sensory breadcrumbs. We can marvel at the magic without needing to know exactly how they do it.

Turtles may have more than one set of maps in their magnetic location system, as if they have a macro map for the oceans and then a micro map for their native coast line which has their own specific magnetic signature – just like a homing pigeon only needing sight for the last yards of the journey home. Does the turtle switch gear to a different system when close enough to the coastal signature of her home?

Neil Shubin has written a fascinating book, *Your Inner Fish*, which Oliver Sacks admires as a *story that will change forever how you understand what it means to be human*. Shubin immediately had me captivated with his comment about other creatures: *Let's not focus on what makes them distinct, we need to focus on what different creatures share*. If only we could repeat this phrase with religions instead of creatures, we could truly say Amen.

---

[27] Nathan Putman, a researcher at Oregon State University in Corvallis.

As Neil Shubin has recently taught me, our ancestors left the ocean and walked on land about 375 million years ago. With my early trade-off between senses of hearing and sight, it was interesting to learn the evolution of senses we share with ocean mammals – how *our sense of smell contains a deep record of our history as fish, amphibians and mammals.*[28] What struck me as quite extraordinary was two-fold. Firstly, that *fully three percent of our entire DNA, our genome, is devoted to genes for detecting different odours.*[29] Secondly, the *genes involved in the sense of smell are present in all of our cells, although they are active only in the nasal area. Our ability to smell enables us to discriminate among five thousand to ten thousand different odours.* Yoav Gilad discovered primates that developed colour vision tend to have large numbers of 'knocked-out' smell genes. We humans are part of a lineage that has traded smell for sight.[30] Through our evolution it seems that we have made trade-offs between different senses, and our sense of smell was 'de-emphasised'.

This again reminded me of Martín Prechtel's first visit to my house in London and his comments at lunch about the 'animal spirits' in my home. How there was a good feeling of exotic animals which had been 'looked after'. My neighbours had told me of a variety of small animals from different zoos which had had been restored to health by the two retired lady vets 40 years previously in the 1950s. Martín never spoke about this subject again until about eighteen months ago, at a public talk. Then he mentioned that first day in London. He remembered walking into my basement and *smelling lion cubs.* Malidoma Somé, in different discussions, has also mentioned smelling what had happened years before. Is it possible that indigenous shamans have access to a much greater part of their sense of smell than the rest of us? That they have somehow reopened sensory doors which our culture 'de-emphasised' for us? As they sometimes say, animals can smell what you are thinking. Experience has taught me to avoid any scented products when shamans stay at my home.

Jonathan Balcombe has also written a fabulous book about fish, entitled *What a Fish Knows.* His writing exposed my ignorance of ocean creatures. Despite studying physics at Oxford, I had forgotten the extent to which water is a much better conductor of sound, taste and smell. Fish have

---

[28] Neil Shubin, *Your Inner Fish.*

[29] Buck and Axel shared the Nobel Prize in 2004 for this discovery as noted by Shubin.

[30] Neil Shubin, *Your Inner Fish.*

more ways of making sound than land animals. The range of their hearing makes ours very rudimentary. Perhaps, as Balcombe writes, fish responsiveness to infrasound as low as 1 Hz allows them to navigate with ambient infrasound, hearing distant ocean currents as 'sea-marks'. Fish can communicate over greater distances than any land animal due to the quality of sound transmission in water.

Carl Safina writes *How baleen whales can produce sounds as loud as a medium-sized ship. Whales such as finbacks swimming hundreds of miles from one another can migrate 'together'.* As he adds: *The animal kingdom is symphonic with mental activity, and of its millions of wavelengths, we're born to apprehend the minutest sliver. Killer whales can be talking 150 miles apart.* [31]

The American Eel can apparently *detect the equivalent of less than one ten millionth of a drop of their home water in an Olympic swimming pool.*[32] Salmon have evolved abilities to detect whether their prey have developed a taste for them or not. This is quite handy. Balcombe reminds us of the extent to which our sense of smell is important in sexual intimacy. He adds that catfish have about 100 times the number of human tastebuds, so that in addition to sound and smell, they can 'taste their way around'.

Despite being underwater, fish can also use the sun to navigate. Like birds they 'record' the sensory information on their initial migration so that all systems can be active to help them return.

Balcombe then offers 'the world of electroreception' as another sense for fish to find their way around. In the UK we are not allowed to have an electric socket in a bathroom due to the strong electrical conductance of water. In imagining that fish had other senses beyond our comprehension, this one had not occurred to me but should have been obvious. *What the Fish Knows* taught me that the electrical sensitivity of a catfish enables him to 'pick up' the heartbeat of a tasty meal hiding six inches under the sand.

The fishes can transmit electricity to bounce off other objects and navigate around, communicating with high speed electric organ discharges of up to a 1000 pulses per second. Amazingly, they often deferentially turn this system off while swimming through a neighbour's territory. No wonder our creation myth needed a whole day just for birds and fishes with such elegant communication and navigational systems.

---

[31] Carl Safina, *Beyond Words – What Animals Think and Feel.*

[32] Jonathan Balcombe.

The cognitive and social abilities of ocean creatures are no less skilled than some of their airborne friends. Culum Brown suggests, as Balcombe writes, that wrasses may be the fishes' answer to the primates among mammals and the corvids among birds in the extent of their tool use. A quarter of all fish species devote caregiving to their young. Whales and elephants share the premier league of a social structure under a matriarch. Our planet's largest creatures are also low on the aggression index. Dolphins remember and recognise other signature whistles their entire life.

A few weeks ago, whilst in the National History Museum, there was an exhibition of cetaceans. These are the mammal family of whales, dolphins and porpoises. Just as my education on our arrival from the ocean 375 million years ago had been recent, so was the learning that the cetaceans came out of the oceans when our ancestors did. But, about 50 million years ago, they decided to go back. For 325 million years they lived on land, sharing some traits with animals such as the hippopotamus. Perhaps, having watched the extinction of the dinosaurs in the dust clouds and firestorms following a giant asteroid hitting Mother Earth, the cetaceans decided that underwater was a safer place after all. Hence, we could consider cetaceans a particularly smart family species.

Because we are both mammals, both have experience of life at sea and life on land, and have evolved many abilities together, there should not be a surprise that humans and cetaceans can communicate so well together. Carl Safina's wonderful book has a whole section on our relationship to whales. He writes that *Killer whales seem capable of random acts of kindness, acts that defy explanation.* In the newspaper, just a few weeks ago, was the story of a marine biologist, Nan Hauser, who during her research in the Cook Islands was protected from a tiger shark by a 50,000-pound humpback whale. He 'tucked' her under his pectoral fin and looked after her for over ten minutes. What we are labelling a 'random act of kindness' could instead be referred to as something between our species and the cetaceans which we do not fully understand. But they might know exactly what they are doing.

The kindest way for us to proceed would be to honour them without trying to find out what or how is going on. This reminds me of porpoises in the Pacific Ocean.

In Kiribati, on Butaritari Island, there was an *utu* – a clan of consanguineal relatives – which could 'call porpoises'. Arthur Grimble spent time with them at Kuma.[33] He wrote in his notes that the *unimane*, or elder, was called Kitina and could call the porpoise at will. Reading his story makes me wonder whether Kitina was a Pacific shaman. Grimble wrote: *This clan belongs to Mone, the land under the sea. When a member of the clan dies he does not go to the land of Bouru or Matang, to which other I-Kiribati go, but to Mone, his spiritual home under the sea.* The funeral practice of this clan is unique in Kiribati. *For this rite there is a deep shaft-like hole in the reef which seems to connect by some subterranean passage with the sea. The dead body is dropped feet first, in a standing position, into this hole, and is said to sink feet first. No weights are used. If the body floats to the surface after a few days, it is left to drift away. This utu is descended from an ancestor who was a famous voyager.* Kitina could bring porpoise to shore at any season of the year. During Grimble's visit, Kitina was asked by the high chief to call the porpoises. He went to lie down in a special place with feet to westward. At some time later, Grimble learned how *he had passed into a natural sleep, during which his spirit left his body and went west to the islet of Bikati before diving straight down to the spiritual replica of Bikati in Mone.* Here were the porpoises. *Once Kitina was sure the porpoises were well on their way to Butaritari lagoon he hurried back to his sleeping body.* Waking up, he rushed towards the lagoon singing *E tau, a roko raomi, nakoni katauraoi te maie*, 'all right, your friends are coming, go and get ready for the dance'. The whole village decked themselves out with mats, garlands, and scented oils, while heading to the beach. Soon the porpoises arrived with Kitina standing knee-deep in the shallow water to welcome them. Once they were close in, and he gave a sign, all the villagers descended into the sea. Each one chose a porpoise and, standing beside them, fondled and embraced them while leading them ashore.

Having the honour to have spent so much time with shamans, it would be dishonourable for me to even question or wonder about such a beautiful experience. Acceptance and joy are the only sensible responses. There is a large part of my mind available for that which *cannot be understood.* Grimble's story reminds me of Mongolian nomads described in *Wolf Totem* by Jiang Rong. In particular, the relationship between the nomads and wolves needed to protect the grasslands. Could this be why their ancient funeral ritual was to return a deceased naked body to the steppe to feed predators? Were the *utu* from Butaritari likewise returning their body to the source of their natural dependence?

[33] *A Pattern of Islands* by Arthur Grimble and Tungaru Traditions (Grimble's notes edited by H.E. Maude).

Arthur Grimble had a little more British reserve. His writings say: *Whatever may be the truth of the caller's descent into Mone, there is absolutely not the shadow of a doubt that if you ask one of this utu to call the porpoises, the porpoises can be made to arrive that very day. Hundreds of witnesses say that, whatever may be the cause of their arrival – they swim into the shallow water in such a condition that a man may go down and clasp them in his arms without difficulty.* The relationship of this *utu* to nature is wonderful.

Perhaps this might make it easier for us to appreciate what Carl Safina wrote about an elephant and a whale. He writes of an experience witnessed by Lyall Watson on the cliffs of South Africa while watching a whale.

The whale had submerged and I was still feeling something. The strange rhythm seemed now to be coming from behind me, from the land, so I turned to look across the gorge… where my heart stopped. Standing there in the shade of the tree was an elephant… staring out to sea… A female with a left tusk broken off near the base… I knew who she was, who she had to be. I recognised her from a colour photograph…. as the 'last remaining Knysna elephant'. This was the Matriarch herself…

She was here because she no longer had anyone to talk to in the forest. She was standing here on the edge of the ocean because it was the next, nearest, and most powerful source of infrasound. The under-rumble of the surf would have been well within her range, a soothing balm for an animal used to being surrounded by low and comforting frequencies, by the life-sounds of a herd, and now this was the next best thing.

My heart went out to her. The whole idea of this grandmother of many being alone for the first time in her life was tragic, conjuring up the vision of countless other old and lonely souls. But just as I was about to be consumed by helpless sorrow, something even more extraordinary took place…

The throbbing was back in the air. I could feel it, and I began to understand why. The blue whale was on the surface again, pointed inshore, resting, her blowhole clearly visible. The Matriarch was here for the whale. The largest animal in the ocean and the largest land animal were no more than a hundred yards apart, and I was convinced they were communicating. In infrasound, in concert, sharing big brains and long lives, understanding the pain of high investment in a few precious offspring, aware of the importance and the pleasure of complex sociality, these rare and lovely great ladies were commiserating over the back fence of this rocky cape shore, woman to woman, matriarch to matriarch, almost the last of their kind.

I turned, blinking away the tears, and left them to it. This was no place for a mere man…

Thank you Carl Safina, and thank you Lyall Watson for sharing such an experience.

Twenty five years ago my life was in crisis. I was trapped on the horns of a very painful personal dilemma and unable to decide which way to jump. Neither option seemed manageable. Nobody seemed to be able to advise me, or maybe my instincts were to reject all advice. However, with my love of elephants combined with 'deaf-sight', I was sure I could ask an elephant for advice. As it happened, my schedule was about to include a workshop on leadership in Johannesburg. This enabled me to plan a visit to the game park at Pilanesberg. I decided to drive over there on my last day before flying back to London, imagining that I would simply find a suitable elephant to ask. Thus assured, it was easier to enjoy delivering my workshop.

On the last day in the early morning, having rented a car, I drove the 220 kilometres alone to the park. Slowly I meandered around looking for elephants. But there weren't any; none at all. Every other animal was about. I was very sad and started to feel rather foolish at the same time. Why had I ever imagined such a plan might work? Time started to run out. Glancing at my watch, there was no option except to give up and make my way back to the airport in Johannesburg, feeling hugely disappointed. It had been a quiet weekday in the park. I hadn't seen another car either.

Making my way towards the exit, about a half mile from the gates of the park, I came around a corner and slammed on the brakes in terror. I only just managed to stop a few feet from a large female elephant in the middle of the road. The shock completely cleared my mind. She just stood there and looked at me. I couldn't move and all my energy was focused on her left eye. At first, neither of us moved a hair's breadth. We were both gripped by the moment. Without words, and just by looking, I asked her my question. She seemed to understand. She started to move very slowly across the road while maintaining our constant eye contact. She stopped with her head against a mid-sized tree. She was still looking at me. There was no break in our interlocked gaze. For a fraction of a second I wondered what she would do next. She hardly moved. What was she doing? Did she need to scratch her trunk? Then, I realised that the tree was moving very slowly. Although I could not see any pressure from her, she must have been gently pushing the tree. Slowly the tree continued to move effortlessly, and move more until the soil next to the road broke. Roots appeared. She moved a little more to continue her very gentle and slow push. Our eyes never left each other's constant gaze. Soon the tree fell completely, but quite softly, with roots right out of the ground. Still watching me, she walked alongside the tree until she could eat the leaves which had been at the very top. Her eyes moistened and softened. At once I understood her answer. She seemed to be saying to me, *If you want to taste the juiciest uppermost leaves, you have to push the roots right out of the ground. No fanfare of destructiveness, just a very gentle push.* I thanked her in my gaze. She understood, her eyes moistened, and she walked on. We must have maintained eye contact for every millisecond of twenty minutes. Smiling, I left the park and drove calmly back to the airport, certain that her answer was sound. She was right and will always have my gratitude.

Dolphins have much else to teach us. They even have spiritual lessons for us. In particular the importance of echoes from others; echoes to find a school of nourishment in a vast ocean. But, once we grasp the extent of our spiritual imprisonment, they can teach us how to swim fast enough to break the ocean surface and taste fresh air.

One of the most interesting lessons in Shubin's *Inner fish* is how we remain the same individual despite the continual turnover of all our parts. All our cells are constantly being replaced. Are we still the same person? Shubin's explanation that *Our House comes together spontaneously because all the necessary information is contained in all the bricks,* is brilliant. *Every individual cell or brick has the plans for the entire building.*

Like birds, ocean creatures find their way home using an array of navigation and communication systems. Together with advanced cognitive skills, they have full use and access to their intuitive and instinctual systems. Relying on their internal and unconscious programming, they can always find their way to an ancestral *home.* They can instinctively enter the place they need to find, a place and state of their birth, a home to prepare for successive generations.

Earlier in this chapter, Neil Shubin said: *Let's not focus on what makes them distinct, we need to focus on what we share.* My thought was to apply this philosophy to different religions. For birds and fishes, one navigation system is insufficient to find their way home. Once several navigational systems hum together in pointing the way they can find the sea-marks and air-marks easily.

My loss of hearing, as an infant, gave me an insatiable hunger for re-connection. Having wandered through so many cultures and religions, my excitement is greatest when finding something that different religions share. Throughout the next chapters, whenever referring to any religion, my purpose is to highlight similarities. Different metaphors and legends may help navigation. There is no intention to suggest that any navigational system is better than another. We can learn so much by focusing on what we have in common with others. If we can concentrate on this first, we might find that our differences don't actually matter.

Having set on the table some light blue jigsaw pieces for the sky and some dark blue ocean pieces, it is time to examine a totally different colour; the dark pieces with red streaks.

Anatomy of Violence

Adrian Raine studied psychology at Oxford and York universities before working as a psychologist in two high-security English prisons. In 1987 he emigrated from the UK to California to continue studying violent offenders. Because the state had the potential death penalty for violent crimes, a number of defence attorneys referred clients to him in the search for mitigating circumstances which could be documented. Thus was created a very unusual, perhaps unique, opportunity to study possible causes of violent behaviour from many different angles. Perhaps he will not mind if referred to by his first name in this chapter. After all, we are both Brits and studied at Oxford in 1975.

Due to the importance of the outcome, Adrian was able to probe in great detail including many types of brain scans. He compared these with 'normal controls' to seek possible deformities in different parts of the brain. Many other physiological attributes were analysed. He sought links with genetics and the possible impact of the offender's childhood nurture. He found other surprising indicators. Twenty-five years of experience and perspectives have been illuminated in his book, *The Anatomy of Violence.*

With such a specific focus on one aspect of human behaviour, combined with the depth and breadth of the research, perhaps it was reasonable to hope for some very clear answers. However, the findings seem to raise as many questions as answers. None-the-less, the questions raised are extremely valuable for a number of signposts and pointers. Adrian's work has generated a germ for some ideas which we take forward in subsequent chapters. Reading his work changed a few of my paradigms and produced some pieces of the jigsaw puzzle needed in my inquiry. Many of the lessons were answers to different questions which had not occurred to me. The information which he has shared is too important to ignore.

My hope had been to learn more about the different effects of the two giants: our genes and our environment. If these two giants could be understood when it came to violence, then perhaps we could apply the conclusions to other aspects of human behaviour.

There has long been the question in Western society of the pendulum swing on the nature versus nurture debate. Adrian's research concludes by telling us that the tug of war in gene versus environment comes out essentially as a tie. There are interesting nuances though. What was a greater surprise for me is the effect of other aspects in our life stories. For example, it turns out that our journey in the womb plays a part, as well as the birth experience herself. What we have eaten, or ingested in the womb, is important. Damage to a part of the brain can make a big difference. Overall, however, the conclusion seems to be that the interplay between the different factors is much more important than the individual factors themselves.

Trying to make sense of this, it helped me to think again about birds. They have several independent navigational systems. If one navigational process is at variance with others they can usually still find a safe way home. However, if two or three of their guidance systems are awry, it would be hard for them to set a safe course. It seems as if Mother Nature has provided us with a number of safety checks and back-ups to compensate for possible difficulties on our life courses. In this sense, the fact that the nature v. nurture tug of war comes out as a tie could be seen as one of our safeguards. We can overcome the challenges unless there are too many of them, or if they inter-react and reinforce in particular ways. For me, the good news is that the more we know ourselves, the better we can understand the interplay within our own guidance systems and therefore make wiser and more spontaneous life choices.

Much of what Adrian found might seem logical to the layman's mind, but it is helpful for some of us to see the evidence.

In support of the biological side of the debate, Adrian tells us the fascinating but awful story of Jeffrey Landrigan who never knew his father. He stabbed a friend to death, received a 20 year prison sentence, escaped from prison, and committed another murder in Phoenix for which he received the death penalty. Whilst on death row in Arizona, another inmate told him of Darrel Hill who was his spitting image. Darrel had likewise killed not once but twice and had also escaped from prison. It turns out that the similarity was more than their looks and crimes. Darrel Hill was Jeffrey Landrigan's father who had left the home soon after his son's birth. And that's not all. Jeffrey Landrigan's grandfather was an institutionalised criminal who was shot to death by the police.

Other cases are put forward to highlight what seems to be a clear genetic influence. In particular, examples are shared of identical twins brought up apart in very different families and environments but who left home as teenagers and turned to similar crimes. However, as Adrian makes clear, biology is not destiny. There is none-the-less a modest increase in probability of becoming an offender if one's ancestry has committed violent crimes.

Adrian dives into the question of whether there is a 'killer gene', or multiple genes that, either on their own or in an intricate conspiracy with the environment, shape killers like Darrel Hill and Jeffrey Landrigan. His findings are compelling and the research proves the case for the genetic giant in our psyche. So far, so good, as long as we do not forget that biology is not destiny and there are other giants affecting our psyche.

My difficulty with focusing too much on genetics is that the argument of the evolutionary biologist's ship is holed below the waterline. Whilst sharing Adrian's admiration for Richard Dawkins' landmark book *The Selfish Gene,* we know that genetics cannot explain the recent increase in suicide, self-harm and other forms of self-destruction – particularly among the younger generation. We can accept the force of genetics in its entirety as long as we accept other forces which are not genetic. We need a greater understanding, or a model to repair the hole under the waterline, before travelling too independently with genetics.

The increase in propensity to violence can be similar if a child has suffered a violent and traumatic upbringing. On its own however, the increase in probability is also modest. But when a child has both a genetic history of violence and suffered an abusive childhood, then the probability of becoming a violent offender goes up exponentially. This was my first 'aha' moment from Adrian's work. On their own, either the genetic giant or the environmental giant can be more easily managed by most of us, but when they conspire to work together it is much harder for us to tread a safe path. Moving onwards, we find that there are other giants and a few dwarves.

The example which was most compelling for me, and changed some of my earlier paradigms, was a study published by Adrian and others in 1994.[34] This involved 4,269 male births at the Rigshospitalet in Denmark in 1959. It was recorded whether these boys had suffered birth complications or subsequent maternal rejection within their first year. Maternal rejection was defined as to whether the mother had not wanted the pregnancy, had tried to abort, or the boy had been placed in a public institution for any reason exceeding four months in early infancy. Eighteen years later the court records were studied to see which of these males had been arrested for violent crimes. The conclusions were dramatic, and supported by other studies in North America.

The percentage that became violent before the age of eighteen was similar if they had neither maternal rejection nor birth complications, or had just one of these two indicators. However, among the boys who had suffered both a complicated birth and maternal rejection the percentage becoming violent was three times higher. Moreover, even though the percentage of the boys suffering the 'double whammy' was only 4.5% of the population, this small group accounted for 18% of all violent crimes perpetrated by the sample of 4,259 births. Interestingly, Adrian's study found that the increase in the effect only applied to violent behaviour and not to criminal behaviour in general.

Before reading Adrian's work, the idea that the birth experience was so important would not have occurred to me. This discovery has given indications which may also open doors in the quest for a greater understanding of our self-destruction.

Perhaps, thinking about this dispassionately, it should not surprise us that the 'double whammy' of a traumatic birth and an unwelcome reception could leave a scar suggesting to the new-born arrival that this world was not such a good place. As Adrian says, he did not find a direct path between birth complications and problem behaviour. Instead, '*social processes are critical, seemingly acting as a trigger for the dormant birth complication risk factor*'. This last comment applies to many of his conclusions. Whether it is our genetics, birth, early acceptance and acknowledgement, early nurture, or other factors, it is the interactions between them as well as the 'social processes' which need to be considered.

---

[34] Raine, A., Brennan, P. & Mednick, S.A. (1994) Archives of General Psychiatry 51, 984-88.

It was interesting for me to learn that, in our upbringing, the parental influence fades relatively quickly. By the age of nine years, children are much more directly influenced by their peers than their parents. This reminds me however of that old adage that one of our greatest responsibilities as parents is to help our children choose the right friends. Perhaps some of us are secretly doing more than the research statistics would give us credit for.

Adrian goes into great detail to explain different parts of our brain, sharing with us the roles of different parts. Again, the unique spread of his research enabled him to make more precise discoveries and connections.

The front part, just behind the forehead and above the eyes, is known as the prefrontal cortex. Some call it the brain's 'Chief Executive', which plans and maintains vigilance on our other impulses. Having the opportunity to scan many brains of criminals, Adrian found that 'one off murderers' show a striking lack of activation in their prefrontal cortex. The reduced prefrontal functioning diminishes control over more primitive parts of the brain, such as the limbic system, which generate raw emotions like anger and rage. A more sophisticated pre-frontal cortex keeps a lid on these limbic emotions.

Adrian's research shows that damage to the prefrontal cortex can result in more risk taking, irresponsibility and rule breaking, greater impulsivity, loss of self-control, less ability to formulate non-aggressive solutions to difficult social encounters, less social skills and poorer problem solving skills. As he suggests, these impairments can result in school failure, unemployment, and economic deprivation, all factors that could predispose someone to a criminal and violent way of life.

On the other hand, serial killers can be very active in this part of the brain. Good prefrontal functioning enables a serial killer to improve his technique and protect against capture. Adrian finds that cold bloodied killers share some traits with British Army bomb disposal experts. They both seem to manage, or put to one side, the fear of danger. They both share a low resting heart rate. Apparently there may be a fine line between psychopaths and national heroes. The role of 'snipers' in war came to my mind.

Adrian has a great deal of experience from a study of children in Mauritius. A link was found between low heart rates in children aged three and future anti-social behaviour. It is impressively backed up by 40 publications with 5,868 children. Antisocial kids really do have lower resting heart rates, as he says. Further, the sex difference in heart rate starts just before the age at which differences in anti-social behaviour begins to emerge. Apparently this even applies to rabbits: the more aggressive ones have lower resting heart rates. The idea seems to be that low resting heart rates may predispose a child to stimulation-seeking behaviour. But, as Adrian also points out, in the Mauritius study the outcome can be quite different. One such boy became a vicious psychopathic thug who did not know fear but craved fear in others. By contrast a girl with similar characteristics went on to become Miss Mauritius.

Adrian admits, despite having found many signposts warning us of a propensity towards violence, neither biology nor early childhood nurture are destiny. Whereas he concludes that we need to help those who might be pre-disposed to potential violence, my conclusion would be wider in suggesting that we need to help everyone in society to find their place. We all need to know more about our aptitudes and talents to find our place for the benefit of society. Otherwise we could be stigmatising Miss Mauritius with a fear of her potential criminality. Adrian's suggested solutions provoke us to look at the state of our society with respect to violence. They helped me on my quest for the source of self-destruction.

Another critical area of our early nurture turns out to be the domain of 'fear conditioning' which is a critical role for the amygdala within the brain. By this is meant the way 'our young children are scolded for stealing a cookie'. If well managed, the parental reaction elicits upset and hurt. This triggers a conditional response which prevents theft in future. Adrian explains that an early impairment in autonomic fear conditioning is linked with a predisposition to criminality in adulthood. Poor fear conditioning as early as three years' old can predispose someone to crime twenty years later. He reminded me of an experience whilst a toddler. As a family we had been to stay with my great-uncle Arthur in Lincoln, where he was the sub-dean at the cathedral. Having just left to drive back to Cambridge, my confession that I had some of my cousin's toys elicited a look of horror in both of my parents. The car stopped, we returned, I was made to apologise for having taken them. Looking back, my parents had managed it very well. I was not hit or punished, but their look imprinted me with an indelible image of fear conditioning.

Even now the image of my sitting on the back seat of the car, as we turned around, is quite vivid.

Another part of the brain which patrols the dangerous waters of emotion, making links between a specific place and punishment, is the hippocampus, which also helps fear conditioning. Apparently embarrassment, shame and guilt are provinces of the prefrontal cortex. It was interesting for me to learn how all of these fit together and how different parts of the brain work in unity to watch over and prevent our potential misdemeanours. It was enlightening for me to learn all about these diverse roles in the parts of our brain construction.

Before leaving the analysis of the brain, another of Adrian's findings which fascinated me was his description of the increased white matter in the brains of adult psychopathic liars. This predisposes them to deception and cunning. But he asks the question the other way around. Could the act of lying increase the white matter in the prefrontal cortex, thus making future lies easier and more probable? It has been shown that the white matter increases in liars, just as the hippocampus expands in birds and London taxi drivers needing to remember where places are. He reminds us of Pinocchio whose nose grew with each lie. In this example, behaviour affects the brain and then predisposes the brain to more of that aspect of behaviour.

Adrian's research into parts of the brain is thorough and well explained.

Considering all of his data and conclusions led me to the following thoughts: In the nature versus nurture debate, or the tussle between these two giants, it seems we could consider the possibility of a third giant. We have all experienced moments when something triggered us to behave completely 'out of character'. Something happened which was, without any doubt, completely beyond our control or predictions and which 'threw off' our guidance system. This 'third giant' could be considered a sudden event, something extraordinary, for which we have neither sufficient evolutionary experience nor the nurture guidance. As such, the situation is neither well managed by our genetics nor our cognitive mind. A story involving the misguidance of birds might make it easier to illustrate this.

Jennifer Ackerman, in *The Genius of Birds*, describes just such a case. A pigeon racer, Tom Roden, saw a bird with a pale tail flutter to his pigeon loft near Manchester in April 2002. Having checked the registration ring he realised it was his own racing bird which had vanished five years earlier during a race across the English Channel. This bird, Whitetail, was no ordinary bird. He was a champion, winner of thirteen races and veteran of fifteen Channel crossings. Whitetail became lost, in June 1997, during the Royal Pigeon Association's centenary cross-Channel competition. The prestige of the race had attracted more than sixty thousand entrants. The homing pigeons were released at Nantes, in North Western France in the early morning. By the early afternoon, fanciers in England, such as Tom, waited at their lofts for the fastest birds to arrive. The champion bird, along with tens of thousands of other experienced racers never made it home. Only a few slower birds arrived.

Jennifer says this became known as The Great Pigeon Race Disaster because of its rarity. Years later Jon Hagstrum put forward theories on the use of infrasound by birds in navigation.[35] Hagstrum, intrigued by the loss of sixty thousand pigeons many years previously, had looked for unusual sound events coinciding with the race. It turns out, just as the racing pigeons were heading out across the English Channel, their flight route crossed underneath the path of a Concorde's supersonic boom. Hagstrum suggested a *sonic boom carpet* could have completely disoriented the pigeons' infrasound navigation.

On that fateful day, it was only some slower pigeons that found their way home. Is it possible that, being significantly behind the champion flyers, they arrived at the English Channel after the sonic boom had passed and did not suffer the disorientation?

We cannot be sure. But something disoriented the birds, or at least all the faster ones. Perhaps Jennifer Ackerman has inadvertently suggested to our inquiry that, sometimes, an effect can trump both sides of the nature versus nurture debate. Our prefrontal cortex and our genetic navigational system can both be thrown awry in terms of guidance. Neither giant can cope adequately. Mere chance or another outside influence takes over, it seems.

Interestingly, just like Saroo Brierley, Whitetail eventually figured out the way home, piecing together other navigational intuition.

---

[35] Jon Hagstrum, a geophysicist at the U.S. Geological Survey as quoted by Jennifer Ackerman in *The Genius of Birds.*

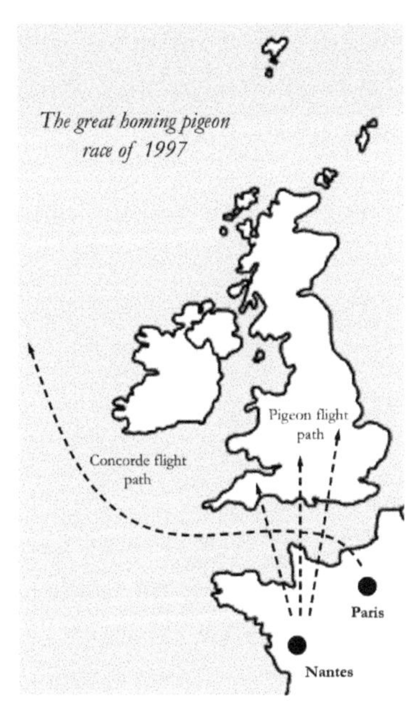

When we read of natural or terrorist disasters, our culture's reporters seem fascinated by those who 'missed' the event 'due to luck'. Or by other victims who were there but should not have been. Somehow we are particularly gripped by these aspects of the trauma. Could we feel as if we have more control over how we might cope within some disasters than on our chance of being there or not? Thus the unlikely chances of our either being there, or not, make a deep impression on us – that there is a fear, or an excitement, of how we or our loved ones either missed or were caught up in a disaster. This giant must affect us.

Adrian begins the introduction to his book with a traumatic event while on vacation in Bodrum, Turkey. He tells us of an attack in the night, seeing an intruder at his hotel bedside: *It was just after three a.m. when I became aware of a stranger standing above me.... In the milliseconds that it took my visual cortex to interpret the shadowy figure and signal this to the amygdala, which jump-starts the fight-flight response, I leaped out of my bed. In little more than a second, I had instinctively grabbed the intruder. I was on automatic pilot.*

Adrian informs us that information from the senses reaches the amygdala twice as fast as it gets to the frontal lobe. Before his frontal cortex could rein back the amygdala's aggressive response he had embarked on his instinct to fight.

His story reminded me of a night in my two-storey house soon after arrival in the Gilbert Islands. My bedroom was the first door on the left at the top of the stairs with louvre windows overlooking the sea. With the humidity always so high, it was most comfortable for me to sleep naked under a mosquito net. The ceiling fan whirled slowly, just enough to keep the air moving gently but not fast enough to make a sleep disturbing sound. Suddenly, in my slumber, I became aware in the moonlight of a man armed with a machete standing in my bedroom doorway. Screaming at him and instantly leaping out of bed, he backed off. It gave me an instant to throw on a pair of shorts and chase him down the stairs. He jumped into a cupboard which I immediately locked, but knew was only a simple bolt on the outside which would not keep him there very long. I ran into the village to get help from others. Coming back with reinforcements, we found he had escaped. But, with my description of his red shorts it did not take long to find him in our small village. Soon he was under arrest in the Bairiki police station.

Adrian asks whether, in his case, it would have been better to have feigned sleep. But the reality is that something else kicks in and makes us react differently and immediately. He subsequently describes that the experience had *broken through his outer façade of liberal humanitarian values and put him in touch with a deep, primitive sense of retributive justice.*

The outcome of my story was completely different. A couple of days later, the police told me that my intruder had been drunk on toddy, a fermented coconut juice. He was now feeling desperately ashamed for having approached me with a knife, particularly since he had threatened an Imatang; a man from the land of the ancestors. A trial was scheduled for just a week later. But, on that morning, the police advised me it had been cancelled. "Why?" The police said he had hanged himself in his cell the night before. It left me cold. His shame moved into me. The thoughts which ran through my mind were that it was not my place to be in his country. As a white foreigner, an Imatang, it was perhaps his misfortune to have stumbled on me rather than on one of his fellow islanders with whom there would have not been the shame. Then his suicide would have been avoided. It made me wonder about my role as a British administrator in a Colony.

For some time, a part of the responsibility for his suicide lingered over me. Looking back now, it is probable that the experience affected me in respect of feelings towards my subsequent responsibilities on the island. Being so far from home, and without traditional support, this may have influenced my leaning more on Reuben for advice. In the difficult weeks afterwards, Reuben was particularly supportive in explaining that the event had been beyond my control. Thus, it is likely that my conduct in deferring to the elders on the islands was enhanced as a result of my traumatic experience. This made me more humble, and energised, to help them achieve more of their aspirations. Thus Adrian's work has helped me discern the relationship between an event and the way, in my mind, it was processed afterwards. Similar events affect each of us differently because of who we are to begin with.

It begs the question as to when our nurture begins and ends. Surely, we undergo nurture all our lives? Unusual experiences affect us unusually. Nurture does not only belong to childhood. Perhaps we are a work in progress and a fresh movement in our nurture crops up from time to time. But, of course, the earliest nurture might have the deepest effects unless there is something extraordinarily traumatic in the later events.

In the case of Adrian's night attack, he writes that c*ompletely unknown to me in the midst of that mismatched contest was that the assailant had been holding a knife. Quite a long one, with a red handle and a six-inch blade, it turned out. But I was lucky. As I warded off his blows with my arms, the blade of the cheap knife had snapped off, leaving only a few millimetres of metal on the handle. So when he attempted to cut my throat, the damage was far less than it might have been.*

In my case, I had no conscious awareness in the pale moonlight that my intruder was drunk and probably unable to successfully wield the machete had he swung it at me.

Had the knife not broken in Adrian's case, or had my intruder been more violent and sober, the outcome could have been quite different. Our genetic programming in terms of how we both reacted might have led us instead into serious injury or death. We were saved by details which we hadn't seen. In Adrian's case he was also lucky because his hotel was next to an Army barracks and the police came quickly. But this is with the benefit of hindsight. Our cognitive minds did not have complete information to make choices which could have overcome the instinctive and reactive leap from our slumbers into self-defence or attack.

Replaying the scene, which can easily be conjured as a fresh memory, it is possible that my deepest unconscious instantly knew I had the upper hand when the intruder backed off from my scream. Otherwise there would not have been time or inclination to throw on a pair of shorts. Or would Richard Dawkins suggest that my selfish genes were ensuring that their reproductive capacity was protected from a machete?

In many of our life's challenges we are encountering technologies for which our evolution has not had time to prepare us. Steel knives of the kind used in the attack on Adrian, or the machete I saw, are recent inventions in human evolutionary terms. The instinctual responses have not been as well-honed as the sharpness of the steel blades. The fight or flight instinct in animals does not have to take complicated weaponry into account.

What happened that night is unlikely ever to be repeated. These were 'one off' life events for both of us. Since the stories do not discuss our aggressors' behaviour but relate to Adrian's and my reactions, could we consider here the effect of a third giant? The 'scrambling sonic boom carpet' which disorients our navigational system, so that neither our genetics nor our nurture nor our cognitive mind could be seen to have sensibly prevailed? Perhaps we could just summarise by admitting we are both lucky to be alive. Lucky, because a cheap knife and a less than sober assailant, together with the proximity of reinforcements, had tilted the battles in our favour. Thus, to my mind, the third giant trumped the other two giants in terms of influencing the outcome – something which occurred beyond our knowledge, beyond our prophecies, beyond our comprehension in that moment which resulted in something which cannot be explained. It reminds me of Michael Meade's comment: *Animals don't trouble themselves with future grief, because that's not the grief that's coming.* They react to what comes.

In indigenous culture much is made of this 'third giant'. Somehow the third is completely beyond any attempt at understanding. One of my observations in traveling around the world is that calmer societies seem to accept more easily what cannot be understood. Indigenous cultures are more humble in accepting fate. Western culture struggles much more with the idea that there could be something beyond our control.

With gratitude for Adrian's well explained research and the germs of many ideas derived from his work, in the next chapter we explore the birth experience herself.

Midwife

Adrian's research identified several factors in our propensity for violence. The birth experience will be considered here.

In the 1990s, with other leaders of the UK men's movement, we organised a number of workshops led by overseas teachers. One of these, with about eighty men and women, was a 'rebirthing ritual' with Sobonfu and Malidoma Somé, both shamans from the Dagara tribe of West Africa. The Dagara arise from where Ghana, Ivory Coast and Burkina Faso meet. During our workshop, Sobonfu acted as the 'midwife'. She prepared a birthing canal in nature with the assistance of four ladies who lay on their backs with knees bent. Under these eight legs we each and all had to squeeze on our backs along the muddy floor against the resistance or contractions of the eight legged delivery canal. It was much more difficult than expected because there was nothing to grab on to, and the tunnel was dark under the weight of many plants.

Once we had all emerged, been received by midwife Sobonfu, and were cleaned up, we gathered again in a large community setting. We had no idea what was going to happen next. But Sobonfu stood up and started looking at a few people, maybe 13 or 15 of us and she said gently, "You, you, you, you… you all did that for the first time." At first nobody knew what she meant. They asked: What do you mean? We did it for the first time? She replied: "Well, you have never been down a birth canal. You must have been born by caesarean section." She was right with every single one.

It was quite extraordinary. She went on to describe how some people's mothers hadn't wanted them and she was right. Others were luckier. Sobonfu and Malidoma were on hand to process the intensity of feelings that flowed. We learned how our individual birth experiences, and the way we were received into the world, are somehow clearly imprinted in our body or psyche – sufficiently clearly that Sobonfu could still sense them more than twenty to fifty years after the event.

Reading Adrian's work reminded me of this workshop with the Somés. In particular, how Sobonfu had been able to see aspects of both our journey in the birth canal and the quality of our initial reception.

Wishing to learn more about the birth experience led me to have the following discussion with Stella, a friend who is also a Chelsea supporter! However, it was much more interesting to learn about her midwifery experience than speak about football. Stella has assisted in the delivery of five or six thousand babies so knows a thing or two. My preference for her first-hand experience led to recording the conversation. We sat on the grass in a park, just next to Euston station, as Stella's brain and memory was picked to help me understand more about birth experiences. We began:

Mark: "You have often said that when a child arrives, they have a character from the very first instant of arrival. Whatever may happen afterwards, they come with a character. I've had this feeling that in our culture, we ignore their individuality. We just stamp them with a new label or a name from a selection of labels, rather than acknowledging 'who' has arrived. Can you tell me about some of the different characters you deliver?"

Stella: "From the very first moment, I feel that they immediately react to the kind of birth that they've had. If they had a natural birth and the mother had no drugs, they're usually born much calmer. Their characters are calmer. They are alert. They look around and are inquisitive. Some of them look right through me; I always get that feeling. I always know when a baby is looking right through me."

Mark: "What do you mean, looking through you?"

Stella: "They know…"

Mark: "They know what?"

Stella: "They come with a history, their spirit, I don't know what to call it, Mark. They see more of me than other babies do."

Mark: "You mean they understand you?"

Stella: "Yes. It's a very deep emotional feeling that I get when a baby looks right through me."

Mark: "So, you think they reach you somehow."

Stella: "Yes, they really see me and I feel warm and humble. They're not all like that. It's usually babies that are born naturally and lovingly, without any distress, without the mother having drips and drugs and monitors, you know. Nice environments, like a home birth or a water birth. These babies are filled with endorphins because their mothers have got very high endorphins. I'm sure that has an effect on them and that calms them.

The babies that move me the most are the ones that are born naturally, where the mother has had a completely natural uninterrupted physiological labour and birth. It hasn't been medically managed. These babies are very calm, they're very loving, and they see me. They are swift to feed as well.

The first thing is to help the mother have skin to skin contact with the baby, and when a woman has a natural birth, we don't cut the umbilical cord; we leave it attached until the placenta is separated, so that might be ten to thirty minutes. The baby gets all their stem cells back. As this happens the baby gets more alert and vibrant. They start to interact more.

The babies that are born naturally, I call them little wise old men, the boys anyway. They've been here before. They know where they're at. They're here, and they're going to have a good look around. They look at their parents, and they're bright as a button really. It's humbling to see babies like that, because that's how we should be born, naturally like that and uninterrupted, leaving nature alone, leaving her to do what she does so well because we just interfere way too much and that's when things often go wrong."

Mark: "What are the different character traits you notice, assuming they've all had a similar natural birth."

Stella: "It's the boys that are the most different. The boys can become angry; they might have a few minutes when they're just looking around, seeing and acclimatising to the outside world. But then, when they start crying, they get angry and they don't stop. Male infants are angrier than female infants. But the boys, once they start, sometimes it's difficult to appease them; they get cross. It is like they're saying: put me back... where am I? It's as though they're objecting and they don't like their new environment. They want to go back."

Mark: "More than the girls?"

Stella: "Much more."

Mark: "That's interesting. Do you have any idea where that comes from?"

Stella: "Not unless its nature, because of the differences between the sexes, and men are angrier, as a rule, than women. The boys can exhibit anger regardless of the way they're born. I don't think I've ever seen a baby girl angry. I feel that the boys are frustrated; because wherever they were, they were quite happy in the womb and now they're born, they're saying, 'I don't like it, put me back'."

Mark: "So what other differences do you find in children, infants, in terms of their nature?"

Stella: "Well, you've got the extremes. The placid babies – they have got a soft tone. Babies generally have a flex tone. You touch them and they flex, even if they're asleep. There is a normal tone for a new-born infant to have. But some babies are very relaxed and chilled, so they've got a soft tone, and they don't necessarily flex when you touch them, they'll stay flaccid. And then you've got the other extreme with the angry babies again, the fractious babies.

Babies that are born fractious just won't stop …they can't be consoled …are irritable. They are shaking rather than having normal movements, flexion and extension. It's not because there's necessarily anything wrong with them physiologically or that they've been deprived of oxygen or anything. It's like a temper tantrum, almost."

Mark: "Is there anything you can see instantly that's genetic as opposed to as a result of the birth experience?"

Stella: "Well, I think it's fascinating that Mother Nature always makes the first-born look like the father."

Mark: "Is that right?"

Stella: "Yes. It's quite well documented. As a midwife I see it all the time; first-borns look like their dad. It's like nature knows what she's doing and she's really clever, and she's designed us like that, so the man will stay with the woman and help nurture and raise the infant. Whereas second-borns don't as much; they often don't look anything like their dad. They're all born with different characters. They've got a personality, there's no doubt about it, and like I say, I've spoken about the extremes – the calm, relaxed ones as opposed to the fractious, irritable ones. Obviously it's all non-verbal, because I'm just looking at behaviour and posture and attitude."

Mark: "And eye contact."

Stella: "And definitely eye contact, yes, and attitude. Some babies will make eye contact, but lots of babies are born with nystagmus when the eyes wobble."

Mark: "Wobble?"

Stella: "I can't simulate it because I'm wearing contact lenses, I'll probably lose one, but their eyes wobble."

Mark: "What does that mean?"

Stella: "It can happen in disease processes later in life. In babies it might only last an hour or so while they're acclimatising to life outside the womb. Because you can't get eye contact with them, they look a little bit lost.

What I also do Mark, that you're probably not aware of, is all new-born babies have to have a new-born and infant physical examination, within the first 72 hours. That's when we check their eyes for cataracts, we listen to their heart for murmurs, we check their hips for development. And I do those examinations, so I might be seeing a baby that's a day old or two days old and I'll spend half an hour examining this child top to toe before they go home. That's a good time after the birth event so then all their chemicals and all their hormones and their adrenalin and the cortisone and everything has settled, so then you've just got the child away from the birth event, and..."

Mark: "That's a much better time for giving an idea of differences?"

Stella: "Yes, and that's when they're profoundly different. Obviously, I've got a way of handling the babies because I have to test their reflexes and do things like that and look in their eyes and listen to their hearts and things, so I've got a way of handling them to keep them calm. I know, I'm always on autopilot at work."

Mark: "It's Mother Nature doing her work rather than the autopilot, isn't it?"

Stella: "Yes, I mean instinctual."

Mark: "Allowing your instincts to guide you. Which, as a midwife, must be such a precious career?"

Stella: "It is."

Mark: "Maybe there's no other more joyous experience when it goes well, and yet there must be some real heartbreak when it goes wrong."

Stella: "Oh, yes, there's some serious heartbreak. But my instinct tells me that the babies that don't make it aren't meant to. I've seen babies that have made it against all odds only to succumb to cot death four weeks later. Sometimes when babies have been resuscitated after a traumatic birth experience and then have passed away soon after, it's as though they weren't meant to make it in the first place. But we've just helped them to live a bit longer.

There are big differences when it comes to feeding. Sometimes I see male infants that are dry. They haven't quite got the knack of it or the patience. They get fractious, irritable, and become poor feeders. Usually girls feed better. Females seem to have more survival instincts than males."

Mark: "Maybe that's a form of selection. Just like the Spartans left their male babies out on the mountainside to see how they managed. They did not invest resources in the weaker males."

Stella: "Babies can crawl to the breast. It's a reflex that they're born with. If the mother is lying on her back and her baby is put on her abdomen, the infant will crawl to the breast. It might take half an hour, but the infant will go and find the breast, and the mother can just lie on her back. The baby is born with this reflex. All new-born, full-term infants are also born with extra fat. It's called brown fat under their scapula and around their flanks. It sustains them for the first 24 hours so the mother can recover from the birth.

There's something I hadn't thought about. Well I knew it, but I have never discussed it with anybody. The females are stronger, feed better, are more robust, less likely to get dehydrated. It's the males that get sick and are more likely to get dehydrated from poor feeding. As far as their character goes, the boys are more likely to be frustrated and irritable and the girls are more likely to be relaxed. I know I shouldn't stereotype them, but I can because it's so obvious."

Mark: "It's interesting because we haven't gone down the direction I thought of. We've gone down a different one which has been more interesting. Maybe it was too much to expect us to be able to determine their character because we've got so little go on apart from reflex."

Stella: "I can give examples though. But the examples seem to relate to the birth experience itself rather than what they had in utero."

Mark: "That is very interesting. It reminds me how some indigenous cultures come to listen to a baby in the womb to find out why they are coming. Perhaps by asking this question of a midwife we are biased towards characteristics that come from the birth experience itself. It would be very interesting to have examples where you think a character relates to the birth experience. Maybe this will confirm one factor that Adrian was suggesting."

Stella: "I remember a case of a boy born by forceps delivery. It was a very traumatic birth for both the mother and the baby, both physically and emotionally. The mother was late and was induced. She was given lots of drugs. The birth was very violent and very swift, a quick labour. During the birth the boy didn't make the descent and rotation that he was meant to, so they had to help with forceps, not regular forceps, but forceps that are now banned."

Mark: "Why are they banned?"

Stella: "They are called Kielland's. They have long handles and blades. They are to get babies that are very high up out and they're banned now because of the risk of injury to the child or mother. It is quite a violent way to be born. The baby boy was born very fractious and irritable. He stayed that way for about six months. He used to vomit violently. There was nothing wrong with him. It was because he got himself so worked up. We couldn't placate him despite our best efforts. It was because he was fractious that he would end up vomiting violently. I think, once he started moving, he became calmer when he was about eight months old. But before he got some independence he was quite fractious."

Mark: "What's difficult is we don't know how much of that is the birth experience as opposed to the nature of the child, do we?"

Stella: "We don't. It's not measurable. But women talk, as you know, we're good at talking. Women talk about their birth experiences with each other. Let me give you another example, but it is a long time ago. This is a baby girl and she was a footling breech. She was born feet first and the first foot was hanging out for four hours. Four hours. Nothing else happened, so the doctors gave the mother an epidural and just waited for the rest of the baby girl. She turned out to be a very fractious child. Very angry and she was always stamping her foot as a toddler. Stamp, stamp, and throwing things. Actually she's the same as an adult. She's got no patience, stamps her feet, she gets really worked up. It's like her whole personality might have something to do with the way she was born, because she had to wait with her foot hanging out for four hours before the rest of her followed. You can imagine how cold she was… her foot must have been really cold."

Mark: "This is very interesting. My mother told me that every time our doctor or GP visited towards the end of her pregnancy he said the baby was breech. He tried to turn me around in her womb but I resisted. Several times he tried but I always turned back. At my home birth the doctor was not there early enough. I was too quick for him and came out head first. He made some excuse later that he must have felt a bony arse, but luckily he hadn't succeeded in turning me. Now it makes me wonder if Sobonfu had also noticed that. Perhaps it led me to trust my own instinct and intuition rather than other experts. My birth experience might have given me robustness. Or, was the determination already there, which is why the doctor was resisted… we will never know. In any case instinct won and the doctor's judgment was definitely second best. Could this have made me more stubborn though? There is so much we don't know. Apart from that aspect, my parents told me later that my birth had been easy."

Stella: "But there is something else. If a mother has a traumatic delivery, it's obviously much harder for her to bond, because some mothers can be angry with their babies. It's not uncommon for some women to get angry with their baby if they've felt violated or hurt by what happened to them. Some mothers have an immediate bond and immediate love. Others are different. It might be cultural... can I talk about cultures?"

Mark: "Sure."

Stella: "In all the hospitals where I work it's diverse, but I notice specific differences by the part of the world the mother comes from. Some mothers don't want to hold their baby skin to skin, they don't want that attachment. It's like they are saying, 'The baby is out, I've done my job, I'm the good woman that the culture has demanded of me, now you look after the child.' So the sisters, aunts and grandmother take over with feeding the baby formula although the mothers will breastfeed eventually."

Mark: "Really?"

Stella: "Yes, and so somebody else is holding the baby – they just want to recover from the birth event. The mother is playing the victim card and just lies there to recover, but they don't seem to show much interest in their baby initially. I think that, in their culture, they believe that the first milk is dirty so they should wait three days."

Mark: "Which cultures show the greatest interest in holding babies skin to skin? I would have imagined, maybe it's a bias, the African mothers would."

Stella: "Oh, they're brilliant. African mothers have their babies on their breast in a flash. The English mothers and the American mothers need more support with breastfeeding before they try it. Are you with me? That's how difficult it is for them – you know, they get themselves so worked up that they can't breastfeed. The African mothers do it instinctively, naturally... they're boom. They don't even give it two thoughts, it just happens."

Mark: "Can you say something about babies born by caesarean?"

Stella: "Babies born by caesarean haven't gone through the physiological changes that they go through when they squeeze through the birth canal, and statistically more of those babies born by caesarean sections are admitted to the neonatal intensive care unit. They have problems compared to the babies born vaginally. Now that's because we practice breathing quite young. I'm not quite sure when we start practise breathing, probably about 30 weeks. So, when a woman's reached the 30th week of pregnancy, her baby starts to breathe inside."

Mark: "Breathe what?"

Stella: "Amniotic fluid, the fluid they're floating in – they will start to use the chest muscles, start to exercise and inhale the amniotic fluid into the lungs and exhale it, okay? So, therefore, when a baby is born and squeezed through the pelvis, all that extra fluid in the lungs is squeezed out, back out. Then, when they are born they can take a first gasp of air and be fine.

A baby born by caesarean hasn't had the opportunity to get all that fluid squeezed out, so they're born with something nicknamed wet lung. Not all of them, but a lot of them. They can develop transient tachypnoea and have trouble breathing. They start grunting, they quite literally squeak, and it's not nice. Usually it's transient, but the baby is immediately admitted to the neonatal intensive care unit for observation until they've got rid of this excessive fluid in their lungs. These babies suffer and it's quite distressing to see them in this condition. They use all their energy reserves, if they've got any left, to try and get fluid out of their lungs. It's very distressing for the parents, and that can affect bonding as well.

Paediatricians would tell you, it's not ideal to be born by caesarean section. We were designed to be born vaginally, through the pelvis."

The conversation with Stella was so fascinating that it went on for a long time and she almost missed her train home. Stella taught me quite distinct cultural differences between mothers from different parts of the world. She convinced me that Adrian was right when he adds the mix of the birth experience to our genetic mix and early nurture to determine one of our propensities for violence. The effect of the birthing experience can be traumatic for both mother and child. Thus the birth experience has an effect on the early bond and subsequent nurture. Finally, Stella had her own stories of a mother who had suffered violence during pregnancy which she was certain affected the unborn baby's character. Again, this is one of Adrian's findings.

One of Stella's conclusions was to urge caution in what we seek to change. Mother Nature is too powerful for us and we shouldn't mess with her too much. What's happened is that the more we mess with her, the more that can go wrong. This is a tough one, as on the other hand we can clearly help so much through our medical discoveries. Stella reminded me how a baby born vaginally is colonised by their mother's flora which makes the baby stronger – that recently we've realised that babies born by caesarean section might have a propensity to all sorts of weaknesses and allergies because they're not colonised by their mother's flora. It is only in the last few years that the benefit of giving the baby a wipe of her mother's vaginal flora has been realised and applied. Somehow we take so long to figure out what Mother Nature always knew.

Stella's descriptions of a naturally born baby 'looking through her' stayed with me. The feelings fascinated and intrigued me. There was clearly much more to it than our conversation was able to explore. Neither of us could understand this initial eye contact, the 'humbleness' she felt as well as the instant 'acknowledgement' which my mind chewed on for quite a while.

Some help came from a different source, so we must make a short detour before returning.

In Neil Shubin's book, *Your Inner Fish;* he says: *Let's not focus on what makes them distinct… we need to focus on what different creatures share.* He is reminding us how we evolved from the oceans, emerging to live on land about 375 million years ago. Within each of us is an ancient core known as the reptilian brain. Virtually all of our nerves are present in sharks.[36] The parallels go deeper still: equivalent nerves in sharks and humans supply similar structures, and they even exit the brain in the same order.

Dolphins and whales, like all mammals, have hair, breasts, and a three-boned middle ear. Shubin tells us how, in 1837, the German anatomist Karl Reichert discovered that two of the ear bones in mammals corresponded to pieces of the jaw in reptiles. The same gill arch that enables a reptile to chew enables a mammal to hear more finely. The way my mind chewed on Stella's observations was perhaps not such a foreign use of words after all.

Then Carl Safina writes of a whale, named Luna by his observers, who became separated from his family.[37] Luna showed up alone, barely more than a toddler of two years old, in British Columbia's Nootka Sound. He was strangely lost and also apparently at a loss for company. His gaze *had need in it.* People saw *an awareness, a presence, a longing.* When a workboat cook encountered Luna and looked into his eyes, she saw something so astonishing and deep that, she said, *I could not breathe.* Another observer said that Luna could *look through your otherness at you.*

Could this be what Stella felt? A very deep part of our mind which we share with whales and can be communicated though eye contact? Who transmits as we emerge from our nine-month float in mother's womb? From swimming in amniotic fluid having exactly the same salinity as the world's oceans to remind us of our shared ancestry? It seems that, in the flash of an instant, we can connect our humbleness and our acknowledgement with another species or with one of our own. And this ability is with us right there at birth, reaching out for our first soulful connection.

---

36 Neil Shubin, *Your Inner Fish.*

37 Carl Safina, *Beyond Words – What Animals Think and Feel.*

Malidoma and Sobonfu taught how babies are welcomed to their Dagara village. A 'hearing ritual' takes place six months into pregnancy when a pregnant woman sits in the middle of a circle of elders who listen to what the baby is bringing. This enables a name to be chosen for each child which encapsulates information provided before birth. The village prepares for a baby's arrival so that they can be honoured, witnessed, and acknowledged as someone positive and profitable to the community. Once a mother is in labour, young children are gathered. Each child knows that they have to stay quiet until they hear the voice and cry of the new-born, and then they must cry back as an echo to confirm the new-born has arrived in the right place.

My heart yearns for just such a welcome. Martín shared a similar story of a new-born Mayan baby fed on the breast of several lactating mothers thus receiving a sense of abundance. Of course, my active mind immediately jumped to thinking how this gives a baby extra flora for immunity. But this might also be a mind jump on my part caused by my inability to stay in the feelings of a warm loving pool which greets such a fully indigenous arrival. The depth of my hunger makes my mind get up and go for a walk, a wander or wonder. Perhaps, the hunger for what we have lost has made the Indo-Europeans among the most destructive towards indigenous society. It is distressingly easier to destroy than it is to learn about the hunger within ourselves.

This first relationship once we depart from our amniotic ocean to arrive on land has to be incredibly important. This reminds me of ancient stories of a whale who married a woman long ago and that is why they can still speak together. Western societies treat these stories as 'myths'. But our Darwinian theory of evolution, and how we emerged from the oceans, is not so different. We share the same myth, which is actually the same reality. Indigenous societies have legends similar to many of our more recent scientific discoveries – as if those who are in touch with their nature know what science seeks to find. By contrast, having lost an oral tradition to share the flesh on the bones of our culture's traditional stories, it is then much easier for us to toss the dry bones away.

Cain and Abel

Chewing and digesting the last two chapters generated a fresh line of thought. Adrian Raine convinced me, with his detailed data, that the interplay between different factors within us was more important than these factors themselves. Stella convinced me of the importance of the birth experience as well as the initial bonding with mother. The reminder that Sobonfu could 'see' our birth experiences many years later should have alerted me to the significance of the physical birth experience and the quality of reception. As recently learned from Raine, the relationship between these two is more important than either of them.

Using the analogy of the birds, if two important but separate navigation systems were clearly pointing south there would be no hesitation in flying that way. But if one said south and the other west or north then other factors must be brought into consideration to resolve an internal conflict – unless of course the system had been scrambled by a 'sonic boom carpet' and the internal guidance conflict could not be resolved. In the case of birds they fly around and sense fine alterations in navigational strength to improve their choice. Perhaps our minds try to do the same. Except that for many of us, because we remain stationary in our anxiety, we don't have any fresh air to help improve our directional guidance. We just go around and around in mind circles.

This chapter seeks a shorthand for the interplay between our natural instincts and the effect of our culture.

Stella captured my imagination with her humbling warm observation of the new born ability to look through her, communicating with eye contact, 'speaking' like a whale. This reminded me of the ancient meaning of the word 'beneficence'; to promote a feeling of wellbeing in others. The young of all species are specialists in beneficence.

In the womb we cannot communicate with our eyes. But, from the instant we emerge we can reach out to others with the language behind our eyes. An ability and a language which can be understood by fellow creatures, humans as well as other species. Perhaps even with the same language which is referred to in Genesis as; *the whole earth was of one language.*[38] Much of our earliest communication is with eye contact. On my journeys, there is always a pleasure to greet young children this way. The smiles in their eyes reach my heart easily. All over the world the eye contact language looks the same to me.

I have chosen to refer to this instinctual genius as the part of me from birth which is 'able', or Abel. Abel 'speaks' the common language and can offer up his communication with other first born creatures. Abel thus stands for my 'essence'.

Our cultures affect us in many diverse ways. Soon enough we are able to start internalising the demands of our culture in exercising self-control. The part of us which plans and maintains vigilance on our abilities and impulses is the domain of the pre-frontal cortex, but includes more. Over time our self-control restricts and constrains the Abel part, or canes him to ensure cultural compliance. This other brother can be called 'cane' for short, or Cain for simplicity.

The interplay between our spontaneous and instinctual indigenous soul and our surveying planning controlling mind could also be a role of the ancient story 'Cain and Abel'. A grown up deaf child, with accentuated sight, can 'see' the story that way. This story never made sense to me as the first murder in the Bible, or the first jealousy, or the first fratricide. My imagery recorded how *both* Abel and Cain receive a Holy blessing, but in different ways. The story had to be about something else.

In some versions of the Genesis story, Abel is not killed. In any case, killing in mythological terms is not fatal. The possibility of returning or rebirth is just around the corner. Many translations of the story have the question: *What hast thou done? The voice of thy brother's blood crieth unto me from the ground.* Are this voice and the way Abel's blood *crieth* from the ground clues that he is quite alive? Subsequently, Cain is not severely punished for the 'murder'. On the contrary, he is promised sevenfold protection, but with a destiny as a wanderer. However, a wanderer is a wonderer or a thinker, and that is what the pre-frontal cortex does.

---

[38] The Book of Genesis 11.1.

It is helpful of the Hebrew scribes to have written down these ancient stories for us. Bruno Bettelheim, in *The Uses of Enchantment*, explains that our oldest fairy tales are of two brothers. He adds that there are over 770 versions of this story in different languages during the last three thousand years. In all variations he suggests the two brothers symbolise opposite aspects impelling us to act in contrary ways; the nature/nurture interplay in shorthand. Bettelheim concludes that a successful existence is only permitted following a thorough integration of these contrary tendencies.

Following on from the brothers Cain and Abel, there is a similar theme in the twins Jacob and Esau. In this case Esau acts impulsively and Jacob studies in tents. This story is also about how the struggle for supremacy between the brothers begins in the womb. Bruno Bettelheim explains: *Cain and Abel, Jacob and Esau are Biblical examples of one brother being suppressed or destroyed by the other.* The two themes of nature and nurture seem clear. In the earlier story Abel offers up the first born animals whereas Cain offers up the cultivation of the land. The animal spontaneity or 'first born animals' is linked with Abel. The culture, or cultivation, is linked with Cain, just as Jacob's 'studying in tents' belongs with culture while Esau's 'impulsivity' belongs with nature.

James Kugel, in his outstanding scholarly work *How to Read the Bible*, gives us other clues about the Cain and Abel story. In particular, the reference to Cain's pleading: *Behold, thou hast driven me out this day from the face of the earth; and from thy face shall I be hid; and I shall be a fugitive and a vagabond in the earth; and it shall come to pass, that every one that findeth me shall slay me.* As Kugel reminds us, a literal reading of the story has only four persons on earth at that time, Adam, Eve, Cain and Abel. Once Abel is 'murdered' only two apart from Cain remain. If Cain is worried about being slain by his parents why doesn't the story say so? Further, in the reply he received: *anyone who kills Cain will suffer vengeance sevenfold*, Kugel informs us that the literal words translated as 'anyone who kills Cain' would be more accurately expressed as 'every killer of Cain'. This is even stranger since he can surely be killed only once? Moreover, there are only two possible killers to fear in Adam and Eve. Why refer to his parents as 'every killer of Cain'?

Samuel Noah Kramer was a world-renowned expert in Sumerian history. While Kugel alerts us to the significant number of Mesopotamian stories in the Book of Genesis, Kramer explains how Sumerian stories written down on tablets in the 4th millennium BCE were almost entirely adopted by the Babylonians. Thus, much of Genesis has Sumerian roots. For example, Kugel makes clear that the story of Noah's flood is based on the much earlier Sumerian poem.

Kramer suggests the ancient Sumerian stories were designed as philosophical treatises on the human condition or to address humanity's place in the world. In the 'disputation of silver and copper', copper retorts: "Silver, only in the palace do you find a station… If there were no palace, you would have no station; gone would be your dwelling place... In the ordinary home, you are buried away in its darkest spots, its graves, its places of escape from this world… When winter comes, you don't supply man with the firewood-cutting copper axe; that's why nobody pays any attention to you… When the harvest time comes you don't supply man with the grain-cutting copper sickle; that's why nobody pays any attention to you…"[39] This 'disputation' story seems to be referring to an aspect of our humanity in the difference between the two metals.

The Sumerian creation stories recorded on clay tablets include the debate between 'Summer and Winter' or Emesh and Enten. Kramer suggests that the Cain and Abel story can be seen as an abbreviation of the 'disputation' between the two brothers Emesh and Enten. There are many similarities.[40] In the dispute between Enten and his brother Emesh, they came before Enlil, the Father of the Gods, in the House of Life with their offerings. Among his arguments, Enten says "Father Enlil, you gave me control of irrigation; you brought plentiful water. I made one meadow adjacent to another and I heaped high the granaries." Enten is declared the farmer of the Gods as he is 'in control' of the life-producing waters and irrigation on which Sumer depends. Apparently Culture always triumphs in the old stories. Following the pronouncement of Enlil, Emesh bends his knee before Enten, offers him a prayer, nectar, wine, gold, silver and lapis lazuli to acknowledge his superiority. However, unlike Cain and Abel, the two Sumerian brothers then dwell in unity representing winter and summer respectively.

What is exceptional in Kugel's account of sacred texts is his generosity and openness to explore many possible interpretations of them. Maybe the stories are meant to have several meanings. Kugel shares how they

---

[39] Samuel Noel Kramer, *The Sumerians, their History, culture and character.*

[40] *Idem.*

were understood at different times and leaves his reader the choice to adopt one of several possibilities. We cannot be sure which interpretation is right. Maybe they all are. Kramer's linking of Emesh and Enten with Abel and Cain suggests some justification for another reading of the Genesis story.

Michael Meade explained that the Latin etymology of 'religion' is from 're' and 'legere' meaning to bind together again. My greatest need, as a result of my silent years, is to bind together these two brothers within me. Thus it helps me to understand the Abel story this way, just as it delights me to read Psalm 133:1 – *Behold, how good and how pleasant it is for brethren to dwell together in unity* as if representing Cain and Abel's successful reintegration. Maybe 'unity' is beyond my aspirations but 'dwelling together' might be achievable in due time.

Maurice Nicol also suggests that *sacred writings contain both a literal and a psychological meaning so they can fall in a double way on the mind.* Maurice adds that *The East* represents the rising of the sun and the source of truth. Thus the story of *in the land of Eden, to the Far East, where man was first put* means to Maurice that for each of us, when *first put* on earth, we are at our *furthest east* or most true. In this interpretation, Abel represents the truest part of our mind, the indigenous soul with which we are 'first put'. The effect of our culture afflicts that which is true in us. Thus, the interplay between Abel and Cain can represent a very important early dynamic in the psyche. Perhaps, the fact that so little else is said about the relationship between these brothers leaves the space for us to find our own internal relationship in some of the subsequent stories. In later chapters, some of Nicol's ideas help to put 'flesh on the bones' of other sacred texts.

It is not my wish or intention to suggest that the Cain and Abel story *must* be understood this way. Only to share with my reader how this sacred story helped me to get my brain around the subject matter. This is how I choose to use the story as shorthand for the very different relationships, and interplay, observed between the farmer 'Cain' and the shepherd 'Abel' in different global cultures. Since the nature / nurture dynamic is so fundamental to our psyche, and so different in each of us, this may reinforce the need for a plethora of religions as well as other alternatives to offer pathways towards unity.

Before taking this forward in subsequent chapters there are greater implications than the choice of story herself. Adrian and Stella convinced me of the importance of our birth experience. The knowledge that a shaman as wise as Sobonfu can sense this within us had fascinated me. But, the subsequent surge of adrenalin and excitement from putting these pieces of the puzzle together was a different one. Having initially not realised the importance of Abel's birth experience and initial reception, there was a 'double, double whammy' for me in realising that both Abel and Cain had distinct and separate birth experiences and receptions.

Abel's birth experience could be our bodily emergence from the womb, together with our first reception. Cain's birth, as the effect of our culture, can be quick or long and be compounded by complications around reception. His birth can also be traumatic. Thus, within our psyche, we have two birth experiences to explore. They both take place before our objective consciousness and before we have a cultural language to express the experience. Thus, one of the gifts of the sacred texts might be in giving a possible language for them. Perhaps the different sacred traditions reflect these two birth experiences in different cultures, as well as the way in which those cultures imprint themselves on each of the next generations.

The story of the twins, Jacob and Esau, whose struggle for supremacy began in the womb, reminds us how the effect of culture can begin to influence our nature before birth. This reminds me of Adrian's observations of the effect on unborn children when their mother had suffered violence whilst pregnant, something which Stella had also witnessed. Adrian's research also documented in detail the effects of different cultures' diets during pregnancy.

There is another interesting aspect of the fairy tales of two brothers in their instant forgiveness. We might be tempted to suspect that Abel remains furious because of his suffering at the hand of Cain. In the stories, this is not what happens usually. There is instant gratitude as well as forgiveness following their recognition. We can look at their reunion from another angle. If Abel is very calm and submissive by nature then his taming by the culture will be easier. Cain would thus be experienced as a gentler brother to him. If, on the other hand, Abel is very fractious and fiercely independent then Cain will need to be even firmer in some way. Thus Cain's personality is, in many ways, a reflection of Abel's temperament. Cain may be responsible for Abel's imprisonment but, at the same time, Cain is also guarding Abel in the culture. Abel is both imprisoned and protected. Perhaps Abel knows this somewhere or somehow and is thus able to forgive immediately when they dwell again in unity. Could the fear of Abel's possible reaction or fury – when actually he might be forgiving – be linked to the fear of elephant spoor? Could we have a fear that our nature will not forgive the suppression, and thus it is safer to keep him underground?

Before exploring Abel's prison, we need to learn more about the prison guard. In the next chapter, starting with elephants, we seek to learn something about Cain's birth experience.

Elephant Domestication

My favourite animal is the elephant. Somehow she always was. The calmness of her power, the grace of her movement, the essence of never having to prove her size to anyone else sets her apart. Even though there should be no other animal to fear, she still exhibits fear as if humility is one of her virtues. The delicate way she protects humans, sometimes, in ways most other animals don't. Except that she also seems to share this gift with the 'sea elephants', dolphins and whales. There are so many extraordinary similarities between her consciousness and ours. She is a great teacher.

My experience of elephants comes from both continents where she still lives. During my many journeys in Africa, occasionally we walked closely together. We stopped and looked at each other for a while. As mentioned in the earlier chapter on ocean creatures, we exchanged conversations as a boy who was deaf could. Sometimes when people asked me how many languages I spoke they were surprised by my reply that English is my second language. "What is your first language?" they asked, to which my reply was "silence" (but spoken of course). My explanation was how most of my first seven years were silent, and that the hospital tests told my family that, "He does not hear anything at all, absolutely nothing." But silence is a language. It is a language we all begin with. *In the beginning there was one language.* Animals also understand the same language. Different species have different calls, but the language of silence is common to all species; all animals use opsins to see. After all, hearing is only one of our senses. The other four senses do not need words or sound. Sight and smell might be just as powerful in the collective 'common language'.

Having promised myself a return to Sri Lanka especially for elephants in the Kandy Perahera, the possibility came just a few years later. By this time, my oldest friend Bahu was married. But there was something he had not told me; his father-in-law was responsible for the second elephant procession starting from Natha Devale. There was more excitement in discovering that his extended family now had three elephants; Raja, Rani and Podda. His mahouts taught me about these large family members living in the back garden. Not just elephants but ones trained for Kandy's religious processions also known as The Festival of the Tooth. The word Perahera means a religious procession. Sri Lanka's oldest procession, the Esala Perahera, originally began about two thousand three hundred years ago in the 3rd century BCE as a series of ritual dances to pray for the annual rains. Several centuries later, when the tooth of Buddha was brought from India by Princess Hemamala and Prince Dantha, there was another procession, the Dalada Perahera. These two processions then became combined into an annual festival in Kandy, where the sacred tooth of Buddha is kept. Had the tooth been brought right away after Buddha's passing, instead of eight centuries later, he might have arrived just before the Esala dance rituals began. Perhaps different dances would have taken place. Such is the evolution of ritual.

Together, these festivals have given us the second largest annual procession in the world, second only to the Rio Carnival which is somewhat younger. In terms of size and antiquity, the Kandy Esala Perahera stands head and shoulders above all others. The Rio carnival procession might be longer, like the neck of a giraffe, but giraffes have nothing of the weight and power of the giant tuskers in the Kandy Esala Perahera during their ten day festival.

Just like birds, elephants have an invaluable contribution to make concerning the understanding of our human minds. Some of the teaching is incredibly sad, but we have to face it. Hopefully my reader might not mind as we jump between Zimbabwe and Sri Lanka, between African and Indian elephants. The differences give us more clues.

A few weeks ago, in Zimbabwe on 24th July 2017, a thirty-year-old 'domesticated' bull elephant called Mbanje had just been giving rides to tourists. One of the guides, Enock Kufandada, was preparing to put Mbanje into a paddock for grazing with another female elephant called Nkanyezi. Suddenly the bull elephant turned on Enock and killed him. Zimbabwe Parks and Wildlife Management Authority rangers were called and they shot and killed the *raging* elephant. My italics as Mbanje

Sri Dalada Maligawa in Kandy (temple of the tooth) on my first visit to Bahu, 1972

was only *raging* in the account of *The Independent.* In other accounts Mbanje 'charged'.

The Adventure Zone managing director Brent Williamson told *The Independent* that the investigation into the death was *coming up with blanks.*

Since both Enock and Mbanje had died they could give no clues. But maybe the female Nkanyezi might have witnessed something. Was she involved? Obviously they could have requested the assistance of Agatha Christie's Hercule Poirot, or even better could have called upon the more local Mma Precious Ramotswe of the No. 1 Ladies' Detective Agency in Botswana. They could also have called upon a very experienced Asian mahout.

Some in Zimbabwe made comments that *the African elephant cannot be domesticated.* The situation reminded me of conversations with the Sri Lankan mahouts. Perhaps the answer is not that simple. In India and Sri Lanka the relationship between mahout and elephants has developed over a great many generations. The oldest evidence of captive use of Asian elephants can be found on seals of the Indus Valley civilization during the third millennium BCE. The mahouts revere the lessons received, often from their grandfathers, as this seems to be a hereditary profession. The mahouts told me: "We have to develop a very close relationship with our elephants. A milking elephant can be trained in two weeks but a mature wild elephant can take five years to train."

What they taught me was a mixture of a very warm and loving relationship as well as a considerable specific knowledge which compensates for the difference in size between the two of them. After all, the elephant may weigh one hundred times more than his mahout. The mahout has a stick, with a sharp spike on the end. But the stick will be useless against a charging or raging elephant without the addition of specialist mahout apprenticeship, and clear communication between them.

Another mahout and his elephant, Sri Lanka 1981

In order to protect himself, and to be able to train an elephant, the mahout has to learn the role of seventy-two places on the elephant's body known as 'Nila'. There are three types of Nila. Some are soft places which the mahouts use "To help their elephant understand" which seems to be a euphemism for a sort of smack. Then "There are places which cause the elephant sharp pain which we use for punishment". Finally there are also places "Where he can be killed" in case of emergency. They told me an inexperienced mahout might kill an elephant while trying to control him.

On the one hand, this is clearly very cruel. On the other hand the very skilled mahout never wants to kill his elephant and does not desire to cause him severe pain. The better the communication between the mahout and his elephant the more likely the 'domestication' can be accomplished through the training of the soft places. Perhaps this is how a young milking elephant can be domesticated in two weeks. But, how much is this affected by the awareness, in the milking elephant, that his parents and elder siblings are also already domesticated? Of course, just like the way we domesticate dogs, there are rewards as well as punishments. After all, the elephant is so conscious that he needs to see some real benefits from the arrangement, which seemingly there are. Without elephant consciousness, and a strong memory, it would not be possible to build this detailed understanding and relationship with the mahout.

One day, following my question: "What is most interesting about being a mahout?" His reply surprised me. "It is very exciting as you never know if the elephant will turn around and kill you. We are always on edge. Sometimes at night I wonder if he will kill me tomorrow. He is an animal that cannot be controlled. If you ever do anything unjust, he will always remember and punish you when you are weaker or off guard. If you use a Nila which causes him sharp pain when you should have used a soft spot to make him uncomfortable he will always remember that."

Thus it seems that the handler, Enock, in Zimbabwe might have received a fatal punishment from a much earlier memory of Mbanje. Something that day may have triggered a memory of his fury at an aspect of his earlier 'domestication'. Elephants are no different from humans here. We sometimes over-react because of some re-triggered childhood abuse. Perhaps Enock had not learned since he was a young boy, from a mahout grandfather, the lessons of over two hundred generations of elephant handling.

Back in Sri Lanka for the Festival of the Tooth, the mahouts continued explaining the Kandy Esala Perahera which involves over a hundred elephants in procession. During my visit the mahouts even allowed me to help dressing elephants ready for their procession, including a giant member of Bahu's extended family.

The mahouts told me that the elephants are very conscious of the ceremony. "Their behaviour changes. The more senior their role, the more they change their behaviour. The senior elephants carrying the important caskets will not move if one of the belts holding it in place on their back becomes slightly loose. They wait until it is rearranged. The elephant that carries the temple of the tooth casket walks on a white cloth, like a special road. If the white cloth is not straight, or becomes furled, then the elephant will stop until it is straightened out. It needs a very special elephant to accept the role. You cannot push an elephant to take this role. In parts of the ceremony the elephants are in a special formation. They know exactly what to do and do not need a mahout to remind them. If the drummers stop, the elephants stop. If you put a

baby elephant in the procession, she will dance to the drum beat with all the others, but it takes another five years to train an elephant for a role in the processions."

This is clearly a very important position for an elephant, and the elephant knows it too. His pride and consciousness of position is apparent. The tusker elephant, Maligawa Raja, participated in the Kandy processions for fifty years and was the bearer of the sacred casket for 37 years starting in 1950. He was one of the most celebrated elephants and declared a national treasure in recognition of his service to culture in Sri Lanka, with a day of national mourning after he died in 1988 at the age of 75. Raja also featured on a postage stamp and the 1000 Rupee note. It is said that Raja never had any problems with his mahouts and was very obedient to them. He always respected Buddhist priests and liked to be in the temple of the tooth. It is worth remembering that despite Maligawa Raja's considerable qualities, he began as an apprentice in the festival in 1937. No doubt the 13 years of study with other more senior tuskers taught him much more than he learned from his mahout.

Perhaps this is one of the biggest differences with the attempted domestication of the African elephant. Since elephants have a consciousness which seems to be at least the equal of ours, they need to be treated with the respect they deserve. It takes five thousand years to build a five millennia relationship between species. Animals understand human rituals. They can understand their part of the ceremony. The ritual understanding can be passed on from generation to generation in both human and animal species. These elephants in the Kandy Esala Perahera must be learning from other elephants having held the role for years before them.

The last night procession is lit by open oil torches, borne by the elephants. In years past, one of these torches sometimes fell and spilt burning oil. When elephants stepped on it, and felt the sudden fire underfoot, a stampede might rapidly ensue and people died. But Bahu told me it was invariably people who trampled on and killed other people in the melee of the stampede. Despite their own distress the elephants were light enough of foot to avoid crushing people. It would be hard to think of another heavy animal we could give the same credit to. For such a heavy beast they are extraordinarily nimble. Carl Safina, in his chapter on Elephant Empathy, suggests a similar virtue. He writes of an elderly, half-blind Turkana woman who'd wandered off a path and fell asleep under a tree. She woke, terrified, to find elephants sniffing her, but covering her delicately with branches until she was rescued in the morning by a herder. Joyce Poole also tells of a herder with a broken leg gently moved and propped up under the shade of a tree by an elephant.[41]

The mahouts also shared with me how one or two days before giving birth a mother elephant, or another matriarch, summonses female relatives to create a safety area. Any males known to be potentially dangerous are chased away.

These experiences have left me without doubt that the elephant has a great deal of consciousness, and has awareness of himself as well as of his relationship with the mahout. The ability to participate in ritual procession is special as is the way of reordering society before a new birth, and following funeral practices. We do not know if the elephant has more consciousness than other animals, but this would not surprise me.

These episodes taught me that consciousness alone is not enough to explain the uniqueness of man, if indeed there is any uniqueness. There has to be something else, particularly if we do not ignore the facts of the increase in suicide. Just recently the UK press has reported a 68% increase in self-harm of girls between the ages of 13 and 16. We might have to admit that what stands the human species apart is not consciousness, but self-harm. Some social insects may exhibit individual suicides in order to save their society. But the waste of suicide and self-harm among our young without any obvious design to save the community is unique to our species. As Carl Safina says,[42] *Self-loathing seems uniquely human.* The question is not going away.

My thoughts from here evolved in two directions. Firstly, what can we learn from elephants in terms of human domestication. Secondly, what

---

[41] Carl Safina, *Beyond Words – What Animals Think and Feel.*

[42] idem.

can we learn from elephants in terms of our relationship to nature. They might even be connected.

We begin with domestication. During 2015, while consulting for a steel mill in Asturias on the north coast of Spain, the easiest way to get there was to fly from Madrid, landing at the smallish airport of Oviedo. My travels took me there regularly and the airport became very familiar to me. Let me describe her: Oviedo or OVD for short.

OVD is open for landing and take offs about 15 hours a day with 17 flights. That is a plane landing every 53 minutes using the mathematical average. But, this doesn't set the scene properly. The schedule is not so regular. It is more like number 9 buses; after waiting almost three hours for one, two or three then come along at once. The airport has two siestas and two naps each day. Nothing is happening for half of the 15 hours she is 'open' and then planes flutter or flock into activity with pairs or triplets of flights within a few minutes. During the long pauses, initially with a blank TV departure screen as if there are no more flights today, she suddenly springs to life with the announcement of seven flights in the next hour. We have imminent departures of: Iberia 479, British Airways 7171, Japan Airlines 6960, American Airlines 8714, LATAM 5464, AVIANCA 4079 and Qatar 6899. This little airport is soon to be connected with Asia, the Middle East, Northern Europe, USA, Chile and Colombia with her far flung connections. Then, as quick as the firework is lit, it fizzles out as it becomes clear that all seven of these flights are going to Madrid and all at the same time. It was a mirage. Iberia 479 is going to fly and the six other 'codeshares' are riding on the fuselage giving the impression that they also fly this way, or do they? In any case the number of passengers arising from the mouth of the single narrow climbing escalator only warrants half a plane, it seems.

The check-in and security are downstairs. The security lane only opens occasionally to sieve the impending departing passengers in their waves. Various bottles and other items are captured in their net. The check-in hall is large, much too big for the daily traffic. The size and frequent lack of activity can give the impression that 'something has happened' as if there will not be any more flights that day. Once upstairs, having passed security, there is a small bar, a newsagent, some seating and a few departure gates. The views of the country around are pretty though.

Arriving early one afternoon, it was necessary to wait over an hour for the security team to return from somewhere to relaunch the X-ray machine and body scanner. Having admitted me first, all alone, and after the quiet ride on a very narrow escalator upstairs, the bench at the top of the escalator became my vantage point for the best view of the countryside outside the airport and all that was going on around me. The task of checking emails on my laptop occupied me initially. It was quiet as I waited for the other passengers.

Many of us enjoy 'people watching'. Perhaps my first language of silence ensured that it was a common and very detailed activity for me too. A few people appeared. Their manners, anxieties, enthusiasm for a future destination or their grief for someone left behind, their distractedness or wholeness as apparent as if they had been given a coded check-in badge. Perhaps in those first seconds after successfully passing the security and being whisked upstairs by the narrowest of escalators was like a form of birth canal bringing them up to the light and views upstairs. On my bench, perhaps like a midwife, they all had to pass me first that afternoon.

A family appeared; two young parents and a little girl. She must have been between eighteen months and two years old. She was in quite a temper, stamping her feet and crying. The parents looked quite distracted although they seemed to have a plan. Was this premeditated, or just agreed on the escalator, with the particular design of Oviedo airport facilitating their scheme? What had happened downstairs in security?

Suddenly both parents dropped to their knees in unison, wagging their fingers and yelling at the little girl as they both screamed: "If you don't stop that crying right now we are going to leave you behind right here." It wasn't the first time that such a phrase has been uttered to a small child, but this time was as if – in the front row of the stalls – the second act of a play had just begun and I was almost on stage. The little girl had not yet been called by her name. To her parents she had become 'you'. Let's call her Anna since she could not be a 'you' while in distress so close to me.

Almost instantaneously another family arrived with several children walking through the same space which was occupied by Anna and her parents, causing a momentary confusion to the plot. Anna's parents took their chance in the disturbance to make a getaway and hide behind two pillars about eight or ten yards further on. From my bench all participants were clearly in full view. The second family regrouped and continued on past Anna, seemingly oblivious to the theatre unfolding before me with Anna's plight.

Suddenly it was as if the earth had opened up before me and all adults spread wide. Anna was left instantly alone in space and unable to see her parents behind the pillars. She was standing only a few feet away from me, and still in intense distress. My instinctive feeling was to reach forward and scoop her up, to console her. She was almost within reach without even rising from my bench. But, being very aware that both of her parents were watching Anna closely from behind their respective pillars, this didn't seem wise. It seemed as if the parents were watching to make sure Anna did not run off or be picked up by someone else. That made me sure Anna should not be rescued by me. It seemed that both parents had the same detailed plan. They watched each other carefully as if to give each other assurance that their scheme was sound. In alternate glances, they were monitoring what was happening with her, the 'you'. In a flash it was easy to see the 'brilliance' of the parental plan. They were in a secure area of an airport gate where their child could not easily disappear. They knew she was effectively 'fenced in' to their domestication corral. It was a well-chosen theatre set as they did not have the worry of losing her on a railway station or in a supermarket. In OVD they had a place where the parents would suffer no fear from the apparent 'separation', but Anna would feel it all. The extent of the parental cunning surprised me. They seemed completely unaware that my observing mind was taking in every gesture as their plot unfolded. Watching them all intently, it was interesting how much both parents seemed to need each other for support during the critical unfolding moments. As if neither parent could have hatched the plot, or seen it through, alone. They also seemed scared of what they were up to.

The next seconds were like a lifetime. It was hard not to intervene. Realising she was alone, the terror soared diagonally across Anna's chest as if she had been struck by lightning. The lightning strike took her breath away. No air remained to continue her temper. No air was left to cry. It was as if the deluge had disappeared into a drop, vaporised by the lightning. Everything dried up. Then, just as suddenly, a different soul emerged. She took 'charge of herself'. As if this was another sister. Anna was still looking around, still unable to see her parents (who were watching her intently), but now it seemed as if a new Anna was armoured to cope with whatever happened next. Anna stood slightly taller as she surveyed the departure lounge. If she still imagined her parents might be there this was not obvious at all. Anna seemed instead to have broken through a fear barrier to a different place altogether and although still frightened she was otherwise calm.

Once Anna had been calm for a little longer, both her parents reappeared. The joy of their reunion was muted, at least on the parents' part. It seemed more of a dog biscuit's reward for the successful act of self-control. All of the reward was for the aspect of Anna which had 'taken charge of herself'. The other, distressed part of Anna, was thus forgotten by all of them. Anna had acquired a ripening defence system like a sword in her mind with which to commit hara-kiri towards any unwanted gut feelings, and so fast it was almost instant.

Those seconds left a very strong impression on me. My mind was flooded with many images and subsequent thoughts. Empathy for her made me wonder about my domestication as a child. But my mind was also flooded with sacred texts. Such as, *The veil of the temple was rent in twain.* The temple is a very specific part of our head. Could the veil of the temple be a metaphor for our mind? For the mind to be rent in twain, perhaps one part of the mind 'takes charge' of the other. In that nanosecond, this is how Anna seemed. She shook at the same time. Could that be a reference to 'earth quakes', or the shaking of the earth? Have our sacred writings captured the essence of these earliest moments of our domestication for which we have, as intact souls, no vocabulary?

Unlike parents that domesticated, as a mahout does, with a long stick and sharp points that can unerringly find the 72 weak or 'Nila' points on the elephant's body, Anna will probably not be able to remember this scene as she grows older. There was no blood on the floor tiles, no sick on the carpet, no memory of the lightning and thunder. Twenty five years of therapy will not help her memory to cough up this aspect of her infant domestication. Unless, that is, she has a two-year-old daughter of her own and she catches herself doing the same while wondering where that came from. That might be the best way to find out how we were domesticated, by 'observing ourselves' as we go through the same developmental stage with a child of our own. Maybe this is how we can also find our culture's traits. The traits which are not genetic at all, but are cultured habits passed along as the wild spirit of every generation is broken in and tamed to suit the cultural demands.

Martín Prechtel had mentioned to me how all animals when tamed become passive aggressive, just waiting to explode. Hence, he prefers his horses which buck and thus get some of this out of their system before he rides them. This reminded me of the domestication of elephants. Having shared with him how the mahout had said the elephant never forgets when a severe pain 'Nila' is used when a discomfort one would have sufficed, he reminded me that our 'indigenous soul' never forgets.

This made me think; if Anna could retain her memory like an elephant, she would recall this moment in OVD as an occasion when her parents had used a 'severe pain Nila' when they should have used a 'discomfort' one, or taught her differently. She could have, like an elephant, paid her parents back when she was a little older and they were 'off guard'. Perhaps this puts a spin on some of our teenage behaviours.

But, this also made me wonder something else, particularly if we think back to the birds. Migratory birds are hatched with a set of migration instructions, such as the distance, direction, altitude, timing and preparation of flight. But they are also born with 'space on their hard drive' to record all their sensory inputs on the first migration to make subsequent migrations easier. As if there is a record of their lives to supplement the encyclopaedia at birth. Why should we not be the same? Perhaps we are likewise born with a special 'space on the hard drive' to record our lives. Could this be connected to the part of our 'indigenous soul' which remembers everything? It could then explain how, in near death experiences, many have spoken of their life being replayed before them at high speed. Martín asked me a very interesting question; it is important to learn 'why you cannot remember'. The question preoccupied me for a long time. At first an idea came up that my indigenous memory had been struck by lightning, or zapped, in my domestication. Martín tossed that idea away as a 'cop out'. It seems more likely on reflection that our indigenous memory is out of reach because we don't allow ourselves to reach it. This is a jigsaw piece to be explored.

Applying to Anna's experience the characters of Cain and Abel, the incident happened just before Cain arrives to take charge of her indigenous Abel. Thus, the part of her psyche represented by Cain has no memory of it. Cain was born together with the lightning at the peak of Abel's trauma.

It is only fair that my reader should know that this critical age in our development as children is something which has often fascinated me during my journeys around different cultures. The way in which a culture is passed on, between the age of 15 and 30 months, is particularly observable to a non-hearing child. We under-estimate these differences between cultures at our peril, but more at their peril as we can do them incalculable harm. There are anti-dotes too, which we explore in Greenland. But, a major difference between our species is how elephants remember every aspect of their domestication. For humans it seems that only the shamans have access to this memory. The memory must be there in all of us. So the question is whether we can find the narrow gate which leads to that garden from whence we were taken, or jolted out of, so rudely.

Unlike birds and elephants who can easily access their life-drawn maps, in entombing Abel our Western culture has buried many of these earliest maps out of reach. We will explore more of Abel's entombing in a future chapter. Our indigenous memory is always there but, for many of us, out of reach of the conscious mind. For us to have full access to the navigational systems, given to us by Mother Nature, we need both Cain and Abel to be fully alert and communicating easily.

This might explain the language of shamans like Malidoma talking of the 'other world'. As if there is a barrier of some kind that keeps these brothers apart. It might explain our culture's expression of 'the need to sleep on it' so that we can retrieve files from the entombed Abel via our dream-world.

This could also explain why some of us find it so hard to access our relationship to nature. Abel has our purest relationship to nature. Cain manufactures a relationship to nature too, using his culture's guidance. But this is not the same at all.

Concerning a relationship with nature, the late Prince Prakitish Chandra Barua of Gauripur in Assam, India, was a legend in Asia due to his mystical affinity with elephants. He chose his daughter, Parbati Barua, to follow in his footsteps.[43] Parbati is unlikely ever to be surpassed as a lady mahout. She often provided services as a veterinarian, finding through her own senses which organ of an elephant was troubling them and then riding into the jungle to see what they ate. From this, she learned the medicinal effects of individual plants chosen by the elephants when suffering from different ailments.

---

[43] Mark Shand, *Queen of the Elephants.*

Just like the birds, elephants have a botanical encyclopaedia. Parbati explained how elephants showed her the medicines they needed whilst loose in the jungle. She would collect these plants and have them analysed in Calcutta. Based on the analyses, several pharmaceutical companies received knowledge for plant extracts to serve as new medications for human use. Parbati's father had taught her how the forests were medicine boxes, but the elephants could show her which plants are needed for what.

Having observed both carefully for many years, this is something that elephants seem to share with indigenous shamans, an 'unconscious knowledge' of medicinal plants. Is it possible that we are all programmed with this information but most of us cannot access it? That it would take a shamanic training and education to find that part of the mind, the part which can communicate with nature directly? Only the shamans know, and they might not tell.

In working with two indigenous shamans, Martín Prechtel and Malidoma Somé, their phenomenally detailed memories always astounded me. Sometimes they might pluck a verb from the third sentence of the fourth paragraph of a conversation twenty years previously to explain how my use of that verb then in that context could teach me something now. I would have to stop and think, yes, that was the verb I would have used. It was a pleasure to share my knowledge of elephants with Martín and my observation that shamans had such memories that they make elephants look as if they have Alzheimer's.

On one of Martín Prechtel's earliest visits to London, I asked if he would be willing to give a talk on medicinal plants to the Chelsea Physic Garden. This garden was established as the Apothecaries' Garden in London in 1673 with collections of plants from all over the world. The knowledge was jealously guarded for 310 years until the garden was finally opened to the public in 1983. The hall was packed with 'friends of the garden' for his talk, sharing his knowledge of all their medicinal plants as well as how to benefit from them. We all had a delightful evening. He also warmed us by saying how he felt "...the English soul had been saved by their love of plants."

Many animals know which plants to eat when sick. Thus, they too, have the apparatus to unconsciously seek out and eat what their bodies need. How could we all have evolved otherwise? One of the effects of our western 'civilisation' is that we have severely damaged this link. We sometimes eat what the mind thinks it wants, and not what the body wants. But the link is still there when guided towards him. As an example, during my teenage years many days were spent clearing and preparing our family garden. My mind was in complete command, focusing on an objective, and seemingly unaware of my physical tiredness or hunger. Coming into the house exhausted, with a headache, my father would alert me to my dehydration. He would advise me to drink water with a teaspoon of salt. If I could not taste the salt then I should drink more. Eventually, once the salt was tasted, no more was necessary as my 'salts were back in balance'. This taught me how the body, through taste buds and other senses, knows what to take in if we listen.

As Carl Safina writes, *Just outside the high elephant grass, five adults and four young babies are selecting a shorter and far less abundant grass. It's more work; it must taste better. They haven't read a treatise on the nutritional content of grass.* He suggests that their subconscious tells them what to do. True enough, except we could also say that their 'indigenous nature' tells them what to do. It is only a matter of the gap in our understanding of them and of us. We cannot be sure whether it is conscious or subconscious or unconscious to them. We can only be clearer of what is conscious in us. However, the word conscious is used in so many different ways, and different cultures attribute totally different meanings to the word. Perhaps this causes us much confusion.

We need to go back to Anna. Let us assume that the OVD experience is retained by her indigenous memory. Abel remembers but Cain has no understanding apart from the need to 'be in charge'. The question is: how might this experience affect her, or what might be the consequences? This is the quest of the next chapter.

Quiet

This chapter is titled 'Quiet' in recognition of Susan Cain's exceptional book by the same name. To avoid any confusion with Abel's brother, she will be referred to by her first name. My wish in this chapter is to bring in a number of factors Susan found. She has provided additional insight and significant jigsaw pieces for our inquiry. My reader will not be surprised that a deaf child knows a thing or two about 'Quiet', maybe too much. It enables me to add a twist or two to some of her discoveries. We can also more confidently examine Susan's work through the lens of the most recent chapters. Anna from OVD will continue to journey with us.

Susan writes a great deal, and very wisely, about introversion. Early on, in her introduction, Susan introduces the distinction between shyness and introversion by saying, *Shyness is the fear of social disapproval or humiliation, while introversion is a preference for environments that are not overstimulating.* This is a very helpful definition.

Susan suggests that introversion is a temperament, naturally inborn. This feels right, just like some animals that are nocturnal, and others prefer a quieter life. Stella saw the quieter babies immediately. Abel can be 'introverted', why not? As discussed in one of the conversations with Meredith, the Minnesota twins study found that a family could influence a child to make them more or less timid. But they would be unlikely to make a timid child brave. Susan goes further and clarifies that we can confuse shyness with introversion because they sometimes overlap. She introduces the idea of four quadrants, either calm or anxious introverts and either calm or anxious extroverts. Susan gives the example of Barbara Streisand as a shy extrovert *having a larger-than-life personality and paralysing stage fright.*

Susan's model would imply that Abel can be either introverted or extroverted, whereas the effect of the culture upon him, the Cain effect, produces the shyness and anxiety. Maurice Nicol reminds us how the word in Greek for anxiety, which we find in the sacred texts, is *merimnao.*[44] This contains two Greek words 'merizo' which means 'divide' and 'nous' which means 'mind.' Thus, anxiety also means a divided mind. It is only when there are 'two of us' that anxiety intrudes – like a table tennis game of two brothers conjuring different situations and different outcomes in the mind. By contrast, when the two brothers 'dwell together' we are 'whole' and feel fear only if there is a real challenge to warrant fear. For many of us, anxiety is 'manufactured' in the divided mind by Cain planning or imagining future events. Without anxiety, Abel might be killed the next time he crosses the road. So Cain is essential to protect him. But, before Robin Skynner helped me find a way through, my anxiety was of a different order. My Cain was going wild in imagining all kinds of dangerous traffic while Abel was nowhere near any roads.

Susan had sought to understand more about the biological origins of human temperament. She chose Jerome Kagan's work as one of her references, whereas one of my choices for the same question had been Adrian Raine. We can compare what we both learned.

Susan informs us how Kagan hypothesised that infants born with an especially excitable amygdala would wiggle and howl when shown unfamiliar objects – and grow up to be children who were more likely to feel vigilant when meeting new people. In a number of experiments led by Kagan, four-month-old babies were exposed to a set of new experiences such as new voices, balloons bursting, the inhalation of alcohol on swabs and much else. These babies had wildly varying reactions to the new stimuli. Kagan predicted, counterintuitively, that the most highly reactive ones would become the quietest teenagers. He found that the highly reactive ones were more likely to develop serious, careful personalities and be introverted. By contrast a low level of reactivity in a baby led to a more relaxed and confident personality, a more extroverted one.

Susan wonders: *Perhaps I've been asking the wrong question. Maybe the mystery of what percent of personality is nature and what percent is nurture is less important*

---

[44] Gospel of Matthew 6:25-34, Gospel of Luke 10:41 as examples. Also, Maurice Nicol's *The New Man.*

than the question of how your inborn temperament interacts with the environment and with your own free will. She also found that our positioning on the introversion – extroversion axis also comes out pretty much as a tie between the genes and environment. She adds, *To ask whether it's nature or nurture, says Kagan, is like asking whether a blizzard is caused by temperature or humidity. It's the intricate interaction between the two that makes us who we are.* Kagan and Adrian have brought Susan and me to the same conclusion; the interplay or relationship between nature and nurture is more important than either of the factors themselves. It seems we came to a violent agreement.

Just like Adrian in his Mauritius study, Kagan also measured the infant and toddler heart rates. Kagan found the more reactive a child's amygdala the higher the heart rate. Whereas Adrian had been more concerned with those having a lower resting heart rate, Kagan had focused on the opposite end of the spectrum of higher heart rates.

Susan introduces to us the work of Dr Elaine Aron on 'sensitivity'. Aron made the connection between a child's sensitivity and the phenomenon of 'high-reactivity' described by Kagan. Perhaps Kagan had discovered something else in his experiments, an indicator for sensitivity – that his tests had picked out the most sensitive and alert children to stimuli in general. But Aron goes further in suggesting that the 'highly sensitive' tend to be philosophical or spiritual in their orientation. They notice many subtle cues that others miss; their observations of others are very keen. Perhaps this trait is a feature of psychotherapists who combine their sensitivity and empathy. Being more aware of lapses in their own behaviour, they are attracted to helping others with their personal problems. Without doubt they sit on a different end of the spectrum from those studied by Adrian.

Aron's observation of the link between high sensitivity and spirituality was borne out in a conversation with Catherine Wilson. A dear friend and a fellow student of Martín's teaching, Catherine is an art therapist but she also has considerable interest in animal behaviour. She told me how important it is for animals to explore their territory. How they are instantly alert to anything new in their neck of the woods. This seems to link with a natural 'high reactivity' in some animals to new objects and smells on their patch. In looking at her patients' art, Catherine was attentive to which part of the paper, or territory, they had used. Some only drew in a corner.

There is a museum in Prague which is well known to both Catherine and me – a museum of children's art commemorating those deported between 1942 and 1944 to the Terezín ghetto, just south of Ústí nad Labem in the Czech Republic on their way to subsequent camps. Most were sent on to Auschwitz. Very few survived. During their stay in Terezín, Friedl Dicker-Brandeis had organised art classes to help the children with communication and a way of channelling their imagination and emotions. Before Friedl was herself deported to Auschwitz she left two suitcases of the children's drawings which are those displayed in the Prague museum. Under each picture is recorded the fate of each child artist.

Catherine's work had sometimes alerted her to see deeper spiritual meanings in patients' art. She shared a connection whilst visiting the art in this museum. She had sensed a greater curiosity and meaning in some of the drawings which she couldn't explain. Subsequently she was able to read each child's fate. In over 90% of cases this spiritual sensitivity corresponded with the few children who survived. Since we are sure that all of this art predates their transport to the concentration camps, do Catherine's senses tell us that the more spiritually aware might have more highly attuned survival instincts?

Catherine also reminded me that in the play of young animals much of it is mock fighting. This seems to offer an environmental development enabling the honing of preservation skills. Perhaps we can relate this to human play. This might enable us to improve our ability, while walking through life, to have a greater sense of people bumping into us – to know if they represent a real fight, a mock fight, or just an accident. Could this be similar to the role of the 'blank map' at birth in the birds? The map on which they record their first and subsequent migrations? Thus, we can also combine our genetic programming with a record of our life experiences as a double reference to call upon in future events.

Returning to Kugel's earlier hypothesis linking an excitable amygdala to later vigilance, to my observation and intuition this is not counterintuitive at all. Let us remember Anna, and think about her experience. An easy going infant might be able to shrug off the parental misdemeanour in hiding behind pillars at OVD, like 'water off a duck's back'. By contrast, a much more sensitive and reactive child would pick up on the parental betrayal, their initial scheming, on the realisation that her parents were apparently able, at ease, to follow through with their threat of abandonment. The indigenous soul of the 'highly sensitive' and 'highly reactive' infant would see it all.

In the nanosecond of Cain's birth during the lightning strike he comes as a saviour. Cain's first act is one of protection for Abel, guarding and preserving Abel from abandonment by his family. Perhaps this also explains why, in the Genesis story, Cain is reassured with the Holy answer: *Every killer of Cain will suffer vengeance sevenfold.* Cain's burial of Abel in the ground was all he could do, instinctively, to protect and preserve Abel. This is the opposite of fratricide or jealousy. Perhaps this is why Abel always forgives him. In the next chapters we could see how, if Cain's protection of Abel becomes too frequent and habitual, Abel can become buried too deep and forgotten. Sometimes Cain can 'over-protect' Abel when there is no longer a threat. The 'daily burial' of Abel becomes unconscious.

There is no doubt in which reactive category my infancy belongs. Apparently, on my first birthday, whilst playing with my mother, she left suddenly to answer the telephone. She told me many years later that my being so enraged had triggered a seizure. It terrified her. As a consequence she became scared of my rage. Much older, and during the analysis with Claude Pigott, this came back to me in two dreams. On both occasions the dream was of a son who had lost his mother and suffered a seizure. The son frothed at the mouth and lapsed into unconsciousness for a moment, then recovered. It seems that my one-year-old birthday experience was still there in my indigenous soul's memory. Having described the dream to my mother, this was exactly as she had remembered my seizure.

In this case, the telephone call was not an attempt by my mother to domesticate me. She deserves no responsibility or blame. Instead this shows how powerful the responses can be in a hyper-sensitive or 'highly reactive' infant. In Anna's case we do not know enough about her reactivity. But, in those few seconds at OVD she 'took charge of herself' at lightning speed. She was not slow to respond to an awareness of her new reality. This is a pure survival instinct, quite separate from her level of reactivity beforehand. Remembering Anna taking charge of herself made me wonder about Malidoma's comment in a ritual over 25 years ago, in telling me how my deafness had been *'my first achievement'*. Perhaps he saw it as the way in which I had quickly taken charge of myself in *'finding the mute button'*. It was not a part of my nature, but a very fast birth of an aspect of Cain. Could this explain why watching Anna's experience made such an impression on me? Perhaps Anna will also be lucky to remember her OVD experience much later in a dream?

Some of my readers will find my next suggestion a bridge too far, but it is only an idea. There was much controversy around the subject of the onset of autism and the MMR vaccine.[45] Major lawsuits ensued. However, the link could be quite different from either side's argument. There is a 'third way' in which the MMR vaccine could be not responsible and be responsible at the same time. The MMR vaccine was typically given during infancy at the peak of the age when autism first presents. Some suggested that there could be a causal link because of the synchronicity of the timing in both cases. But, because there is a correlation between high reactivity in infants and autism as well as introversion, maybe the link could also have a different cause. Suppose a highly reactive infant picked up the parental anxiety in their discussion about the vaccine. Such a child would then associate this unknown fear and anxiety with the vaccine. This infant's reaction might be influenced by anxiety around their parents' feelings, and nothing to do with what is inside the syringe. It is not impossible in a few cases, and we cannot repeat the experiment with a controlled sample of only saline in the syringe.

Since my hearing was lost at the age of fifteen months, my 'first achievement' according to Malidoma, this would suggest that it is indeed possible for a highly reactive infant to become instantly withdrawn from the world at the same age when the MMR vaccine is given. It is just a thought. The irony is that I was bedridden for three months having contracted measles, German measles, mumps, chickenpox and whooping cough all within the same period. The hospital assumption was that my aural nerves had been damaged by the intensity and coincidence of the afflictions.

On a different note, having learned from Claude that we can use rage to displace fear, this can help us with other childhood indications. For a child who cannot safely express rage because the family are also frightened of it, they would have to find another solution – such as to turn the fear inwards and 'split' the mind, or suffer night terrors, or become destructive. In my case all of them were present. Don't we use the 'terrible twos' to describe these reactions? The terrible twos are not

---

[45] The MMR vaccine protects against three separate illnesses – measles, mumps and rubella (German measles).

mock fighting, they are a furiously real fight for supremacy between either Cain and Abel or Jacob and Esau. A battle that rages within us until either the brothers dwell in unity or one has to give in, becomes buried or lost. The stories tell us that culture nearly always wins in the battle with nature, but the same struggle continues in subsequent generations.

In the story of Cain and Abel, the Lord appears to both sides. He favours Abel's first born animals, hears Abel's cries from the ground, but promises vengeance on every killer of Cain. The story of Jacob and Esau speaks of the children in their mother Rebekah's womb: *And the children struggled together within her; and she said, If it be so, why am I thus? And she went to enquire of the Lord. And the Lord said unto her, Two nations are in thy womb, and two manners of people shall be separated from thy bowels; and the one people shall be stronger than the other people; and the elder shall serve the younger.*[46] The one who subsequently takes charge is Jacob. Like the story of Cain, it is the brother representing culture who wins. Our nature has to be subservient to our nurture in both stories.

What cannot be denied is the level of fear which Anna might now have of any expression of her temper and her tears. She has learned to fear being abandoned at random somewhere if she cannot keep these feelings repressed. This might lead her not to want to stray too far from home. At least, any abandonment would then leave her somewhere familiar. Very much also depends on which other feelings she has to repress, and the extent of the fear associated with their repression. Perhaps only a few feelings cannot be expressed in her family? Perhaps she can enjoy love and joy but not grief and anger? Perhaps laughter is allowed but not jealousy? There are so many possibilities in terms of when Cain may be called upon for repression and protection. Most of us, in the Indo-European culture, have some feelings repressed to some extent. Anna's experience however makes the cultural process easier to understand. Some children suffer terrible violence instead of the parental 'hiding behind pillars'.

There are so many possible outcomes for the Abel and Cain relationship.

One possibility is a Cain who easily assumes command. Abel becomes submissive and retreats. Cain grows up to have a 'happy childhood' with the occasional nagging thought about what might happen if he dropped

---

[46] Genesis 25: 22-23.

his guard. But all his friends are similar so they find ways to help each other avoid the risk. Abel is almost totally absent. This reminds me of a James Hillman expression: *The most beautiful moments of our life are when we are out of control, but we spend the rest of our life trying to be in control.*

Some cultures, by contrast, have processes or rituals to continually repair the bridge between the two brothers. They focus on ensuring that Abel is still alive and well in their communities. This healthier case will be outlined in the chapter 'A bed-time story in Greenland'. By considering the luckier cultures, we can learn more quickly where our own culture measures up on the scale.

Here, with Anna, we will continue to explore the less fortunate.

If a very significant number of Anna's feelings cannot be expressed, and if the fear of expressing them is very great, then something else can develop of a quite different order. In this case Cain might become so active continually repressing feelings that he may try to 'catch the problem at the source'. Instead of simply inhibiting a feeling which arises, he tries to stop the energy underneath. In this case Cain learns to inhibit Anna's life force which gives rise to all her emotions. Literally, he has to find a way to break her life force or spirit somehow. We will also explore this extreme which might be contained, perhaps, within another early Genesis story – a story of two women, and like the story of Cain and Abel, both women receive a Holy blessing but in different ways. This story will be explored in the chapter called Shame.

A critical aspect of Anna's domestication is how quickly she learns, or how easy it is for her to maintain self-control. Is she compliant or rebellious? The conclusions are not hard to fathom. This might explain the challenge of those born with a greater determination and higher reactivity. That's me too. This leads to a wrestle between giants. If a child is a compliant and quick learner, especially if she has low reactivity, she will find her domestication more easily digested.

For the moment, while leaving the details of a 'broken spirit' to a subsequent chapter, we can consider these two unhealthy roads. The first is a case when only certain feelings are firmly and continually repressed. The second case is when even the life force or spirit under all feelings is repressed. The former may also be a mild form of the latter.

The exploration might help resolve some other questions which Susan raises. For example, the anxiety felt by some public speakers. Susan even refers to this as one of her own afflictions. As she writes *I can't sleep, and I want to die... What if my mouth dries up and I can't get any words out.* Susan explores some theories of public speaking anxiety such as, when our ancestors lived on the Savannah, being watched only meant one thing – a wild animal was stalking us. Whilst my story cannot speak for others, it may help to share the root of my anxieties. In my case there were, and are, two sources of the anxiety and of a totally different order.

Both fears in my case were a huge surprise. They are connected, but sometimes one part is easier to find. The clue which came to me first was a fear that what might come out of my mouth could be very good and heartfelt. My reader might now be raising their eyebrows, but hang on. Anna might even develop this. Let me explain how, with a highly reactive child, this can come about without any violence at all – even imagined violence is enough. Claude helped me to find the roots.

Anna had instantly found a way to control herself, particularly in respect of the difficult feelings of grief and rage. Her survival instincts made such a discovery imperative. She does not know how it happened that she became suddenly controlled by a fierce force during the lightning. But a part of her, Abel, was suddenly struck down by another part of her we can call Cain. As time goes by, the afflictions of Abel by Cain continue, even in quieter moments when Anna is alone. She continues to practise, perhaps even with her dolls. But Abel is still alive, and becomes more furious in the repression. Abel, having developed the fear of being murdered by Cain develops a counterpart feeling. A feeling of aggression sufficient to defend, sufficient to kill Cain even, grows from nowhere. Perhaps this seed of self-preservation was always there but it is now fully activated in the mind. This new fear becomes attached to these aggressive feelings of self-defence, which are now focused on the persons Anna depends on most – in particular on her 'other half', Cain, and her mother. The fact that a part of Anna would defend herself to the death becomes ever more frightening to her, as this part, if not controlled, might even be strong enough to kill her mother. What could be worse than knowing that within us there is a desire to kill the person on whom we depend the most? Over time this battle rages internally until the Cain within Anna's mind completely shuts Abel down. She has transformed a repression of an emotion into a repression of her life force. And then she has to keep her life force down as if her life depends on it. The ultimate oxymoron. She has become her own worst enemy.

As long as the public speeches made are bland there is no problem. But if Anna was to deliver a really important speech, the speech of her life, a career changing speech, a true speech from her heart, this early unconscious battle for survival might be awoken again in the previous night. After all, such a speech has elements of Abel's rebirth, Abel's own achievement but helped by the education Anna has received. The more important the speech is, the more the Abel / Cain initial lightning might be reactivated with all the related fears. In short, to deliver a speech of a lifetime requires Anna to relive moments next to the two pillars at OVD. Perhaps this is why so many do not bother. Depression or withdrawal is a much simpler option, or a few mediocre speeches. We mustn't take too many risks. Some call it the fear of success, which if the life force has been repressed can feel like overcoming strangulation. This fear may never disappear completely, but it helps to know whence it came.

It was only when all of this imagery came to me that Malidoma's comment finally made sense. How he had instinctively called my deafness 'my first achievement' an achievement of mastering the flow of one's life force, but this had come at a huge price, the price of silence.

I have to confess to my reader the memory which came back to me when my daughter, Alika, was 'Anna's age'. She was in a 'stroller', suddenly full of anger and with a fierce spirit. A strong and sudden urge rose in me as if to hit her hard on the temple. The urge was controlled and nothing happened, but a sensitive and hyper-active child would have seen everything – not just the rumble of the thought of it, and the lightning in the sky announcing the inevitable, but also my terror in realising the need to choke even an idea of my rising fist. Perhaps for a child it is the last part that increases the terror and withdrawal – not only the fact that one's parent is capable of a violent blow but more that they are terrified of doing it too. The child's fear is doubled as even our parent is scared. So we would need to develop even more hara-kiri to keep these gut feelings away.

In Anna's case, there was no sudden violence, or raised fist. But, the sudden withdrawal following a sharp remark or threat is just as painful and just as effective in the domestication. Remember how scared Anna's parents were as they 'corralled her'; they constantly needed to look at each other for reassurance as they followed their plan through. We forget the degree to which a child is sensitive varies enormously. A very sensitive child has the risk of *seeing* much more during her domestication.

She may thus become much more withdrawn in horror at the 'potential she saw' within her parents to do her harm. During my analysis in Paris, with Claude Pigott, this was a regular theme. While wondering why a struggle with the fear of death persisted, Claude had replied, "It's not so simple. Sometimes people are ready to die, like a soldier in battle who feels that he is going to die as a hero... but just imagine if you felt that you were going to die because of some violence from the person in the world you loved the most. What could be worse than dying at the hands of the person you loved?" The important message is that an over-reactive child can easily imagine all of this even if no actual violence is suffered by them.

Claude had taken me to the point of discovering my fear of being murdered by my mother. This is only one of the two fears. The other took me many more years to find. This is the equal and opposite counterpart; the fear of a part of us which has instincts of defence. A part of us which, to survive, may have to kill our mother first in order to defend our life. This is a possible origin of the greatest fear of our own life force, a fear of our own potential and a fear of 'our success'. This could be why, giving the speech of a life-time, from the heart, could reawaken this trauma in the night. In my experience, Susan's expressions of a dry mouth, words not coming out, wanting to die and being unable to sleep would be a signpost of worry of 'drifting towards these two terrifying and complementary fears'.

Let us not forget that, for Anna, her indigenous soul will never forget how her parents had decided to abandon her after the threat. And abandon her they did. She did not then have the mental apparatus to figure that they were 'kindly' preparing her for a culture. Not that it was a 'small challenge' to stop her tears. And by the time she figures that out, the terror of the lightning and the earthquakes are already consigned as deep scars to a memory she can no longer access. But, lest we forget, please remember that this relationship to the entombing of the indigenous soul is specific to some cultures only. The Indo-Europeans like myself, who are specialists, make a terrible error in assuming this to be universal. It is my good fortune to have spent some of my life with cultures for whom this experience is alien.

It is important not to leave my reader with the idea that we are blaming Anna's parents. After all, they were probably domesticated this way too, and Anna will likely do the same in her turn, unless she grows some self-knowledge in the meantime. Blaming the parents is a phase of therapy which it is best to pass through as quickly as possible. Robin Skynner used to say that the parts of our parents we could not tolerate are the parts of ourselves we hadn't yet found. This comment was immensely helpful – not helpful to the parents, but helpful to us, his group members, to find quicker the parts of ourselves we didn't know.

A Bedtime Story in Greenland

Sometimes thoughts come like thunderbolts, or may arrive like a gloriously speckled butterfly in the spring warmth landing on a hand. This one came in July 2012 with bright summer sunshine insufficient to melt the icebergs still hovering in the bay of Kulusuk, in Kalaallit Nunaat. The world's largest island is however more familiarly known by the name she received from early Viking settlers, Greenland.

A year previously, needing a one-way ticket from USA to London, my search found that the cheapest option was to fly via Reykjavik, Iceland. Having made a delightful stopover and explored beautiful landscapes, the time came to continue my onward journey. Also waiting beside me in the airport departure gate was the pilot for the next flight to London. Having complimented him on the beauty of his homeland, he replied: "But the most beautiful place on earth is Greenland. Nature is at her most overwhelming there." My interest was obvious. So he explained to me that the simplest way to visit would be to make the short flight from Iceland to the east coast of Greenland in summer. Several months later the opportunity again arose to travel across the Atlantic via Iceland and include this additional detour.

The Air Iceland pilot was not exaggerating. Nature is breath-taking here. The winds create sculptures all by themselves and then float them down from the Arctic Ocean.

A Danish anthropologist shared with me how he experienced the annual Inuit rituals as always telling the same stories, and cracking the same jokes year after year. Yet, they still fell about themselves laughing even more. My response was not thought out, emerging from my mouth spontaneously: "But of course they would, that's how connectedness works."

The comment surprised both of us and we spoke about the subject at length. Chewing over and digesting thoughts led to new ideas as we worked through the implications. Having also spent time with indigenous society and remembering my experience of their rituals enabled us to share our experiences. We combined the anthropologist's way of watching with my childlike style of observations. We agreed that recounting the same story allows the conscious mind to be less active and sleepy, so spontaneity is freer to get up and dance. The well-known story becomes a frame and a known canvas so that the participants can add their own colour. We can all enjoy ourselves more and be more connected. In my travels, when lucky enough to join in tribal rituals, this appeared a universal phenomenon. In some cases, having also been able to attend more than once and hear the same story again, made me feel more connected internally. Somehow my mind allowed the more spontaneous part of me to live as there was less need to be on guard against something unknown – less need to concentrate on the words of the story to understand what was being said.

But then something else came to mind, remembering my daughter Alika's desire for the same bedtime story night after night. There seemed to be a connection. A colleague had suggested perhaps she had wanted to 'master the story', but this is clearly insufficient to explain the joy in listening to her favourite bed-time story. Only Cain would want to master a story. The joy was too full and alive to be a tick for mastering something. The 'mastering of the story' had to have another aim or benefit. The idea which came was, once every page and picture has been captured in Cain's memory, she can allow her spontaneity to change a word for fun, or to be pronounced with a different feeling and laugh. The story thus becomes a safe container for the dancing spirit. Abel comes out to play. Perhaps this is one of the most valuable lessons of the teachings of primordial ritual, or the purpose of some rituals more generally.

Through a difficult second birth of the elder brother Cain, our access to the spiritual parts of ourselves in Abel may become more difficult and tricky. But, through stories holding the tensions between all the characters, the bridge back to a time when the spirit can dance is continually rebuilt in indigenous society.

In a sense, with a successful existence of Cain with Abel, once an indigenous ritual was about to begin, Cain could go and 'fetch' Abel. In English the word 'fetch' has a second meaning. The word also means 'to arouse the feelings of' as used in a 'child who is fetching'. So for Cain to fetch Abel both meanings are implied.

After the 'conversation' in Greenland, the memories of reading bedtime stories to my daughter make sense in a different way. She wanted to hear the same story over, and over, and over again. In so doing, her nature was alive. Our looks, laughter and spontaneity in those stories were the connection, and the story was not the point at all. Once our children know the story, the active thinking part of the mind is able to relax, and a child can fully enjoy the interaction with the storyteller. A child that knows, and loves the story-teller, can feel so connected and full of delight, so happy and whole. They can invent and enjoy a spontaneous variant as even more delightful.

The sadder part is that, by encouraging a child to leave their favourite story for a new one before they are ready, we may extinguish the flame of their spirit before they have the strength to let the flame reignite. Or we let them know that, in our culture, a new story would be better. Hence we devalue connectedness. Thus, we complete the domestication of their wildness just as easily as if we had smothered them with a pillow in the night. We don't even see ourselves doing it.

By following our culture's need for more 'consumptive entertainment' we write off what the older stories gave us. Since each culture has its own ancient stories, such stories bring forth the healing balm for each culture's traumas and disconnections. Just as in many parts of the world one can find plants which cure many of the local diseases, so the ancient stories are the healing plants. Thus, we must treasure all religions as they each have their stories which may help their culture to become whole. And who are we to criticise another religion when their plants may be different because their culture had undergone different afflictions.

As Michael Meade had reminded us, the word religion has its etymology in re: for 'again' and legere: for 'bind together'. We can apply this at two levels, to our internal selves and to our culture. Thus each religion has the task of enabling her culture to reconnect herself. It makes as much sense to offer our religion to another as to ask them to take the medication we have been prescribed. Instead, we should focus on reconnecting with our self, to become more whole.

We have lost so much of the deep art of connectedness that one finds in primordial society. Through much of history, when a cracked culture found an intact indigenous existence, they sometimes massacred them though uncontrolled jealous urges to bury the pain for what they had lost.

One evening just before leaving Paris and talking with a very dear friend enabled me to become progressively calmer and more affectionate. Suddenly the telephone rang, and the sudden loss of contact made me feel tight in the chest with difficulty in breathing. It made me wonder if the sensation that follows a sudden loss of affectionate contact is like a sudden loss of air. Could that be why we sometimes try to catch our breath? Out of a fear of losing it? Could that be part of a sigh of relief; letting out the air that one had hung onto because of the fear of the loss of breath?

If there were any doubts about this, my mind was convinced one evening when Alika, aged four, was restless and having difficulty in sleeping. I had tried to console her with a long fairy story. But, suddenly catching sight of the alarm clock, and realising how late it was, I told to go to sleep, with a sharpness and anxiety in my voice. Alika immediately put her little hand on her neck telling me she couldn't breathe. She asked desperately for some ice to cool her neck down, and I rushed to the kitchen to get some. She held the ice on her neck and followed my suggestion to feel calm, not to think about her neck. All she wanted was another story. Having begun a new story very softly, quietly and calmly she soon fell asleep.

A little later, lying in my bed to try and sleep, this made me shiver and shudder. My own little daughter had been unable to breathe because of my sudden withdrawal of affection from her. I had witnessed a strangulation of the heart.

In the morning other aspects made sense to me, including the idea that the beginning of our mortal existence was *...a long time ago in the days when wishing was having.* In Bruno Bettelheim's work *The Uses of Enchantment* he suggests that our mother in this earliest stage of life is the fairy godmother. She only reappears when the Prince or Princess is in extreme need and willing to open up to receiving her help. As the Prince grows, and his mother coldly brushes him aside, she becomes the stepmother. He cannot totally accept this cooler figure as his real mother, because she is no longer unconditionally available. Then, when the stepmother expresses her anger or other negative feelings, she becomes the witch. Bruno Bettelheim stressed how important it is to read these stories to young children, because it gives them images to process difficult and violent feelings towards their mother. If the parents are comfortable with the extraordinary and violent imagery in the story, it comforts the child that everything is normal. This helped me to understand the value of these stories. I resolved to help Alika with as many readings of the fairy stories as she wanted, and she wanted a lot. Sadly, looking back, the significance of the spontaneity during her favourite stories was not understood by me at the time.

Armed with this knowledge has helped me notice something else when listening to public speakers. Sometimes, having noticed when a speaker approached feelings of affection but suddenly stepped back from them, this could make many in the audience yawn suddenly. Like a sudden and collective need for extra air because the speaker had constricted his own heart. It was amazing that the physical response was so sudden and simultaneous; too coincidental to be simply a common tiredness among the audience at that instant.

The information helped me to reconnect with myself and my audience during my own public speaking engagements. When several people had a tickle in the throat and coughed, it made me wonder if perhaps my voice had been avoiding something. The cure was to share, in the next sentences, a familiar aspect of myself. This enabled me to reconnect better and perhaps my audience to be more comfortable too.

This consciousness can be overcooked though. We can over analyse our audience, or overestimate our power. In 1993, the year before Mandela became President, I was in Johannesburg to give a two-day workshop on leadership and empowerment to an audience of about two hundred. The entire audience seemed unsure of everything concerning the future. Half was black, including many union leaders. They knew that they were about to assume power but seemed unsure about the implications for them. The other half, all white managers, seemed anxious about their impending loss of office. It was as if the lecture hall was a giant hourglass about to be turned upside down so that the sand could flow the other way.

Holding my nerve, and sharing the same stories illustrated in my favourite cartoons, it seemed that the audience were all enjoying my observations on empowerment, engagement and leadership. Everything seemed to be going well. Suddenly a large Zulu Union leader stood up looking uncomfortable. He half looked at me, turned and walked out. My anxiety spiked, wondering what had upset him. Was it something said, or the way it had been said? He did not return and, despite the workshop proceeding normally, my mind kept returning to my doubts about my delivery. What could have happened? Was everything about to fall apart? Would others abandon me? What could be done?

But, in the morning, he was back. Being emboldened, and having sought him out in a coffee break, I asked him whether something had made him uncomfortable, or whether my delivery was inappropriate. Not at all, he said. Having found a few different ways to engage him in helping me understand my failings, it seemed he became puzzled too. When we both became stuck, clearly trying helpfully to discover something, he asked me why I had asked. Having explained my concern at his sudden departure from the hall the previous morning, he laughed. "Oh, I was uncomfortable as I just needed a shit." It was a valuable conversation in warning me of the dangers of 'over-processing' the reactions of my audience. But it was just as valuable in highlighting the benefit of being open and sharing my perceptions with the others.

Hopefully, from then onwards, my relationship with my audiences matured. As if an aspect had been understood including my relationship with my little daughter on the one hand and my relationship with a very large audience on the other. Perhaps, for my reader, this is obvious. But, for someone who had a silent childhood, it was a lesson to be found much later on by me.

SHAME

The book of Genesis draws our attention to the subject of shame very early on, through the shock in the Garden of Eden. One possible reading of the story, from among Kugel's several scholarly choices, includes the evolution from naked hunter-gatherers to clothed and cultured farmers. They covered themselves 'from the shame of their nakedness'. The way they were 'being' was 'shameful'.

Robert Bly offered us men a very clear explanation of the difference between shame and guilt. He said that shame is when you feel that your very existence is at fault; that your foundations are fundamentally and deeply flawed. By contrast, guilt is when you think you have done something wrong and are simply waiting for the punishment to arrive. Not the same at all. With guilt, our existence is not in question but we have erred.

In the Garden of Eden, Adam and Eve obtain knowledge of good and evil. Only our rational mind can discern good from evil; the concept does not exist in nature. Undomesticated animals do not think in terms of whether they are doing good or evil. Instead they live in accordance with their nature. From the awareness of good and evil, from rational consciousness, Adam and Eve become ashamed of their nature, their nakedness. The shame leads to hiding and covering. The story of Cain and Abel can be seen as a natural sequitur, highlighting the difference between shame and guilt. In essence, Cain completes the burying of Abel, the part of us representing our nature.

Surely Abel experiences being buried by shame while Cain realises, or thinks, about his guilt and the impending punishment. The Holy question, *What hast thou done?* makes sure he cannot escape thinking of his guilt. He has 'been found out'. Cain's reply includes, *...and it shall come* *to pass, that every one that findeth me shall slay me.* He knows he will have to run away and hide, but punishment will catch him sooner or later.

Whichever way we understand what happened to Abel, without doubt his very existence is threatened. Shame can feel like *a wish not to have been born*; the suffering is beyond our vocabulary. What can be worse than feeling our mortal existence is flawed? That our mortality was an error? Shame is not simply a feeling; more a state of terror, trepidation, consternation, despair, hopelessness, and an abyss of darkness. Shame makes depression seem a picnic in the park; unless depression is among shame's foothills.

Confucius often spoke about shame, even encouraging us to look for shame. His followers wrote that *if people are kept orderly though penal law, they will avoid punishment but will be without a sense of shame. If led with excellence they will develop a sense of shame and will order themselves.*[47] He says that once we find shame we are *close to energy.* This advice always tickled me and let some hope lighten my search. The idea which sustained me was how Abel must have been buried by shame. Therefore, a sense of shame would have to be encountered on the way towards finding Abel again, on the way to letting Abel come out of the ground. Can 'shame' be a 'troubling' state to visit along the journey which both Christ and the Buddha speak of?

In their wonderful book; *Families and How to Survive Them,* by Robin Skynner and John Cleese, Robin introduces the idea that we have a 'screen' in our minds. Because of our upbringing and culture, we have to put some feelings 'behind a screen'. For example, Anna at OVD will learn to keep her anger and her tears 'behind a screen'.

Robin goes on to explain a more extreme example. For these people, he says, *there's so much behind the screen, and the fear of it is so great, that there is no compromise.* This extreme situation is the one which we explore here.

Anna's experience at OVD caused Cain to sprout 'out of nowhere' to fulfil the survival instinct of burying her anger and tears. Once Cain had been born in the lightning, he was armed to prowl for any future hint of these feelings. As suggested in the chapter 'Quiet', a situation can then arise, for some of us, in which Cain becomes much too busy with the frequency of his task as there are many feelings to 'keep under wraps'. Cain, with his planning and foresight, finds instead a nuclear strategy to

---

[47] Analects 2.3.

weaken, divert or bury Anna's life force at source. That way all her feelings are tamed and more manageable, as if the dragon of her life force is 'slain'.

This outcome is an order of magnitude greater than simply 'repressing an emotion or two', or 'popping them behind a screen'. Such a situation deserves another sacred story to help conceptualise the enormity of the distress. But, first, my enquiring scientific mind needed some logical foundation for such a state in the psyche. How did this evolve and why?

Before the agricultural revolution, society was made of hunter-gatherers. About ten thousand years ago, plants and animals became rudely domesticated. Rising like a crescent moon from the Nile in Egypt across Syria and down the Tigris and Euphrates rivers into the Persian Gulf was a giant 'domestication corral'. Having managed to domesticate plants and animals, it is a very small extra step to domesticate other humans. Therefore we should not be surprised that this part of the world gave birth to vicious slavery. Trying to imagine my ancestors between ten and five thousand years ago brings the most horrific images. Having watched, in the last few years, the unbelievably disgusting treatment of the Yazidi population at the hands of Daesh in Syria, it is not hard to imagine the suffering of the first few thousand years of slavery.

This may lead us to a Darwinian explanation for a more recent and rapid evolution of the human mind, starting in one very specific part of the world. In Stephen Mithen's book, *The Prehistory of the Mind*, he takes us on an archaeological journey. Our oldest hominoid records began two and a half million years ago following the development of stone tools. From 100,000 years ago there is evidence of our ancestors burying their dead in pits. Like other species, we have multiple different intelligences. Mithen suggests that around 30,000 years ago our early human minds developed the ability to access and combine the output of several specialised intelligences thus creating an explosion into art and early scientific understanding. He has made a fascinating inquiry. My excitement rose in the hope of finding more answers to my main questions. In his epilogue he explores tentatively the period between 20,000 and 10,000 years ago when there was some domestication of plants coexisting with hunting and gathering. As he says, *Consider the 18,000-year-old sites in the Wadi Kubbaniya (west of the Nile Valley). In addition to charred plant remains indicating a finely ground mush there is a diverse array of roots and tubers which had been exploited possibly all the year around from permanent settlements. Similarly, at Tell Abu Hureyra in Syria, occupied by hunter-gatherers between 20,000 and 10,000 years ago, no fewer than 150 species of edible plants have been identified.* Our hunter gatherer ancestors clearly had a botanical encyclopaedia, just as the birds do. So, the sudden change around 10,000 years ago is not due to 'a new intelligence or knowledge'. He suggests something else going on.

Mithen's most convincing argument concerns sudden fluctuations in climate between 15,000 and 10,000 years ago, from cold and dry to warm and wet and back again. Times of plenty were interrupted by times of drought. This somehow led to *the propensity to use animals and plants as the medium for acquiring social prestige and power.* The evidence comes from a change in burial sites with the addition of important animal bones and plants next to the favoured few. Mithen suggests that we can *...indeed see agriculture as just another strategy whereby some individuals gain and maintain power.* This was how the human mind was already developing before the first 'great civilisations' began, at least in the Fertile Crescent. Reading Mithen's analysis intrigues me. Did the sharp and capricious fluctuation of climate in the five millennia after 15,000 years ago lead the human mind to be enraged with nature? Can this explain the Biblical fascination with the oscillations of droughts and floods? Can this have encouraged some early societies to put faith in a leader to 'get a grip on nature'?

Steven Mithen concludes his epilogue with, *I have treated the origins of agriculture as no more than an epilogue to my book. Nevertheless agriculture fundamentally changed the developmental contexts for young minds.* His book seems to stop just before the finish line.

To an evolutionary biologist, the last ten thousand years is too short a period to account for significant further evolution in our human minds. But the enslavement of animals and plants is huge enough before we add in the earth shattering changes coming from enslavement of our own minds.

My choice is to read many of the earliest sacred texts as the recorded effects on the minds of those who went through this traumatic period. The legends have some history in them which can be verified. But, being sacred, there are many words which can 'fall in a double way on the mind'. The authors have shared with us, out of their suffering, lessons which can help us put our minds back together again. Ancient peoples in this region suffered terribly. They were enslaved a number of times.

Possibly we can imagine, through the 'double reading of the words', how they understood experiences like Anna's at OVD and the need to split their minds 'to get a grip' like the story of Cain and Abel. The sacred texts of the religions born out of the Fertile Crescent are very helpful to me. In darkest moments they can provide faith, hope and guidance. But perhaps they are so helpful because of what my psyche contains as a result of the suffering of my ancestors.

As Charles Darwin told us, selection is much faster than evolution. Like our friends the birds, we had evolved the ability to write maps based on our life experiences and to choose between our instincts and our learnings. Cain, with our pre-frontal cortex, had been created to give us choices; in particular, the ability to override and 'hide' our nature.

In the Fertile Crescent, those who could not get a 'quick grip on themselves' would be unlikely to survive in the new environment of slavery. The independently minded would perish unless they could escape, or deceive their new master. An evolution of weaponry enabled mass killing among the population. The advent of slavery forced a very selective survival of those who could 'control themselves' at once when necessary. The ability which Anna demonstrated at OVD, to get herself quickly under control, is just the trait which would have increased her ancestors' chances of survival in early slavery. In order to be able to self-control, we have to be able to 'divide the mind'. One does not seem possible without the other. Hence *the veil of the temple was rent in twain.*

Slavery was endemic throughout the Fertile Crescent region for millennia, there was little escape. The ancient Middle Eastern cultures of Egyptians, Phoenicians, Hittites, Babylonians, Sumerians, Akkadians, Assyrians, Armenians and Chaldeans, among many others, all had slavery. The Greeks and Romans followed their example. The three major monotheistic religions, Judaism, Christianity and Islam, were born out of this cauldron of slavery. All three religions contain very powerful psychic medicine as antidotes to the situation which befell their people.

Returning to the subject of the worst possible outcome for Anna, a situation in which Cain takes the shortcut by diverting or suppressing her life-force, makes me wonder whether the enslavements made this trait essential. A parent might 'break the spirit' of their child to give her the chance of surviving a cultural enslavement. This brings us to another story in the book of Genesis which appears in the middle between the two pairs of brothers; between Cain and Abel on the one hand, and

Jacob and Esau on the other. The two women, as a pair, share some remarkable features with the other two stories of brothers.

This story, falling in a double way on the mind, includes the effect of enslavement and an emphasis on the relationship to the force which brings fresh life through the feminine. More like Cain and Abel on steroids.

The story mid-way between the pairs of brothers concerns the relationship between Sarai and Hagar.[48] Abel is the first male in the Bible to experience violence and suppression. The first female to suffer such harsh affliction is Hagar. There seem to be connections between these two stories if we consider them in terms of our relationship to our nature in Abel and the relationship to our life force in Hagar. Like Cain and Abel, apparently the Lord also favours both sides in the feminine story. Cain may have buried Abel in the ground but he is neither punished, nor threatened. On the contrary he is promised sevenfold protection. Likewise, Sarai treats Hagar very badly but suffers no criticism for so doing. The rational planning and foresight of her mind is not faulted.

Hagar is an exceptionally distinguished and important woman, no ordinary slave. She is the first person in the Bible to be visited by an angel, a messenger from God. She is the only person in the Bible who addresses God by name. *She calls the name of Yahweh who has spoken to her.*[49] Thus, for me, she glows as a metaphor for the force to bring new life, a true feminine spirit. My first meeting with Sobonfu Somé, with her giant feminine spirit, reminded me of the greatest fineness of Hagar.

The story begins with Sarai's inability to get pregnant. She says to her husband, *Behold now, the Lord hath restrained me from bearing: I pray thee, go in unto my maid; it may be that I may obtain children by her.* These words are not the words of a spirit. They are the words of a planning and foresightful aspect of the feminine mind. The Lord has made her barren so she has planned a way around this inconvenience, by employing her slave.

We should not be too critical of Sarai's scheming. After all, her husband had passed her off as his sister on the way into Egypt. They both seemed to have a matching ability to let the planning and foresight part of their mind take full charge of self-preservation.

---

[48] Genesis 16:1-16 and 21:9-21.

[49] Genesis 16:13 as written by Phyllis Trible in *Texts of Terror.*

Thus, the story offers us the idea of a quartet. On the clever rational controlling part of our mind we have Cain and Sarai, and on the part of our mind which is true to our nature and spirit we have Abel and Hagar. We are provided with a quartet which has two aspects and two genders, very neat.

Phyllis Trible, in *Texts of Terror*, has written an extraordinarily deep analysis of some of the stories of women in the Bible who suffered. In her account of Sarai and Hagar, she points out that Sarai neither speaks directly to Hagar nor utters her name. She is instead 'the maid', an instrument and not a person. If Hagar represents the feminine life force, this is natural. Next, *Sarai took Hagar the Egyptian, her maid, and gave her to Abram.*[50]

Time is of the essence. Hagar conceives immediately. Spirits don't hang about. But, as soon as Hagar is 'with child' she despises her mistress Sarai. For a moment the spirit, being successful, despises the controlling mind. Well, she should, shouldn't she? Sarai now fears that she will be deposed and asks Abram for the return of her prominent position.

Abram, the one who had passed off his wife Sarai as his sister, is on Sarai's side completely. There is no apparent concern on his part for how Hagar might feel about matters. He replies *Behold, thy maid is in thine hand; do to her as it pleaseth thee.* Thus Abram washes his hand of the relationship between the two women. Sarai now *afflicts* Hagar terribly. Trible points out that the verb 'afflict' is a strong one, connoting harsh treatment. She adds that this verb characterises the suffering of the entire Hebrew population in Egypt, the land of their bondage. This comment helps me understand a possible additional meaning of the story, since we now have the entire suffering of the Egyptian enslavement metamorphosed into the internal relationship between Sarai and her life force as an 'Egyptian slave'.

The story continues with Hagar escaping from the affliction by her mistress. *And Sarai afflicted her. So she fled from her. But the messenger of the Lord found her by a fountain of water in the wilderness.* The mention of finding her 'by a fountain' seems another confirmation that she represents the feminine spirit. Fountains are not common in that region, particularly not in a desert along the road to Shur. Just like the story of Cain and Abel, the Lord has a conversation with both sides. The aspects which

---

[50] Genesis 16:3.

interest me are the Holy questions. After all, the Lord should know everything; why ask? Just as Cain was asked, *What have you done*, the questions are: *Hagar, Sarai's maid, whence camest thou? And whither wilt thou go?* When Hagar replies that she is fleeing from the face of her mistress Sarai, the Lord tells her: *Return to thy mistress, and submit thyself under her hands.* The story might be telling us that we can afflict our feminine spirit but she will come back.

To continue the story, Hagar is promised that she will have a son Ishmael, *And he will be a wild man; his hand will be against every man, and every man's hand against him; and he shall dwell in the presence of all his brethren.* At this point, having heard the Lord's words, Hagar *calls the name of Yahweh.* Once again, the double way in which this story can fall on our mind might tell us that the wild spirit will continue, but will always be afflicted. We will have a long line of struggle between the planning and foresightful mind on the one hand, and the wild spirit on the other. Cain and Sarai are going to be busy every day as the combination of nature and the life force will exhaust them. Abel and Hagar will not surrender or give in, but they might wait.

More than twenty five years ago, during my analysis in Paris with Claude, he had helped me to see the masculine split in my psyche between Cain and Abel. Or, a dynamic in which many emotions were repressed and hidden behind 'the screen'. The deeper feminine in the psyche, and the split between her two parts was much harder for me to find.

My daughter, Alika, suffered a tragedy not of her own doing and found herself imprisoned in a cell in Asia. Thirty-six hours of travelling were necessary for me to find her so that I could bring her home. But they would not let her out of her cell until the following day. Not being willing to leave her, I told them they would have to lock me in for the night with her. In the middle of that night we had the most beautiful conversation of my life. She was delirious but delightful and loving. With her 25-year-old voice she spoke of the most loving memories of her earliest infancy. She had known that I was coming, was certain she would be rescued. She described moments of her earliest childhood when I had picked her up and she had put her little arms around my neck and squeezed. This is her story, so no more will be said here. But, on my next visit to Martín, the details of the whole story were shared.

Martín remembers Alika very well; he used to tell her a bedtime story often when he stayed. Her eyes were always on stalks then. Once he gave her a special stone which, when rubbed in the palm, caused one to see stars. He told her that an Indian would give her four horses for that stone. Martín's bedtime storytelling had enough warmth to have melted all of Greenland. Having listened carefully to my recent Asian tale of Alika's troubles, he only said a few words: "Interesting, that to have such a beautiful conversation, you have to be in chains."

The following morning he continued by talking intensely for an hour or more about slavery. I had never felt so alive. My throat was on fire with my heart containing the scream trapped behind. There could be no doubt that my psyche contained deep memories of enslavement, or of being in chains. Martín left for lunch and a nap overtook me. When he returned, I was still lying on the floor so he stepped over me. Leaping up, I said, "We have never spoken about this, but I have two shames. The original shame and the shame about my voice. As a small boy because I couldn't hear I couldn't speak properly. When I spoke people sometimes winced and looked at me as if I was deformed so I also had shame about my voice." He didn't need to think or pause for breath, tossing my thoughts of shame away with: "Just like all indigenous people; the original shame and the shame about their language." His response was surprisingly powerful, and liberating. That morning helped me to find the suffering of the enslaved contained within me. What a surprise. In a strange way, this was an enormous relief. Something unknown and feared could now be named.

He taught us much more about slavery but this was very hard to bear. Having known him so long, and always known him to be right, generated a giant conflict within my mind over this appalling subject. My notebook suddenly broke out in a rash of dark graphite question marks all over the page. How could this be? But then, it must be? My ancestors had been enslaved and ran away from it, but the deepest scars are still there in the recesses of my mind. Every new wave of explanations brought feelings of drowning but somehow breathing continued. Wave after wave came.

Martín has an expression: "If you try to run away from something, you become it." This part of the idea was easier to grasp as it matched something learned from the Oedipus myth. The myth is well known and was a particular fascination for Freud. However, Bruno Bettelheim explains that Freud's understanding of the myth was quite different in the original German from his work in the English translation. The story of Oedipus tells how the oracle at Delphi told him that he would kill his father and marry his mother. Out of fear, and hoping to escape the oracle's prediction, Oedipus runs away from home. He meets a stranger on the road who he kills, *not knowing that he has met and killed his father.* Likewise when he arrives at Thebes and marries Queen Jocasta he does *not know that he has married his mother.*

The irony and the point of the myth is that, had Oedipus simply accepted the prophecy, and his fate, he would have returned home and he could neither have killed his father nor married his mother as they were not there. He had been found as an infant on a mountainside and brought up by adoptive parents. It was his attempt to deny, and his running away from, which made the prophecy into a reality. Just as: "If you try to run away from something, you become it." Somehow this rather critical aspect of the myth is less often taught in my culture... perhaps because we are also too busy running away.[51]

How could I have missed it? Like finding some pieces of a jigsaw puzzle and wondering why they had not been seen as a perfect fit before. A DNA test had already suggested that my Maternal Haplogroup included a strain from Jordan in the earliest times of slavery, but the idea that such feelings were still hidden in my mind was a revelation.

There was, at once, no doubt for me that feelings of a trapped slave and of deep shame had been encountered in my psyche. It helped to make sense of my worst night terrors, a fear that there was another part of me wanting to kill me and of not having the strength to defend myself against another part of my mind.

It took several months for me to digest the enormity of this teaching, and to appreciate the extent of the lessons from my daughter's tragic accident in Asia. But the revelations kept coming. A torrent of different learnings ensued. Allowing some experience of shame back into my life opened surprising discoveries and fresh paradigms.

A door and a different pathway were awakened during a warm July night. Whilst subsequently recounting the experience to my friend Riccardo, who owns an excellent Italian restaurant next door, he was kind enough to record my description on his phone and sent my words back to me.

---

[51] Bruno Bettelhein, in *Freud and Man's Soul*, explains this gap as a loss in translation from Freud's masterly writing in German.

The experience I had was just over two weeks ago. I was in bed and in an extremely deep sleep. A very, very deep sleep. Suddenly, I flew out of the bed sideways and crashed into the radiator underneath the window. It was a good five feet straight. Now, I didn't hit it at the bottom... I must have collided about half way up. I was still half asleep as I hit it. I can remember stopping, helplessly, when I hit the ground, when I hit the carpet below. I was still half asleep – so two hits that were not enough to fully wake me up but able to feel them clearly in my sleep.

I got back into bed to go back to sleep because nothing hurt. I was lying on my back for a few minutes to go back to sleep. I touched my forehead and it was wet. I thought, have I been sweating more than usual? I thought, maybe I should just check, in case I cut myself on the radiator. I went to the bathroom and looked in the mirror. I was completely covered in blood, completely covered. As I looked in the mirror, it was like my spirit brother and me were standing together. It was like we were a pair as one. It was a very unusual and strange feeling. It made me a bit dizzy but also made me quite strong. I looked at him the same way I would have looked at my daughter when she was eighteen months old, as if she's knocked over a tin of tomato soup. I would've thought it wasn't her fault. It was just one of those things. I should clean it up.

I decided to have a shower and see what the damage was. After a shower the mirror said there were three gashes, two on the forehead and one on the nose. Better get those looked at. This was two-fifteen in the morning. I got dressed quickly, just jeans, a shirt and shoes – the two of us brothers walked down the road to Chelsea and Westminster emergency room. Walking together was eerily calm and strong.

The nurse said, "What the hell did you do?"

I said, "You're not going to believe this, I must have been in some kind of a deep dream because I just suddenly flew."

"Were you alone?"

"Yes."

"Have you been drinking?"

"Not at all."

"Well, you're going to need stiches."

After waiting a while, a lovely young lady doctor came and gave me the stitches. I was trying to explain to her that this was clearly a spiritual gift that I hadn't yet digested. I was going to have to work through whatever it was. It had taken away all my anxiety. As if Cain and Abel met again and were reunited.

What's so special for me about it is that within the 770 versions of the Cain and Abel story, in that many different languages, they all say it takes a moment of violence of some kind for the brothers to come back together again. Blood is usually necessary. There you are, Riccardo. I've been aware in the last six months or so that Abel is speaking up for himself a great deal more and saying he's fucking sick and tired of being ignored and not brought back to life as an equal. I may have said this to you, I may not, but there's a lovely piece which you find in Psalm 133, when it says, *Behold, how good and how pleasant it is for brethren to dwell together in unity! It is like the precious oil upon the head, coming down upon the beard, even Aaron's beard. Coming down upon the edge of his robes.* The psalm fitted exactly as the blood ran down through my beard. I think it could mean how good and pleasant it is for Abel and Cain to be back together again in unity.

On the one hand the experience that night was quite alarming to say the least. But on the other hand the mystery was that it felt good and as if meant to be. As if a necessary passage on the mountain pass. My logical mind decided that much more exploration and processing were necessary. A triangle of advice was needed.

In addition to checking with Malidoma and Martín, I sought out the guidance from another very important man in my life, John Schlapobersky. John was my tutor when training as a Group Analyst almost twenty years previously. I owe him a great debt as without his interventions I probably would not have qualified from my training institute. None of these three men blinked, taking such an experience in their stride as if they all knew what they didn't explain. They all reassured me. Malidoma said the absence of pain was important. He added that, "Even when blood is gushing, it doesn't have to do with something very bad. That could be the gift of liberation embedded in the redness of the gushing blood. That's what is really happening to you, you see…"

Martín's first comment when we met again was delicious. He said: "You have never looked better. When I saw you coming in I thought you looked nine feet taller."

I had two questions for Martín, as follows:

"Somehow the experience felt right, but there is something which troubles me all the same. Can I ask you something?" After his nod; "Do you remember the very first mixed ritual we did together and we all met to introduce ourselves in a circle. There was one lady there who was in a wheelchair. She said that she had tried to kill herself by jumping in front of a train. You said to the group: Let's ask Mark, he will know what to do. I had no idea what to do but instinctively I got up, walked over to her and knelt before her, looking into her eyes until I found her. Then I watched her a while until it felt right to return to my space. I want to ask you. What had you seen that evening that made you say that I would know what to do?"

Martín looked at me as if we were still sitting in that same circle that same evening and replied gently, "You come from a people that wrestles with that." In a flash, images of ancestral slavery walked through my mind. Then I continued: "But sometimes when I am on a subway platform I have a fear that there is a part of me that could throw me in front of the train. Sometimes I feel when on a high balcony that there is a part of me which could just throw me off. How can I defend myself against that part of me?" He replied calmly, "You can't. You have to work with someone else, with your hands, and make something of beauty and then you metabolise it."

As usual, Martín's advice was very revealing and comforting. This gave me the courage to explore further. At a psychological conference a few weeks afterwards on the subject of death, I explained those fleeting fears while on a high building or on a train platform and asked how many of the audience had experienced the same. The hands going up were clearly the vast majority. Winston Churchill called this feeling his Black Dog. *I don't like standing near the edge of a platform when an express train is passing through. I like to stand back and, if possible, get a pillar between me and the train. I don't like to stand by the side of a ship and look down into the water. A second's action would end everything. A few drops of desperation.* For Churchill it was part of a dark depression. For me the state is a fleeting one, a flash, like a temporary passing vertigo. Can this fleeting state be connected with that split in our minds when Cain was born? Connected with the lightning, like Anna's at OVD, which struck down our indigenous energy in a flash? Well, according to the number of hands that were raised in response to my question, there was no doubt that we come *from a people that wrestle with that.* It was very reassuring to know how many of my tribe shared the same fears.

It seems the nature of shame, like an abyss or black hole in the psyche, can cause the Cain part of our mind to evolve many avoidance strategies. Nevertheless, we must find shame and 'go through' as Confucius recommends. We are further reminded of the need by Gawan in the medieval romance *Parzival* by Wolfram von Eschenbach: *If a pure heart does not feel shame, it is because death has already stilled its beating.* Just like the magnets in my school laboratories, it is not possible for me to bring the two north poles of a magnet to like each other. My mind is repelled from my own shame. Instead, a skill has developed to keep away from the feelings of shame which surround the pure heart. Perhaps this paradox makes the journey so hard.

The relationship to shame varies enormously around the world – perhaps it is one of the critical defining differences between cultures. Whereas my culture finds shame impossibly difficult, Asian cultures experience shame more easily and in contrast take care to avoid promoting shame in others. Sometimes our Western mind tricks us into thinking we could use superiority as an anti-dote to shame, which was my favoured strategy as Martín reminded me. This doesn't work.

Returning to the example of a split mind where Cain has damaged the flow of spirit, the feminine life force represented by Hagar, to try and limit the power of feelings which cannot be freely expressed, we have found a possible source of the river of self-destruction.

If only some feelings cannot be expressed, Cain can hide Abel by repressing him but the habit may lead to depression. If the life force has to be buried, this may lead to forms of self-destruction. Over time, such a person will fear that their love or life is dangerous and at fault. They become afraid to love, afraid to be spontaneous and thus deeply imprisoned. They have the double affliction of not just a strong Cain repressing Abel harshly, but also a very strong Sarai fiercely afflicting Hagar.

The greatest irony, and perhaps one of the reasons why the source of the mysterious river is so hard to find, is that our self-destruction began as self-preservation. When Cain arrived in the lightning, he came to help Anna survive. He was a part of her survival instinct because her existence was threatened by just 'being herself'. Over time, the 'self-preservation' can become such a habit that we become completely unaware. We don't realise anymore that we are restraining ourselves out of 'habit'. We think that our existence depends on Cain's careful management and that we would not exist otherwise. Instead of enjoying our freedom, we can continue to repeat all alone the darkest aspects of our infant domestication.

As G.I. Gurdjieff explains; *you are in prison. If you wish to get out of prison, the first thing you must do is realise that you are in prison. If you think you are free, you can't escape.*

For each of us who became 'entombed' in infancy, and who 'forgot' that we were imprisoned, the task of plotting an escape is different. But, no escape can be considered if we think we are already free. In my case, it took a great many guides just to discover the depth of my 'self-inflicted entrapment'.

My debt to all the teachers necessary to help me find this oxymoron is incalculable, especially the three shamans – Malidoma and Sobonfu Somé and Martín Prechtel – who have been such patient healers despite all my attempts to sink their life raft as they nudged me kicking and screaming towards a safer and more delicious place. They helped me to find in which direction to travel so that the real work could actually begin; the first two questions had a source at last.

"How does an individual mind become 'poisoned' by a self-destructive tendency?"

Our survival instincts create a way of being as Cain to hide our indigenous nature known as Abel. Our self-preservation instincts cause us, over time, to bury our nature in the ground and to continue our existence as if just the 'other brother Cain'.

"How is the poison hidden, and harboured, in a part of the mind which is 'out of reach' or 'unknown to us' so we cannot simply 'deal' with it?"

The memory of our nature's trauma becomes buried with Abel. Cain had not been born at that instant and has no memory of the unfolding 'scene'. Since Cain had arrived 'as a saviour' his existence is protected by the planning and foresight part of our mind; as if our life depended on him, which for Anna, was originally the case. Cain cannot access this memory, nor can he grasp the idea of the scene at OVD. To find the truth, Cain would have to let Abel rise from his tomb; yet his arrival in the instant of the lightning was to achieve the opposite. Cain's reason for existence is to keep Abel protected and buried, except that Abel becomes forgotten and imprisoned as a consequence.

As Hagar tells us, the male part of our psyche is not the only aspect to be buried; the feminine spirit is continually afflicted harshly until both genders within our mind become buried or cast out.

The irony is that, the more 'successful' one's life, the less one needs to look 'inside'. If Cain has a 'happy childhood' there is no need to look for his lost brother. Success traps us; but failure allows us to look for something more valuable than 'success'. We have a Catch 22 in our mind. All the memory and maps we need to escape are held by Abel in his prison cell. That is also why such a long time is necessary to discover that we have become our own worst enemy.

The fear which is greater than the fear of death is the fear of our aliveness?

THE POOL OF BETHESDA

As a thirteen-year-old, attending my second lesson prior to confirmation in the Church of England, I just had to stop. My inability to continue was because the 'priest spoke with a forked tongue' like a movie which had been 'dubbed'. My two hearing systems were in conflict and, unlike a bird, there was no way for me to fly around to be sure of the right path. My reading of both Testaments of the Sacred Writings was still cherished, but the priest and his Church had to be abandoned. Whilst crossing the Sahara, I also treasured another Testament for protection which had been given to me by tribesmen.

My extensive wanderings embraced the beauty contained by sacred legends in many other traditions, particularly warm cultures more 'intact' and 'alive' than the land of my infancy. My enjoyment while watching their invigorating stories enabled a fresh way to re-examine the sacred stories of my ancestors. Without the help of other teachings it is very unlikely that it would have been possible to understand the depth of my own. My heart had jumped with each discovery of similar ideas. To be fair, as my reader knows, my hunger since infancy was always to 'look for connections'. However, finding what different religions share is much more sustaining than seeking their differences.

As a younger child, not being able to hear the words, their texture was felt by the style and imagery of the particular words used. The more emotional language of the Gospel of John had always resonated with me. Many years later, Maurice Nicoll's work opened a different path into these sacred texts. He taught that words in esoteric writings are designed to fall in a double way on the mind; they have a deliberate double meaning. As a Greek scholar he was able to decipher a hidden, 'other' meaning of the stories. His work 'spoke to me' instantly. Since Maurice had also worked with George Gurdjieff, and knew very well the Eastern traditions, this helped to find yet more connections.

Maurice Nicoll suggests that an awareness of Abel's internal imprisonment is the first step towards re-birth. He says: this awareness is called *metanoia* in Greek. *Meta* refers to a change of state, and *noia* means mind. Together they mean 'a change of state of mind' or 'awareness'. A very specific understanding is meant by *metanoia*, the understanding of imprisonment. Christ taught: *Except ye change state of mind and become as little children, ye shall never enter the kingdom of heaven.*[52]

Maybe 'as little children' could refer to our spontaneous nature; like Abel who offers the first born animals. Christ's phrase, as suggested by Nicoll, implies two conditions; we need a change of awareness on the one hand, and we need to become spontaneous like little children on the other hand. Then we need to be both at the same time, perhaps.

Confucius taught a similar principle to *metanoia* in *referring to the possibility of coming under new influences.* He also implied the need for both awareness and spontaneity in his teaching: *At fifteen I set my mind upon learning; at thirty I took my place in society; at forty I became free of doubts; at fifty I understood Heaven's Mandate; at sixty my ear was attuned; and at seventy I could follow my heart's desire without overstepping the bounds of propriety.*[53] Socrates felt similarly: *when we know fully and completely, suitable actions follow automatically and reflectively. Choices are made without conflict and with full spontaneity.*[54] The 'second sage' of China and prominent Confucian interpreter, Mencius says: *He who exerts his mind to the utmost knows his nature* and *the way of learning is none other than finding the lost mind.* [55]

Nicoll implies *metanoia* is an awareness of a part of us 'which was lost'. First we have to realise that a part of us is lost, before subsequently realising that this part is not truly lost but is instead 'buried' inside us. He writes: *It is clear that if something gets lost in a man, there was a state of him when it was not lost; and that if a man can become alive again, there was a state when he was alive. There is something in us, eternally young, that can understand beyond this visible world, beyond phenomenal reality.*[56] Nicoll's words; *something in us,*

---

[52] Matthew 18:3.

[53] Analects 2.4.

[54] Mark Ettin, *Foundations and Applications of Group Psychotherapy.*

[55] The *Mencius* in Chan.

[56] Maurice Nicoll, *The Mark.*

eternally young, that can understand beyond this visible world remind me of Stella's description of babies 'looking through her', Abel himself.

Maurice Nicoll's extraordinary and wonderful ideas are contained in a lovely book on an interpretation of some of Christ's parables.[57] His book grabbed me like the octopus' younger sister; she would not let go of me and was clearly connected with my struggles. She has been 'on my back', as a friend, for thirty years and for long before the larger octopus of this book snared me. Perhaps the realisation that the little octopus had served me so well released the courage to follow the designs of her larger brother.

The Gospel of John dives quickly into the subject of rebirth; but Nicodemus exclaimed: *Surely he cannot enter a second time into his mother's womb to be born.* A response is found in two parables, one after the other, as if to explain something connected. The first parable is of a *Woman from Samaria,* who had five husbands, and came to draw water from a well. If she really had five husbands, this would be quite a story, but the 'five husbands' seem irrelevant. The second parable is of *The Pool of Bethesda,* which had five porches.[58] Likewise; there seems no reason to mention the five porches. Nicoll says something unnecessary in the esoteric writings must be very relevant. He suggests this imagery relates to the five senses. Five senses which are 'husbanding' something and a 'porch way' to something.

Both parables speak about a different kind of water, a *living* water. In the first, the water spoken of is such that, *once* one drinks, one will *never* thirst. In the second, the pool is such that the *first* person, who steps in after the *troubling* of the water, is at *once* restored or made *whole.* The five husbands and the five porches are 'husbanding' and 'gateways' to the healing in the water.[59] As if we can reach our true centre by going *through* our five senses to *what is inside.* We can almost see the Buddha nodding.

The answer to the exclamation of Nicodemus was, *I tell you the truth, no one can enter the Kingdom of God unless he is born of water and the Spirit.* The two parables follow. Maybe the first is about the water, and the second is about the Spirit moving the water.

Nicoll had been interested in these parables because they only appear in the Gospel of John, and are connected with rebirth. Since the subject of

---

[57] Maurice Nicoll, *The New Man, An interpretation of some parables and miracles of Christ.*

[58] The Gospel of John, chapters 4 and 5.

[59] Husbanding in English has another meaning – to conserve, preserve, or safeguard.

becoming well again is so critical, my interest followed Nicoll's and kept digging with the help of his earlier excavations.

The Pool of Bethesda

1. *After this there was a feast of the Jews; and Jesus went up to Jerusalem.*
2. *Now there is at Jerusalem by the sheep market a pool, which is called in Hebrew Bethesda, having five porches.*
3. *In these lay a great multitude of impotent folk, of blind, halt, withered, waiting for the moving of the water.*
4. *For an angel went down at a certain season into the pool, and troubled the water: whosoever then first after the troubling of the water stepped in was made whole of whatsoever affliction he had.*
5. *And a certain man was there, which had an infirmity thirty and eight years.*
6. *When Jesus saw him lie, and knew that he had been now a long time in that case, he saith unto him, Wilt thou be made whole.*
7. *The impotent man answered him, Sir, I have no man, when the water is troubled, to put me into the pool: but while I am coming, another steppeth down before me.*
8. *Jesus saith unto him, Rise, take up thy bed, and walk.*
9. *And immediately the man was made whole, and took up his bed, and walked: and on the same day was the sabbath.*
10. *The Jews therefore said unto him that was cured, It is the sabbath day: it is not lawful for thee to carry thy bed.*
11. *He answered them, He that made me whole, the same said unto me, Take up thy bed, and walk.*
12. *Then asked they him, What man is that which said unto thee, Take up thy bed, and walk.*

The parable begins with; *There is at Jerusalem by the sheep market a pool called Bethesda.* Just six words; 'by the sheep market a pool' might have a deep meaning. Nicoll's thinking suggests two paths; one to the sheep market and the other to the pool of the five porches. As if living by the manners of culture would be following a sheep to market. The pool is 'by' or 'adjacent' but very different. Cain, or the culture, would take the path to market, but Abel would be in the pool through the five senses. The part of us we need to find to become 'whole' is not a sheep of habit or culture.

Nicoll suggests, in the language of parables, the blind, halt and withered refer to states of self-awareness.[60] Although the word 'affliction' has evolved to include physical illnesses in modern times, this was not the meaning at the time of the King James Bible translation in 1611. 'Affliction' originates in Latin as 'struck down', similar to the suffering of the Hebrews in Egypt and the way the spirit of Hagar is 'afflicted' by Sarai. By the 11th century 'affliction' had evolved to mean 'humiliation' in old French. During the 13th to 17th centuries the word was primarily used for 'self-inflicted pain' or 'self-discipline' and 'a cause of constant pain or sorrow'. The Pool of Bethesda cure of being *made whole of whatsoever affliction he had* implies a cure for humiliation and self-inflicted pain. Anna at OVD describes the evolution of 'affliction' precisely; she had been 'struck down' by lightning and humiliated before rescuing herself with self-discipline.

The word 'impotent' is also significant and surely not referring to something which could be cured by a little Viagra. The story might refer to potency of spirit or of allowing another spontaneous force to rise up and lift us. Abel, or little Anna, needs to rise and 'stand up'.

Canon Beaumont Stevenson, from Oxford, suggested two other aspects of the parable which had been missed by me. He offered the role of the angel is to draw our attention to something beyond our self. In other words, we should not follow the sheep part of ourselves. He also directed my attention to Christ's question *Do you want your health restored?* If the man had been literally blind or lame (halt), then it would not be necessary to ask if he wanted to be made whole. The point of Christ's question seems to highlight the importance of free will; that the man must first decide he wants to become whole. One cannot have the desire to escape Abel's entombment unless one has obtained sufficient self-awareness, or metanoia, of the condition. There is a further clue in the angel descending 'in a certain season', or from 'time to time' which is how this phrase is sometimes translated. This reminds us that the parable is not a 'miracle' since the story happens from time to time, *whenever* the angel troubles the water.

---

[60] In old English, 'halt' means lame or limping.

The *first person whosoever* steps in could also be referring to the part of us which is spontaneous. Just like Abel offering 'first born animals' which could be thought of as 'animal spontaneity'. To be made whole, we need the part of us *whosoever* is spontaneous to stand up and step out. Perhaps this is how we could interpret the sentence, *I have no man, when the water is troubled, to put me into the pool: but while I am coming, another steppeth down before me.* On the one hand, the man thinks he needs a helper to help him to be spontaneous, which is an oxymoron. On the other hand, the phrase *another steppeth down* could refer to a part of his own mind which frustrates him from being spontaneous.

After the metaphors in verses two to seven, there is different mystery in verses eight to twelve. There is yet another 'five' hidden in the words, *Take up thy bed and walk* which appear five times; like a repeated chorus. For a sacred story to include a phrase five times suggests a particular significance or relevance. The conclusion which came from continuing with Nicoll's line of reasoning whilst jostling with the younger octopus suggested that the five times was to underline the importance of this phrase instead of a literal interpretation of the sentences in which the same phrase appears.

Lifting the 'bed' did not initially make sense to me in the story, having immediately provoked an image of a man who has just been to Ikea and has some bits of wood together with Allen keys ready for assembly. Before getting too 'hung up' on the word 'bed', the discovery that other Biblical versions translated this word as 'mat' led to a different thread.

My adventures with native tribal traditions taught me a different imagery from the Cain and Abel story. Instead of a protective *brother*, some refer to the covering of our nature with a special type of clothing. In the Mayan tradition this could be an animal hide and in Malidoma's tradition could be 'armour' for example. The idea of animal hide made my heart jump as the double meaning is obvious; wearing an animal hide also implies 'hiding the animal within'. In a number of native initiations the initiate is instructed to *name the armour so as to walk freely beside him* or *to throw off the animal hide; to jump up and live again.* They do not use the term 'rebirth' but 'walk freely' or 'live again' is rather similar.

Having found some Biblical translations using the word 'mat', I wondered whether the original word spoken might have been closer to a pun like an 'animal hide'. For over twenty years my curiosity was tickled by this 'five time phrase'. Last year, having found an Aramaic version of the Gospel of John from Syria, I looked immediately for the word Christ had spoken in his native Aramaic. I shed a tear of joy, discovering the Aramaic word is a *quilt*. A quilt is both a bed and a covering. But my first image of a quilt is of a series of multi-coloured pieces of fabric patched together by my grandmother. An image of the covering of my spontaneity which had been handed down and woven together by a patchwork of ancestral culture filled me. Both sides of the coin are in this word. We have both an idea of warmth and support as well as something which hides and smothers us so that we are no longer visible.

The parable could be teaching us to lift up our ancestral quilt or protection and become true to ourselves again. The *another* who steps ahead of us might be a part of our quilt; our ancestral inheritance of suppression which needs to be 'cast aside' for us to 'stand up' and walk. The quilt may thus represent our resistance to spontaneity; the image reminds me of those nightmares when trying to run but my legs get all tangled up in the bed clothes.

Anna from OVD will always have my gratitude for providing so many clues while watching her 'domestication'. Reading my notes again, I had written, *Anna had acquired a ripening defence system like a sword in her mind with which to commit hara-kiri towards any unwanted gut feelings, and so fast it was almost instant.* The imagery of a sword while watching her has suddenly reminded me of another Biblical passage which refers to Christ having come to bring a sword: *Do not think that I have come to bring peace to the earth. I have not come to bring peace, but a sword. For I have come to set a man against his father, and a daughter against her mother, and a daughter-in-law against her mother-in-law. And a person's enemies will be those of his own household.*[61]

Anna's suppression of her nature in that instant was seen by me as an image of a sword in her mind. The quilt woven by her parents behind the pillars made her instantly 'lame' in respect of expressing her feelings. In this imprisonment of her nature, *her enemies are those of her own household.* She will not be 'whole' while suffocated by the family quilt. The imagery of Christ coming with a sword now provides Anna with the chance to stand up again; she does not need to stay forever imprisoned like her parents and ancestors. She can be free once she has the *metanoia* to understand how her parents had mistakenly used the 'wrong Nila' of extreme pain to domesticate and bury her.

---

[61] Gospel of Matthew 10:34–39.

Since the quilt was made by our own household, the teaching might be suggesting a sword is needed to *peel off* the inheritance of our quilt. The sword is not to be used against our family but to separate, or free, Abel from the 'quilt' which has smothered him. As Robert Bly taught us, a man needs his anger to cut himself off from his self-pity. As Robin said to me, "You won't be able to reach your feelings of affection until you have reached your anger."

My very first conversation with Martín had been about my struggle *with my daughter's anger*. He had replied, "Of course. She is trying to find your anger. She will not feel safe until she sees the edge of yours. That's why she is angry." The word 'edge' is interesting. Doesn't a sword have an 'edge'? Luckily, at the time, being an organiser of the men's movement, we had a number of exercises to help men become more comfortable with anger. Many men confused anger with aggression, violence, and rage. They were sometimes violent because they could not simply express their anger to defend themselves calmly. Lessons are necessary to learn how to express anger *without overstepping the bounds of propriety.*

Anna, as she grows up, might need some help to express feelings which are completely natural and which should not have been associated in her mind with a fear of death, or of being stuck by lightning. She is no longer 18 months old with a risk of abandonment if she allows these feelings to rise. Then she can peel off, with a sword, a part of her ancestral quilt smothering her aliveness. She will have discovered the 'metanoia' of *not what was done to her, but what she is still doing to herself, with self-discipline, because of what was done to her.* [62] She might even enjoy the African proverb: *a person without their anger is unborn.*

In my case, thirty-eight years were necessary, helped by nomads, indigenous societies, therapists, elephants, shamans, philosophers, birds, ocean creatures and trees before being able to see Anna's plight at OVD adjacent to the beauty in the parable at the Pool of Bethesda. Much of my work still remains; *seeing* the situation is only halfway to resolution.

But there is still much more in the story, another dimension even.

The moving or troubling of the water appears to be rather more than an important part of the parable. The multitude had to wait by the pool for a *moving of the water.* Nothing can happen until the angel comes to *trouble*

[62] A special thank you to Norman Vella, my supervisor and a wonderful coach during my group therapy training.

the water. Healing only takes place once stepping *first* into water which is *troubled*, and *in a certain season*. This imagery seems so deep that a whole chapter is required for her, and a different teacher. The best teachers seem to be trees. Like other friends with trunks who have so much wisdom for us, trees can explain more easily the difference between living water and the rising of sap.

New Sap in the Old Tree

My first teachers from the US men's movement were James Hillman and Michael Meade. James told us that *The oak is in the acorn*; that the acorn can only become an oak.[63] The genetic programming is rather clear on this point; that was easy enough to grasp. But what shape of oak is another matter. Michael Meade taught us how *character* is an ancient Greek word for a tool which makes a groove or scar in stone. He said this was why the word was also used for Chinese characters, made like scars in stone or wood. He added, the Greek wisdom was how a man's character is the sum of his scars; reminding us that the French word for scar was *blessure* with the same root as *blessing*. We are blessed by our scars, apparently. Maybe this was to slow us men down from 'whinging' about all our scars. A delicious memory has just floated onto my mind. One afternoon, discussing with Malidoma my training as a therapist; he responded delightfully, "How interesting that a deaf child is going to make his life from listening."

Ideas began to grow in me, sprouting from James and Michael's seed. The acorn was going to become an oak, come what may; but the strength of the summers and the fierceness of the winter winds would have much to say about the acorn's developing character into a giant oak tree. As, of course, would the influence of the other trees around.

In the beginning, when a sapling is upright and green, his shape and growth are more easily influenced by his immediate environment. Like a plant on a windowsill which develops a particular tilt. As the sapling grows, he must hide his green nakedness with a bark to prepare for the first winter, and to become strong. A dog uses his bark to create an area of defence and safety around himself; our ancestors used the same word

[63] James Hillman, *The Soul's Code.*

because they are the same idea. Once the sapling has a protective bark and becomes a tree, he finds he cannot so easily change his tilt even if moved so the sun or wind comes from the other side. Spare a thought for the sapling's first winter. He doesn't know whether he will ever have leaves again. Can the sight of other trees that have survived be what helps him through? As he matures, with even thicker bark, progressively his shape determines and channels where branches can grow. Over time, the influence of his early development may become 'more rigid' and quite resistant in both senses of the word.

The metaphor of *moving* or *troubled water* did not connect with me until the day Martín started teaching a group of us regularly. He gave our group the name, *New Sap in the Old Tree.* Suddenly an image of *sap* opened my eyes to a different way of seeing; conjuring images of sweet water full of essential nutrients springing up to nourish a tree from within. The idea of sap immediately connected with the two parables but took a long time to ferment. Clearly, sap was *living water.*

The tree, like us, must develop this bark to protect him against winds, storms and frosts; to protect his sap and survive his first winter. His bark conserves, preserves, safeguards or 'husbands' his inner water, or sap. Within the tree, both the bark and the sap are working together like two brethren in unity. Because the sap is within him all year round, and he is in touch with his nature, he can always taste this living water. The tree might not realise that some humans had lost contact with their bodies, or could no longer feel their living water. He has no need to ask a tree therapist to learn that sap is within him; nor to learn that this is a taste that no-one can ever take from him; he has no concept of a thirst for a taste which is his own. This could be a message from the parable of the Woman at Samaria; because we have lost contact with our true nature, we need to develop afresh the natural connection between our afflicted mind and our inner life or living water. Together with our five senses, we must safeguard or husband this living water again.

The tree winked, reminding us that the amount of water he contains is relatively constant all year round; just like us. But the sudden movement of water, the rising of sap, begins spontaneously *in a certain season.* This rising of sap is beyond the tree's control. He must wait for the angel too but that's how nature plays. Meanwhile, he can send out fresh feelers in fine roots to enhance his reach for water; he can extend his reach for water. But, he cannot go hunting for a rising of sap which only comes when she comes *in a certain season*. Only after the angel comes will he have fresh leaves. He knows that sap, and the rising of sap, are quite different. Like the difference between a slowly dripping tap and one switched on fully; they sound quite different as we know. Peter Wohlleben tells us that, just before the leaves open in spring, water shoots up the tree's trunk with such force that we can hear the rising with a stethoscope against the bark.[64]

Perhaps the two parables are necessary to remind us of the difference between sap and the rising of sap. Being able to taste the living water is only the first step, so that we do not thirst again from an inability to feel the living water inside us; and the second step is to be able to accept that the *movement* of *living water* is governed by forces beyond our control. This last part is hard for many Western societies; they want to be able to control everything and immediately. The delicious gatherings and laughter in the Gilbert Islands was an experience which had not been a part of my childhood. The love they all felt for each other; their spontaneity and sexuality was not something which can be found 'by looking for her'.

There are a surprising number of sacred stories in many different traditions which seem to link Spirit with *rising water*. Water which springs, is stirred, bubbles or is troubled all have this additional aspect of moving or troubling water. Fountains have water movement too, as in the story of Hagar meeting the Lord by the fountain on the road to Shur.

Sometimes we refer to someone full of spontaneity as having a 'bubbly personality', connecting with water that bubbles, the opposite of a 'wooden personality'. My language uses bubbling sap and wooden bark as contrasts; opposites which are necessary for the tree's life.

In summary, because the tree is in contact with his inner water, his living water, he enjoys and responds immediately when the sap rises in him. This seems to be the message of the two parables connected as a pair. In the first, the tree will never thirst and he can always drink his water. This living water can be accessed at any time the tree is thirsty. But the moment of rising of sap is beyond the tree's ability to command; the environment around him determines the rising of sap. He can only wait, and then, in a certain season, the angel will trouble his living water so she spouts.

---

[64] Peter Wohlleben, *The Hidden Life of Trees.*

Just like a small child, the sapling needs enough warmth, light, water and nutrients. But above all he needs the sweet water of connections. Without the contact of his roots with the soil and his tree neighbours he can make little use of anything. Recent research, beautifully written by Peter Wohlleben in *The Hidden Life of Trees*, shows that trees have many ways of communicating in the forest. They can communicate by scent, or by electrical impulses travelling twenty-inches per minute through their roots. Thus an hour may be needed to speak to a tree neighbour.

Wohlleben tells us, that like birds and other animals, trees also have a zoological library. Acacias only need ten minutes to pump toxic substances into their leaves to get rid of giraffes. Thc giraffe then moves on to chew another tree a hundred yards away, or upwind, out of the range of tree communication. Trees can match their excretions to repel particular insects which are a nuisance. He says, for a tree, thirst is much more unbearable than hunger. Trees can cry out to each other with thirst, just like babies. But this seems a different thirst; the thirst of a dry well; quite different from an inability to taste *living water* in a normal well.

The metaphor that our core self, or essence, is living water is as old as Father Time. This idea is found in so many native traditions and ancient philosophies. There is a story in the life of Confucius. He had become frustrated with his ineffectiveness with certain rulers and sought advice. Lao Tzu suggested he consider water; *She is very soft, but over time very powerful.* Many ancient philosophers used similar imagery, such as Plotinus suggesting, *We are not bodies but souls resident in bodies*; as if we are not trees but sap resident in trees.[65]

In a forest, when the spring warmth passes through all the trees, each tree responds in his own way. Some trees might 'not yet be ready for leaves'; they might need more warmth and longer daylight. For each tree, the angel who causes the sap to rise comes at a different time.

The teaching which was most difficult for me to grasp in my long search was this difference between living water which should have been reachable by me, so as never to thirst, and the movement of living water which cannot be sought; the angel decides when she comes. One afternoon, while walking home, an old nursery rhyme suddenly came to mind:

---

[65] Plotinus; 204 – 270 CE; In Enneads V iii.13. As quoted by L.S. Hearnshaw, *The Shaping of Modern Psychology.*

Jack and Jill went up the hill
To fetch a pail of water
Jack fell down and broke his crown
And Jill came tumbling after

Immediately after being reminded of the words, a thought came. When have wells ever been on the top of a hill? There must be something hidden in this most popular of English childhood rhymes. The rhyme had to be chewed, like a dog with a bone, until another meaning flowed. In old English; 'to fetch' also means 'to excite the emotions of'. Just like a child who is fetching. 'A pail' has also a double meaning, being either a bucket or a small amount. So to fetch a pail of water can also mean *to excite the emotions of a small amount of life*. But because there is no water on the top of a hill, they must both fall down in despair.

The rhyme is often repeated to our children, like a gramophone record stuck in a groove, reminding us of an aspect of our culture which is to look for love or life where she cannot be found. Like the Woman of Samaria, struggling at the well, it is the 'living water' that Jack and Jill need, not imaginary water from a well on top of a hill. Looking in the wrong place, instead of feeling something inside, is also well described in a poem by Kabir in the early 1400s, which was translated and often read to us by Robert Bly.

> Are you looking for me? I am in the next seat
> My shoulder is against yours
> You will not find me in stupas, not in Indian shrine rooms
> nor in synagogues, nor in cathedrals
> not in masses, nor kirtans,
> not in legs winding around your own neck,
> nor in eating nothing but vegetables
> When you really look for me, you will see me instantly
> you will find me in the tiniest house of time
> Kabir says; student, tell me, what is God?
> He is the breath inside the breath[66]

---

[66] Kabir was born around 1398 of Hindu birth, adopted by a Muslim couple; translation by Robert Bly in *The soul is here for its own joy.*

Perhaps the breath inside the breath should be as unmissable as the tree's rising sap.

The Semitic and Indo-European cultures can have an 'enchantress' which may lead a child to look for a gratifying relationship, or to look for a rising of sap. Somehow this has become a constant and internalised seeking passed on through the generations. Social media has added hyper steroids to the mix. But, we should not forget many other cultures don't have this disease; it is not universal even if rather infectious.

Could this also be what is meant by the Prophet Jeremiah; *For my people have committed two evils; they have forsaken me the fountain of living waters, and hewed them out cisterns, broken cisterns, that can hold no water.*[67] Impatience with the angel and trying to 'beat the system' has been around a long time.

The nursery rhyme provides an example of a culture's teaching which will not easily translate. As soon as the words are translated into French, the double meaning of *to fetch a pail of water* becomes lost. Just as translating the Aramaic word 'quilt' into Greek, then Latin and a few other languages before English loses the hidden double meaning and only a 'bed' is left.

With our sapling, if constantly displaced from water and soil he struggles to survive or grow. Too much transplanting is hard. But what is much harder is a sharp frost just when he started to blossom in spring; nipped in the bud. A few of those and he could be permanently stunted or killed as a farmer knows. Imagine a hot spell with bright light and surging sap followed by a very sharp frost. Wicked and sharp frosts just when he has vulnerably opened up for spring. If this becomes a regular occurrence he may start to mistrust the rising of sap, knowing well what comes next. He might then believe the rising of sap is evil. He could become afraid to live. The rising of sap which would have given him leaves and nourishment has to be stopped. If he could reach a knife, and bend a flexible young branch, he might cut his bark so the sap could leak out; to reduce the risk of the fierceness after her rising. He might live in the terror of having renounced his sap and yet cannot stop her rising; and it's worse because he knows that he doesn't know when the sap might rise next.

Originally we thought that saplings grow towards the light, but then we learned that direct sunlight *impedes and stunts development.* It is the shadow

---

[67] Jeremiah 2, 13

side of the sapling that grows quicker and consequently bends the sapling towards the light. Just like over intensive parents. Enough light is needed, but neither too much nor always from the same direction. If a parent is too intense the child turns limply toward them like a pale green sapling leaning on the window-shelf. Initially this may be gratifying, but unfortunately fragile for the future tree's prospects of withstanding the wind.

Our friendly oak agrees with the Mayan belief that there is no such thing as a man's past because he carries the past with him all the time. He knows about his 'inner rings' as scars marking the strength of all his summers, the fierceness of all his winters. His body bears witness to the winds he has suffered as well as the crowding of his space. Like an elephant, he remembers the branches we 'hacked off'. The oak may be in the acorn, but the weather he will endure is not. Unlike some of us, he has access to his memory of the environment. His trunk contains a memory which his roots can read. Like an elephant he may wonder why we cannot remember our life as a sapling.

The 'metanoia' spoken of by Maurice Nicoll may thus have two keys; there are two doors to open. The first key is our relationship to the *living water* and the other key is our relationship to the *troubling* and *movement* of the water which is beyond our control. Once we find the first key, we discover that a second key is not needed as we can just leave the door open.

The journey to find these keys could be a voyage of self-understanding or self-compassion. The Buddha described his teaching like a raft for crossing over. He said to his Bhikkhus, or disciples: *O bhikkhus, a man is on a journey. He comes to a vast stretch of water. On this side the shore is dangerous, but on the other it is safe and without danger. No boat goes to the other side, nor is there a bridge for crossing over. It would be good therefore if he would gather grass, wood, branches and leaves and make a raft, and with the help of that raft cross over safely to the other side, exerting himself with hands and feet.*[68]

We are all unique with different journeys. The Buddha may have taught this story to emphasise how, once crossed over, we should not be burdened with the raft. He adds, once the raft has been used to cross over: *It would be good if he beached this raft on the shore, or moored it and left it afloat, and then went on his way.* Just imagine how many wars we could have avoided if priests left their raft and went on their way.

---

[68] Walpola Sri Rahula, *What the Buddha Taught.*

Many routes to health share the surrender to waiting in order to discover different internal resistance, while becoming more aware that what we are seeking is next to us all the time. Either surrendering to one's body, through meditation, physical and spiritual Yoga practices; or surrendering one's mind through a spiritual belief; or surrendering to a group process and allowing others to act out one's inner life; or surrendering to shamanic teaching with a voice which calls us 'from the other side'. There is no right answer as we are all different to begin with, and have acquired a variety of afflictions along our path.

As the man steps into the Pool of Bethesda he discovers that he can walk, if he lifts his 'quilt'. He learns that it was his 'affliction' that held him back all along. His problem was caused by his continued self-discipline, by the continued imprisonment of his aliveness. Realising he is his own worst enemy, and he owns the key to his deepest prison, he has taken a step on the path towards freedom. The *living water* can never again be taken away; he will *never thirst* again, because he has learned to trust the water within himself which he had been protecting himself from. And, once he is comfortable with the living water, he might learn later on to accept and then enjoy the troubling of the water by the angel.

Michael Meade explained there is no such thing as happiness ever after. He says this phrase in the fairy tales should be translated as, *The happiness is ever in the after.* However, once we find the story of our own predicament, or affliction, we can keep seeing him over and over again or ever after. Freedom begins by discovering our affliction enabling us to change our state of mind, or metanoia.

As my journey walks through the afflictions of my childhood silence, many others with more spring in their step will pass me on the road. Perhaps you can smile as you listen to music which I don't understand, and drop back once you have found what you are looking for, to give me another nod of encouragement to continue on this mountain pass with rarefied air.

My wish is for Anna to learn much quicker than my tortuously slow discoveries; perhaps she will throw her hair back with gentle laughter as she trades her quilt for the African proverb: "When death finds you; make sure he finds you alive."

Another Lost Mind

Maurice Nicoll speaks of finding a mind which was lost. Mencius says, *He who exerts his mind to the utmost knows his nature* and *The way of learning is none other than finding the lost mind.* Birds, and many other animals, have taught us the wonderful extent of the mind 'of our nature'. Losing our nature is losing access to a large part of our mind.

Anna may have lost some of the mind of her nature at OVD because her parents had inflicted upon her what had been done to them. During the translation of the King James Bible, *halt* in a person meant to walk with a limp. The noun *halt* implied 'a state of inactivity after an interruption'. After Anna's 'halting' she joined her parents as a daughter who 'limps'. None of them are aware of this 'affliction' because the experience is locked in the 'lost mind'. In addition to *halt*, they are now blind or unaware. Having seen this blindness of affliction spread, out of reach of the mind of Cain arriving as a replacement, it was not difficult to imagine how a whole community or tribe can also become *halt.*

Similarly a nation, a culture or even a religion can become 'halted', losing their original nature. Many did. That might have been what my heart had seen, without realising the meaning, when the priest of my confirmation lessons just had to be abandoned with his forked tongue or out of body voice. The answer to the third question; why does a culture do it, might be beginning to emerge from a fog. The mist could be the way in which the culture has also become blind.

Around the time Nicoll first published his work, at the end of the Second World War, an Egyptian farmer, Muhammed al-Samman, found a sealed jar containing thirteen leather-bound papyrus codices near Nag Hammadi; about a hundred kilometres down the Nile from Luxor and the Valley of the Kings. These included 52 treatises of early Christian thought, including the only complete text of the Gospel of Thomas and a part of Plato's Republic. They had been buried for about 1,700 years. Although we do not know why they were buried, it is rather probable they had been struck down by 'lightning' as 'heresies'.

Irenaeus, the 'orthodox' Bishop of Lyons, writing around 180 CE, explained; *the heretics boast that they possess more gospels than there really are.* He adds *especially full of blasphemy is a famous gospel called the Gospel of Truth.* Ironically, the extent of the orthodox writings condemning these heresies confirms their contemporaneous existence in the first two centuries after the crucifixion; long before these texts were made available again for us to make up our own minds. My sadness is that this discovery was just too late for Maurice Nicoll to have digested them all. He would have had a 'field day' with so many early writings supporting his understanding of the parables.

The mid 1990s were a busy time for me in 'painting by psychic numbers' while trying to make sense of the different pieces of the puzzle of my 'Humpty Dumpty' mind. Although Robin Skynner had retired, his loving teachings continued to sustain me. The twice-weekly therapy group, which Robin had first invited me into, continued under Lionel Kreeger's guidance. My 'analysis' with Claude provided priceless insights. Martín stayed at my house for about ten days each three months during which he led a mixed workshop for a long weekend. The amount of teaching which he shared with me is too extensive to describe. Malidoma filled my house with his giant African spirit from time to time, sometimes with his lovely wife Sobonfu and her larger than life presence. Ritual weekends with Malidoma were always deep and intense. Other teachers came across the pond including Michael Meade, James Hillman and Robert Bly. Organising the UK men's movement together with Richard Olivier and other friends enabled us to plough a rich soil together while benefitting from the support of our teachers from the US men's movement. On top of all that my first reading of the Nag Hammadi library was like a 'cherry on the cake'.

In being 'struck down', Anna lost her ability to 'stand up for herself'. The most interesting texts in the Nag Hammadi library concern subjects such as, 'empowerment', 'independence of Spirit', 'not following the advice of leaders on directions towards the Kingdom of Heaven', and 'equality of gender with liberation of women to preach'. These are not small matters. They are all subjects relating to the ability of the people to 'stand up'. Looking back, with the benefit of hindsight, knowing how many people have been killed, enslaved or otherwise brutalised in the name of religion during the last two millennia must make us wonder how this could have happened. As Tolstoy says; *There was only ever one Christian.* Where did it all go wrong? The prevailing culture of the first two centuries of the Christian era managed to strike down the true freedom which had been promised by Christ's teaching. Perhaps, in the light of the male dominated Roman Empire, this should not surprise us. It would be more honest to reflect that, just as Anna was struck down in her earliest years by a pair of *halt* parents, much of the true nature of Christ's teaching was struck down by *halt* priests and Roman Emperors. The seed had been choked by thorns.

The part of me which had been 'struck down' was instantly drawn to the Gospel of Thomas. Reading this Gospel now, it is almost impossible to imagine the words being thought of as heresy, except by those who wanted all the power for themselves in direct contradiction to the teachings.

If you bring forth what is within you, what you bring forth will save you. If you do not bring forth what is within you, what you do not bring forth will destroy you.

Let him who seeks continue seeking until he finds. When he finds he will become troubled. When he becomes troubled he will be astonished, and he will rule over all.

With my hunger to find connections, the greatest joy was how the Nag Hammadi library provided a 'missing link' connecting early Christian thought with other traditions, including the Buddha, Confucius and Socrates. There was thus no need for Dogma. The new possibility was to dream of being myself again whilst embracing all other religious traditions as different homeopathic medicines. Maybe some of the other teachings might suit me better than my original inheritance.

The Buddha suggests that desire for 'water' is one of the main causes of fear. He adds, *looking is not finding* which is deliciously simple. Just like a sapling thinking of hunting for rising sap. His nature would never dream of such a thing. Only if all the trees around him had lost the plot could he become so twisted. He would then have to learn from a very wise old Bodhi tree to accept his nature and that what is coming will come.

My joy flowed from every realisation of how Confucius, Moses, Buddha, Christ and Mohammed together with many Greek philosophers would have understood each other instantly. We can surmise that self-understanding and compassion, together with spontaneity, was a goal shared by all of them. They describe similar ideas using slightly different metaphors. A silent perspective *sees* the links in their imagery. This book is insufficient to include all their similarities. Of course, someone looking for differences will find plenty. But the differences are inconsequential compared to the deepest connections. We are all the same race; we all share the same 'hard drive' of a common indigenous language and we share 'the human condition'. No wonder so many sages found similar ideas 'in the deep end'.

This position of Mencius is further aligned with the Buddhist and Taoist teaching, as well as the Gospel of Thomas when he explains how humans do not need cultivation; they just need to acccpt their innate, natural, and effortless goodness. The object of education is the cultivation of benevolence, otherwise known as 'Ren'. Confucius described Ren as: *Wishing to be established himself, he seeks also to establish others; wishing to be enlarged himself, he seeks also to enlarge others.*[69]

Having been guided by birds and fishes, there was much joy in finding a verse in The Gospel of Thomas which is similar to a teaching of Moses:

The Gospel of Thomas says: *Jesus said, If those who lead you say to you, See, the kingdom is in heaven, then the birds of heaven will precede you. If they say to you, It is in the sea, then the fish will precede you. But the kingdom is inside of you. And it is outside of you. When you become acquainted with yourselves, then you will be recognised. And you will understand that it is you who are children of the living father. But if you do not become acquainted with yourselves, then you are in poverty, and it is you who are the poverty.*

This might be Heaven's mandate which Confucius understood by the age of fifty.

Heraclitus suggested that dogs bark at people they don't know. And people bark not only at others, but themselves they don't know. He added, *I searched myself for truth lies within.*[70]

Many Eastern religions have a philosophy or moving towards 'self-realisation' which can be considered as similar. Even meditation can be considered as allowing the inside self to make himself known. For most western minds, including mine, meditation is extremely difficult. The thoughts invade, are chased or grasped after. Cain remains in the ascendance and Abel cannot get out of the ground.

---

[69] Analects 6:30.

[70] As quoted by L.S. Hearnshaw, *The Shaping of Modern Psychology.*

One of the greatest challenges for me was my misconception that intellectual understanding was true progress. The image of a diving board at the local swimming pool comes to mind. Not the high one, don't be daft; the one just two feet above the water. Standing there, knowing that the water will not kill me, is not the same as jumping and getting wet.

Following this realisation, much help and guidance was still needed to step off with one foot in front of the other. The catch, as identified by Gurdjieff, had been that a map can sometimes trick us into thinking we have already escaped the prison cell. Alas not. As the Buddha suggests, once we have escaped, the map or raft is no longer needed nor of much interest. In the meanwhile we can instead become 'attached' to our maps in the same way that we can become attached to religions and therapists can remain attached to their 'best interpretations'. My worst enemy was, as usual, always myself and often defeated the map.

Abel doesn't need to understand as he knows everything he needs and nature provides the extras. His only need is to be 'allowed out' and then 'welcomed out' instead of only escaping in Cain's deepest sleep.

Whilst in the Namibia desert a few years ago to meet the Himba tribe, I met an English psychoanalyst. Learning of my experiences, she asked me the difference between the traditional analytical approach and a Shamanic approach to healing. Having the time to reflect was useful. My offer was: "Analysis feels like training my mind to walk backwards into myself. But, eventually, a chasm or a river appears which is too scary to walk into backwards and so progress may become slower.

The Shamans are on the other side of the river, or chasm. They can see everything and they call me from the other side. Thus one can find more easily what we might have found if we had the faith to walk over the cliff backwards into our own darkest minds."

Sometimes, when trying to explain something to someone else, the one who learns the most is me. Just after this conversation, and reflecting on my own words, made me wonder what the chasm or river was. On the one hand Cain does look for Abel sometimes, perhaps secretly, but there is something which prevents him looking too carefully; something which makes his task almost unsurmountable. Could this be the fear of what he might 'find' close by Abel; the lightning which had heralded Cain's birth?

Not being sure of the psychoanalyst's 'tradition', I did not explain how shamans are masters of the conditions in which Abel thrives so that he feels welcome. Their ability is to re-infuse Abel with so much life that Cain's ability to contain him is weakened and Abel has more chance of finding a way out. Over time Abel escapes more often and the two brothers become better acquainted. Cain's ultimate task is to open the door to Abel's cell and embrace him; until then we haven't really begun; we have just understood a little more of the problem. We sometimes confuse Cain's 'quickness' with Abel's spontaneity. It would perhaps have been more honest to have told the psychoanalyst that my problems were so deep and so extreme that without shamanic help I would have needed more than one life to begin to see my way out. To have lost my hearing at fifteen months followed by six years of silence was a deep burden. But I have no regrets, as without that scar this book could not have been written. As Malidoma had said to me once, "You have had the life you were meant to have."

The warmest memory of my career is the years in the Gilbert Islands among such delicious people. There was thus no surprise to discover how some great sages extol the virtues of truly indigenous peoples. My eldest friend, Vikramabahu in Sri Lanka, taught me that Buddha based his ideology on indigenous society. Instead of using the language and culture of his upbringing which was Aryan, he went back to the previous

Dravidian society and language. The word 'Buddha' means 'rising' in Dravidian. We could wonder whether he had 'rebirth' in mind. The root has continued into the Tamil language where the word is now pronounced 'Pudiya' and still means 'rising'. Dravidian society explained our responsibility for *Sanahasa* which could be translated as love. Bahu told me there were four sub principles:

Mettha: which means to think of others at the expense of yourself.

Karuna: which means to give to others at the expense of yourself by sharing.

Mudhita: which means to have joy at the success of others.

Upekhsa: which means to tolerate the offence from others.

Whilst on a journey through Turkmenistan to visit the ancient city of Merv, my path crossed that of a very fine and beautiful mare. We watched each other gently. Admiring her demeanour, sporting an apparently gentle 'halter', suddenly reminded me of another 'coincidence' of my ancestors' relationship to the word 'halt'. Just as this word can mean 'lame' in the sense of a loss of spirit in the Pool of Bethesda story, so the word is used in the 'halter' or bind which makes the taming of a horse easier. In both cases, the 'head' is in a bind and the culture has won. But, the relationship to the halter is what matters.

The idea came back again on another wandering, on the other side of the Caspian Sea, in Armenia. Early one Monday morning, in the dewy chill while approaching a monastery at Gosh and quietly circumnavigating the external walls looking for an entrance, I came around a corner and bumped into a priest. We were both shocked and laughed. His smile was radiant and our greeting was warm. He asked my name before imploring me to wait five minutes while he rushed off. Returning quickly, having changed into his sacraments and carrying his ancient bible and silver crosses, he sang prayers and a short service for me in an otherwise empty church. He sang several songs and made special prayers, inserting my name at appropriate moments. It wasn't necessary to understand Armenian to feel the strength of his blessing and a warm glow stayed with me all day.

Later on, reflecting on the joy of meeting him, reminded me how some priests are not 'halt'. They appreciate fully the teachings and can still ride the spirit with freedom.

A key seems to be around the relationship to the 'halter'. Just like a quilt can either warm and protect, or hide and smother, so our relationship to the quilt or 'halter' can be different. Some priests appear liberated with a free spirit by sacraments whereas others appear 'halted'. During my journeys in the Middle East, some women described feeling smothered under a burqa. But others expressed feelings of spiritual liberation as soon they covered themselves; as if the burqa enabled them to feel the part of themselves underneath the restrictions, or under the quilt. Perhaps the danger is in making assumptions about what others may be feeling.

Hypnic Jerks, Sneezing, Kissing and Tickling

In this short final chapter, my interest was aroused by the possibility of thinking about ordinary physical sensations and relating them to the roles played by Cain and Abel in the psyche.

Hypnic Jerks

According to Wikipedia, *a hypnic jerk is an involuntary twitch which occurs when a person is beginning to fall asleep, often causing them to jump and awaken suddenly for a moment. Like the 'jump' experienced when startled, the jerks are sometimes accompanied by a falling sensation. They are also associated with a rapid heartbeat, quickened breathing, sweat, and sometimes a peculiar sensory feeling of 'shock' or 'falling into the void'.*

Tom Stafford wrote about hypnic jerks for BBC future, published in May 2012. He says: *As we give up our bodies to sleep, sudden twitches escape our brains, causing our arms and legs to jerk. Some people are startled by them, others are embarrassed. Nobody knows for sure what causes them, but to me they represent the side effects of a hidden battle for control in the brain that happens each night on the cusp between wakefulness and dreams.*

Hypnic jerks seem to be a sign that the motor system can still exert some control over the body as sleep paralysis begins to take over – we have two opposing systems balanced against each other that go through a daily dance, where each has to wrest control from the other.

Hypnic jerks are the last gasps of normal daytime motor control. In dreams, the planning and foresight areas of the brain are suppressed, allowing the mind to react creatively to wherever it wanders – much like a jazz improviser responds to fellow musicians to inspire what they play.

So there is a pleasing symmetry between the two kinds of movements we make when asleep. Rapid eye movements are the traces of dreams that can be seen in the waking world. Hypnic jerks seem to be the traces of waking life that intrude on the dream world.

Although there has been much research on the causes of hypnic jerks, no conclusion has been found. This gives me a chance to offer my own; and agree with Tom Stafford. My own experiences of hypnic jerks are more like climbing a ladder with old wooden rungs and suddenly one breaks so that my body falls back a rung. They always occur 'on the cusp between wakefulness and dreams'. For me, the deep creative dream world *when the planning and foresight areas of the brain are suppressed* represent Abel's domain. The planning and foresight is Cain's domain. Thus, the jerks occur when Cain gives up his control of the body and mind to let Abel *react creatively to wherever he wanders.* They are a sign that Cain is completing his 'shift' and the baton is being passed back to brother Abel.

Watching Anna at OVD, and in particular the way she shuddered in the lightning strike as Cain was born, makes me wonder if Cain's giving up his daily control is a reminder of the feeling experienced by Abel when Cain was first born. Anna's sudden shake looked to me like a hypnic jerk. Maybe our indigenous soul still retains the psychic memory of that moment. Perhaps the feeling comes, like the 'earth moves', on the way back to Abel's domain. Could our hypnic jerk resemble the lightning jolt when Abel first surrendered control to Cain, even if travelling in the opposite direction? A brave researcher could investigate the propensity of hypnic jerks in different cultures, comparing the Indo-Europeans to more indigenous cultures to see if there is a stronger emphasis among cultures where the domestication is 'sharper', 'faster' and less smooth.

Sneezing

Wikipedia says that *a sneeze is a semi-autonomous, convulsive expulsion of air from the lungs through the nose and mouth, usually caused by foreign particles irritating the nasal mucosa.* Well, most of us know what a sneeze is. Often, having wondered if bright sunshine caused sneezes, someone explained to me that it was more likely that my eyes squinted in the extra light, putting pressure on the sinuses which triggered the sneeze. My inquiry is not about the origin of the sneeze, but more 'how we react to the impending sneeze'.

Some of us fight and resist sneezes. There is even a word for the fear of sneezes; sternutaphobia. My reaction is usually the opposite. They are welcome. As the sensation of a sneeze starts to develop, the part of my mind which is called Cain knows that he can pause for a moment. He can completely trust brother Abel and their shared body to lead the 'sneeze dance'. For a nanosecond in the sneeze an experience is shared between the brothers as if they dwelled together for an instant of shared bodily control. Even though this feeling is short lived, my assumption was always that others instinctively noticed the momentary wholeness of the brothers dwelling together which is why they say, "Bless you."

Of course there are many other explanations of the expression 'Bless you'. In Ancient Greece, sneezes were considered prophetic signs from the gods. Others believe that life is tied to one's breath – hence the word 'expire' which is linked with 'exhale'. Perhaps this link of 'to come to an end' or 'to die' generated the response: "God bless you." But, my preference is for unity of the brothers and their fleeting wholeness. After all, a deaf person only has to watch the way others say, "Bless you" to see that they are open and generous while they express the words and not gloomy as if thinking of our 'coming to an end'.

Kissing

An Indo-European might assume that romantic kissing is universal. But less than half the world's cultures agree. My own travel experience is that, often, the more indigenous the society the less that romantic kissing plays a part. Hunter gatherer societies encountered on my journeys do not seem to kiss 'romantically'. Perhaps they don't in public and it was not my nature to pry.

Rafael Wlodarski, from Oxford University, trawled through records to find evidence of how kissing has changed. The oldest evidence of kissing-type behaviour comes from Hindu Vedic Sanskrit texts from over 3,500 years ago. Kissing was described as inhaling each other's soul.[71] Using the analogy of Abel representing our indigenous soul and Cain representing our planning and foresight mind, maybe we can wonder if this also describes a couple, such as Cain and Sarah, attempting to 'inhale the soul of the other'. Perhaps this is the origin of locking lips to catch all of the breath. As a teenager my memory was of

[71] Melissa Hogenboom writing for BBC Earth in July 2015

calling kisses 'hoovering each other's tonsils'. Could this explain why romantic kissing is more prevalent in cultures which have more difficulty in maintaining their 'wholeness' including access to the part of themselves who 'reacts creatively to wherever he wanders'. Chewing on this idea tickled me when discovering that all cultures in the Middle East kiss romantically, as do 70% of the Indo-European cultures. There appears also to be a correlation between the presence of kissing and the amount of stratification within a society.[72] Researchers say that the kissing urge is not genetic. This all fits and is a timely reminder that, whilst enjoying the kisses, we must not forget how different our paradigms are from those of 'intact societies'.

Another possibility crosses my mind. Perhaps because our sense of smell has been 'supressed' we need to complement her with the addition of our sense of taste.

Among societies who maintain legends and rituals to preserve the bridge to their own indigenous soul, there seems little need to 'inhale the soul' of a partner. Perhaps they enjoy the presence of their partner's soul in other ways, particularly when they are both able to fetch their own souls for the dance. But, we do not know what every culture gets up to in their most intimate moments, and nor we should.

Tickling

The aspect of tickling which interests me here is that of an uncle who provokes laughter in a young nephew or niece, which they both enjoy. Although apparently harmless, this seems a sign in some cultures that the 'tickler' is living vicariously to 'enjoy the uncontrolled laughter of the tickled'. Perhaps in generations to come the interaction will be banned and consigned to an earlier time when physical boundaries were being improperly crossed.

My thought process is that, for some, the part of the mind represented by Cain is so much in control that he yearns for a free and uncontrolled laughter. The laughter of Abel is missing. Since, as Christ says, we have to *be as little children* some might be trying to take a short cut in provoking this feeling in young children in order to awaken the feelings which are otherwise hard to attain within themselves.

---

[72] Melissa Hogenboom writing for BBC Earth in July 2015

The word 'tickled' as in 'tickled pink' refers to being pleased or delighted, and some other animals also enjoy tickling. Charles Darwin noticed that if a stranger tickled a child without warning, catching a child unawares, the child would withdraw rather than laugh. Therefore a basis of trust is necessary first. Darwin continued that the tickled needs to be *surprised* by the part of the body being tickled; hence the tickler is constantly 'on the move'. Perhaps this is why we cannot tickle ourselves as we are unable to surprise ourselves. Notably even Aristotle wondered about the same subject. Really; had he nothing better to concern himself with at that moment? Perhaps it is not fair of me to judge and this thought should instead be taken as a sign that the time has come to move on to the 3rd question of the book and more significant matters. In the next volume of this book, hopefully my readers' imagination will be tickled by unexpected probes into different parts of the globe and more particularly with how some of her cultures might have 'come about'.

EPILOGUE

This journey began with three questions.

How does an individual mind become 'poisoned' by a self-destructive tendency?

How is the poison hidden, and harboured, in a part of the mind which is 'out of reach' or 'unknown to us' so we cannot simply 'deal' with it?

How did our environment or culture develop in such a way that this 'poison' became thrust so deep into our children's minds?

This book has been guided primarily by the first two questions, and so far only alluded to the third question in a way, like an egg becomes a chicken, that the young *halt* children become the adults of the tribe. The tribe thus becomes *halt* and *blind*. This is only a part of the answer and doesn't explain how everything began. Also, the world's cultures are not the same. Some are very different from others. Two neighbouring lands of the same original peoples can have significant cultural differences. Originally this book contained three parts with the third part addressing the third question. But an intermission is necessary. *Mannership III* will address the third question, 'How did our environment or culture develop in such a way that this 'poison' became thrust so deep into our children's minds?'

The first part of this book included a review of the morning of my career up to my thirties. The afternoon of my career included the lessons of coaching leadership in over thirty countries. My watchful eye was fascinated by the origins of cultures around the world. This provided much of the material for continuing my quest in the sequel.

By examining some cultures in more detail, my hope is that my reader will be able to see similarities and differences in a fresh examination of their own. Understanding the cultural history of the land of our upbringing is an important part of healing; hence the importance of legends and sacred stories.

Before leaving this beginning, there is a message about cultural differences which must be the last thought, and should have been the first.

Mencius says: *The way of learning is none other than finding the lost mind.* Nicoll explains metanoia, a change of state of mind, as an awareness of a part of us 'which was lost'. *Something in us, eternally young, that can understand beyond this visible world, beyond phenomenal reality.* The challenge, according to Mencius, is to exert the mind to become aware that we are not seeing something.

My good fortune was two-fold; firstly to have experienced a silent childhood which, after losing a part of my mind, enabled me to know something was missing, and equipped me to *see* whenever a culture was operating in a dimension beyond my own; secondly, having encountered such generosity in nomadic tribes and indigenous societies, I could *see* they had something so valuable which my culture was missing. Without my 'way of looking', I would not have been drawn to begin my working life among Pacific Islands. Having recognised these societies had something so precious helped me to appreciate the wonder of indigenous shamans.

My career began, knowing something was missing and seeing a few cultures enjoying what was lost in me. But, it was not possible to explain exactly. Writing this book helped me to learn something of what I had seen, but not yet understood, all those years ago. This might answer the mystery of the chapter on 'deaf-sight' and 'blind-hearing'; that it is hard for a seeing person to imagine how the deaf might see more, because this would imply that we are all missing some extra light which the indigenous swim in naturally.

This book has explored explanations for some of the more extreme cases of afflictions with a Cain who has to strike down both the nature and the life force, or spirit, of his little brother and sister.

My wish, now, is to leave my reader with some memories of 'intact' culture.

In my global wanderings, the two most important discoveries were firstly how 'intact' societies avoid vengeful motives by trusting; *The sun and the ancestors will do what they will to your ill-wishers*; and secondly the importance to them of a child having pride in himself, and knowing himself, to be a real person.

While writing this book, my conclusion is that these two conditions are only possible when a culture has access to the well of 'living water' as well as accepting the angel's timing on the moving of the waters. The deliciousness of this pair of relationships might lead such a society to prefer drinking 'living water' together and lose interest in any vengeful activity. This seems to be what Christ really taught. Confucius says simply: *Before you embark on a journey of revenge, dig two graves.*

Michael Meade has a wonderful expression: *If the First Layer of human interaction is the common ground of manners, kind speech, polite greeting, and working agreements; if the Third Layer is the area of deeply shared humanity, the universal brotherhood and sisterhood of all people, of the underlying, fundamental oneness of human love, justice, and peaceful coexistence; then the Second Layer is the territory of anger, hatred, wrath, rage, outrage, jealousy, envy, contempt, disgust, and acrimony. And, the Second Layer always exists between the First Layer and the Third.*

Looking for water, Egypt 1973

My 'deaf-sight' taught me to see how much of indigenous society lives in the Third Layer, whereas Western societies spend much more time in the First. Perhaps, whenever the 'living water' of the Third Layer can be regularly tasted, there is less interest to spend time in the First Layer.

In indigenous society, a crucial role of shamans is attending to leaks or blocks in the spirit plumbing; assuring the 'living water' flows or spouts like a fountain.

In these societies Abel thrives.

By contrast, in some of our 'first world' societies, we may think we have been successful in creating happiness but may have only enabled Cain to have a 'happy childhood' by making him comfortable. We may have forgotten about Abel's existence. There is an easy way to tell; only a society which 'makes Cain comfortable' imagines that happiness can really be measured.

We will not have seriously begun the task of turning the tide away from self-destructiveness in our children if the measure of success is 'Cain's comfort'. There is something even more important which Malidoma taught me; our relationship to the feminine spirit is the same as our relationship to Mother Nature. The two crises facing our planet are apparently connected. This will be explored in *Mannership III.*

My last thought is a memory of that night in El Aaiun when my teenage life was saved, in the flash of an instant, in a glance connecting humbleness and acknowledgement with another. And this ability is with us right there at birth, reaching out for our first soulful connection.